The Allure of Capitalism

THE ALLURE OF CAPITALISM

An Ethnography of Management and the Global Economy in Crisis

By
Emil A. Røyrvik

berghahn
NEW YORK · OXFORD
www.berghahnbooks.com

Published in 2011 by
Berghahn Books
www.berghahnbooks.com

Library of Congress Cataloging-in-Publication Data

Røyrvik, Emil A.
The allure of capitalism : an ethnography of management and the global economy in
crisis / by Emil A. Røyrvik. — 1st ed.
     p. cm.
  Includes bibliographical references and index.
  ISBN 978-0-85745-185-9 (hardback) — ISBN 978-1-78238-065-8 (paperback) —
ISBN 978-1-78238-066-5 (retail ebook)
  1. Economic policy. 2. Industrial management. 3. International finance.
4. Financial crises. I. Title.
HD87.R697 2011
658—dc23

                                                                    2011018719

British Library Cataloguing in Publication Data

A catalogue record for this book is available from the British Library

Printed in the United States on acid-free paper.

ISBN: 978-1-78238-065-8 (paperback)
ISBN: 978-1-78238-066-5 (retail ebook)

CONTENTS

FIGURES

TABLES

PREFACE

At the turn of the millennium anthropologist Allen W. Batteau advised that if organizational ethnographers were to approach "the corporate and institutional worlds not as tourists or apologists but as interlocutors in a larger, shared drama of civilization," both a more "thorough self-examination" and a "greater rigor of preparation" would be required (2000: 737). My own journey into these worlds began, I believe, when I conducted my first ethnographic fieldwork in an urban Roma district in Bulgaria as a graduate student in 1996. The vantage point of the marginalized and dispossessed Roma offered a significant perspective of the formal institutional world of power "outside" of their communities.

I spent part of my time in Bulgaria traveling and talking to officials and organizations that were trying in various ways to remedy the tragic poverty of the Roma. For example, I met with emissaries representing the European Union, some of whom were driven by private chauffeur into the gypsy "mahalas," sometimes with both hope and funds. I met with international organizations like the Soros-funded Open Society Institute, national research institutions, foreign investor companies, and recently established Roma foundations. Watching a version of a capitalist market economy emerge in real time—corrupt, warts and all—was at the time both fascinatingly concrete and frustratingly intangible. I learned a lot about the day-to-day trials and tribulations, but also the finely tuned strategies and complexities involved in carving out pockets of possibilities. However, the larger-scale political and economic contexts and more structural causes of the misery displayed in the Roma communities remained distanced and opaque.

After completing my master's thesis I was employed as a researcher at SINTEF, Scandinavia's largest independent contract-based research foundation. Employed as an anthropologist, I was projected directly into the worlds of formal organizations, as our research group focused on the emerging "knowledge society" and "knowledge economy." I went on to work in various research projects, collaborating with both public- and private-sector organizations in which themes such as organizational development and learning, knowledge management, and strategic processes were central. A world of business and industry; a world of consultancy managers in engineering, and in information and communications technology; a world of modern bureaucracies; a world of capitalist corporations, and of professional experts and elites: I entered these unfamiliar organizational environments, engaged in experiences of technical experts and leaders in the modern economy that displayed a variety of interesting themes, contrasts, and dilemmas. But because most projects were confined to Norway, it was not really until my first research project in China that the truly "real" contrasts in terms of economic inequality came into the scope of research again.

By this time I had also formally embarked upon my PhD work in social anthropology at the Norwegian University of Science and Technology (NTNU), focusing on the management of international investment projects in the Norwegian-based "global corporation" Hydro. Among other things, I investigated several of their projects in China, where I found myself, again as a research "student," immersed in global patterns of inequality—but this time from the perspective of the "other side," as it were. In one sense I was an ethnographer "living" the international corporate manager or "expat" professional life: walking past the beggars on the crowded streets on my way to meetings in fancy high-end hotels, or glimpsing street sweepers at work on dusty highways from the back seat of a new, privately chauffeured American car on the way to an industrial plant or business office. Rather than taking small trips to the affluent side of the divide, so to speak, now I made small detours out onto the line of poverty and despair.

The present book is the result of this ten-year journey. The road taught me that it is imperative to link people, incidents, events, and situations with the wider social contexts and connections in which they take place. This is just as significant as situating larger structural factors and "forces" within concrete agential, historical, and social circumstance. Although the corporate and capitalist worlds explored in the present study are an inexhaustible source of new discoveries, I believe my professional journey, comprising over ten years inside of, outside of, and on the boundaries of the multitude that make up the corporate and institutional worlds, at least to some extent offered me a role not as a tourist or apologist, but rather as an interlocutor, both complicit and critical, in what Batteau rightly calls this larger, shared drama of civilization.

The study explores patterns, ambiguities, and asymmetries of contemporary globalized capitalism. The more I was myself enmeshed within these worlds, the more I became alarmed at the wider conjunctures of capitalism. By 2006 I had discovered a system of global political economic relations that was captivated by finance and "financialization", and poised for collapse. Initiated through the central prism of managing advanced international industrial investment projects in a so-called global corporation, the study enabled a close-up investigation of core practices of present-day political economy and cultures of capitalism. It exposes the contemporary core dynamics of value and wealth creation and distribution. Concomitantly it provides an understanding of the production of patterns of global inequality and of the legitimating forms of rationality underpinning these processes.

ACKNOWLEDGEMENTS

The quest chronicled in the present book was fueled by curiosity and a drive to get to the truth of things of importance. Mostly through strokes of luck and intuition over the duration of my ten-year research journey, I was able to carry out my search by engaging with and learning from numerous generous people, communities, and institutions. I want to take the opportunity to thank many of them here.

First, the Hydro organization and its members must be applauded for the way they have constituted a receptive, challenging, and constructive counterpart and research environment, both through various SINTEF research projects and through my thesis work. The many people in Hydro who deserve thanks are to numerous to mention, but you know who you are.

In and around my first research "community of practice," organized by SINTEF "Kunne," where I learned the arts of collaborative research with counterparts in both the private and public sector, I am grateful to several people for contributing to an energetic research culture and providing invaluable dialogues and feedback in my research process: Eric Monteiro, Morten Hatling, Roger Klev, Mona Skaret, Arne Carlsen, Grete Håkonsen, Bjørn-Emil Madsen, Theodor Barth, Truls Paulsen, Merete Molberg, Erling Hoff Leirvik, Bjørn Haugstad, Katja Hydle, Reidar Gjersvik, Kristianne Ervik, Rita Westvik, Grete Wennes, Joachim Breunig, and Kenneth Kongsvold. Ingrid Aalberg made much of the whole community tick. Egil Wulff and Anton Trætteberg have, through the wisdom of their years of experiences and insights, provided invaluable guidance into the fascinating world of engineers, managers, organizations, and corporations. Their holistic and knowledgeable yet notably curious and open-minded approach to research stands out for me as exemplary. A most special salutation is owed to fellow SINTEF initiates Kjersti Bjørkeng and Arne L. Bygdås, with whom enduring relations were forged. Not least did we share an Australian academic adventure that has borne many fruits. Arne lived with this book project throughout all its phases and was unstinting with concise comments on any issue. And to all my knowledgeable colleagues in my new home at SINTEF's group for "work research," kudos for their generous social and scientific exchanges. I also want to thank my research colleagues at SINTEF ICT, especially my long-term friend and research collaborator Torgeir Dingsøyr.

My latest research "community of practice" at the Department of Social Anthropology at the Norwegian University of Science and Technology (NTNU), also has my sincere gratitude. The department granted me the scholarships and positions for both my PhD study and thesis work, as well as the postdoctoral work that made possible the writing of this book. I am especially grateful to Prof. Carla Dahl-Jørgensen, chair of a now-burgeoning "community of organizational anthropology." The anthropology community here, and especially my fellow PhD and postdoctoral colleagues Kirsti Sarheim Anthun, Sigrid Damman, Håkon Fyhn, Marte Giskeødegård, David Hogstad, Hans Hadders, Jens Røyrvik, Martin Thomassen, Flore Singer Åslid, Turid Sætermo, Linda Dyrlid, Cornelius Heyse, Olav Eggebø, and Haakon Aasprong, has contributed to a sense of academic community in the otherwise lonesome processes of writing. Special thanks are due to Stein E. Johansen, a trailblazer who pushes the limits of thought with an exceptional combination of scholarly and imaginative inquiry. Never short of time to explore and share new ideas, he has also managed an academically vital, critical, and open-minded collegial forum throughout my years in research. The academic work of Tord Larsen has also been particularly inspirational. As the chair of the evaluation committee of my PhD, along with the scholarly critique and feedback from fellow committee members Christina Garsten and Michael Blim, he made the public defense of my thesis in 2008—just after Lehman Brothers collapsed and the financial crisis was officially declared—an academic ritual I will never forget. The defense and the aftermath also started the transformation of the thesis into a book.

I am also indebted to Kristin Hestflått and Kjell Stenstadvold for their valuable feedback on parts of the manuscript, and to Eirik Hem for technical assistance. Kjersti Thorbjørnsrud eagerly discussed my ideas and provided discerning feedback on the text. And, to the team at Berghahn Books, thank you for your confidence in, and your professional work with, this book.

During my research work I was fortunate to spend time as a visiting academic at three different institutions abroad. First I visited the Department of Management at the University of St. Gallen, Switzerland, for three months. I am grateful for the discussions and ideas generated in exchanges with Georg von Krogh and his research group there. Second, traveling with my family and accompanied also by my friends and colleagues Kjersti and Arne, I spent six months at the internationally oriented ICAN (now CMOS) research center in the School of Management at the University of Technology, Sydney, Australia. Sincere thanks are due to Stewart Clegg and all the interesting people there who provided valuable feedback on my research and made our stay unforgettable. Last, I spent half a year finalizing the present book at the anthropology department of the City University of New York (CUNY) Graduate Center. To Michal Blim goes heartfelt gratitude for the invitation and help with the book, and the same is owed to his colleagues for their contributions to an intellectually stimulating and vitally important research group. I am indebted to SINTEF, DNV, and NTNU for providing all the necessary traveling grants.

Nonetheless, the most special thoughts are for my networked family, for all their love and support: to Jens and Kakuua, and to my second mother Habiba, for all their laughter, warmth, and vivid discussions. The Sunday dinners are an oasis of rejuvenation. Live and Terje are also thanked for their continuing contributions and support, and warm thoughts go out especially to my three children, the jewels of my life: Ruben, Ylva, and Charlotte, a robust team that has traveled the world with me in the name of research and exploration. And notwithstanding the complexities of the nature/nurture debate and the deepest enigmas of life, I thank especially my parents, Grete and Johnny, who must bear at least some responsibility for my existence and thus for the products of my work. By their own and very different examples, they taught me the essential qualities and importance of independent and truthful thinking. Finally, and probably needless to say: although entangled minds have enabled this book, the responsibility for its content is mine alone.

Introduction

INVESTMENT PROJECTS, CAPITALISM, AND CRISIS

Capital is defined by crisis.
—Michael Hardt and Antonio Negri, *Empire*

Those for whom a great human cause is central can
be in a relationship of alliance or opposition with
a state, but never of permanent identification.
—Eric Hobsbawm, *On Empire*

It was "a dark, rainy day," as the story goes, that particular Saturday in 2005. Nevertheless, it was the evening of the arguably most spectacular popular culture event in Norwegian history. Frognerparken in Oslo, the huge park in the heart of the Norwegian capitol famous for its fantastic stone sculptures by Gustav Vigeland, of nude people in all possible and impossible positions, was the site for the happening. Hydro, celebrating its centennial, on this particular day hosted the most monumental of several cultural happenings and activities. After a hundred years as a company on the world stage, it is undoubtedly Norway's most successful, important, and international industrial corporation, projecting a global outlook since its inception in 1905—the same year, incidentally, in which Norway celebrated its independence from the union with Sweden. By 2007, having recently established two of its three major businesses as separate companies listed on the stock exchanges, Hydro as a dedicated aluminum company had operations in more than thirty countries worldwide and a market value of about NOK 100 billion.

Despite some ambivalence, Hydro had to make it big. An audience of 120,000 people attended, an impressive new record for a country with about four million people, and a city of about half a million. To be sure, it was a band that was attracting the crowds: a-ha, the only truly international pop music success ever to have come out of Norway's music scene. Having conquered the world pop music stage in the late 1980s, they were now a more mature band, reunited and offering new material for the first time since their heyday—an appropriate analogy to the aging but still very viable Hydro corporation. The concert received mixed reviews in the newspaper the day after. Still, the record-breaking ocean of people swinging and swaying collectively to the music is imprinted in the historical book of Norwegian social gatherings.

Later, Hydro's centennial "birthday" was celebrated in various ways on the same day at all its sites throughout the world. But in Høyanger, a small industrial city on the largely rural west coast of Norway, the centennial celebration was canceled. The local community, where Hydro has been a cornerstone company, had recently been notified that Hydro would close down its Søderberg production lines as of 2006. It chose not to reinvest in new production lines when the old lines had to be shut down because of pollution requirements. The same thing happened in Årdal, another of the key rurally situated, cornerstone Hydro production sites. The decisions would affect 120 jobs in Høyanger and 210 in Årdal. No centennial celebration was held at the latter location either. A few years earlier Hydro had decided to closed down its magnesium business at Herøya, one of the sites evoking the pretense of Hydro's history and signifying strongly its "culture and tradition." Simultaneously it was establishing a magnesium plant in China, among the projects investigated in the present work. In all of the instances, employees protested and politicians were capitalizing on the situation, criticizing Hydro's management. The ghost of unemployment was called forth, and huge outcries dominated the media. Hydro was seen as betraying not only the local communities but also its responsibilities as a Norwegian institution.

In 2006, after participating at the annual Hydro shareholder meeting, having recently bought five Hydro shares to get the invitation, I chanced to run into a top public official from Høyanger. "When the decision of closing down was imminent," he said, "we mobilized the people. We walked the streets in protest marches. We made a stir." He left the impression that it was mostly to put on a show so as to make it political. "When the decision came, definitively, then we rolled up our sleeves, and went to work. Our job was then to squeeze as much money as possible out of Hydro." He was very happy with the result. After the media storm, the protest marches, and various politicians' heavy public criticism of Hydro for abandoning its societal obligations, I expected of him to be critical as well, and asked him about that. "No, no," he said, "I have only positive things to say about Hydro. A formidable company, the management handled the process exemplarily. We got the money we asked for and are only very happy." With the money they got from Hydro they established an investment fund and worked on attracting high-tech investments and companies. "Our only problem is to get enough people. We are short on labor in Høyanger."

In Årdal as well, similarly a small, west coast, industrially based settlement and a symbolic beacon of Norwegian industrial modernity, the process seems to have been handled exemplarily, and unemployment never became a problem. This side of the story, however, did not make it to the headlines, and no politician capitalized on it—though they tried. As Eivind Reiten, then the president and CEO of Hydro, later explained: "The very same politicians that were flocking to Årdal and Høyanger to pander to electors, getting their pictures in the newspapers while criticizing Hydro, they came to me later and asked us to give them a podium to praise how we handled the process. It is very tempting sometimes to talk out loud on these issues. However, it would not be very constructive."[1]

Cultural Analysis of Corporate and Capitalist Organization

The present book provides a cultural analysis of contemporary forms of capitalism at the postmillennial moment, when the alleged total triumph of liberal capitalism, seemingly in an instant, turned to tragedy in 2008. After several years of investigating managing practices in a set of industrial investment projects at Hydro, I came to realize that these practices provided a particularistic starting point, an empirical and interpretative springboard, as it were, from which a broader and deeper, and not least a more holistic account of key cultural dimensions of contemporary forms of capitalism could be portrayed.

To briefly contextualize Hydro in the "world of corporations," we might first notice that among the 100 largest economic actors on the global stage in 2004, compared in terms of value of GDP and sales, 28 were countries and 72 were corporations (Clegg et al. 2004: 457). The world is home to more than 60,000 "transnational" companies—most of them, however, with origins in just a few developed countries. In a world in which the processes of "globalization" so far have produced global economic systems and cultural exchanges on a global scale, while politics still is largely national and regional, these companies are an immense power container and source of global forms of authority. Indeed, a "transnational solution" to the situation of managing across borders has been proposed (Bartlett and Ghosal 1989). Simply by acknowledging this situation I agree with Burawoy and will avoid treating the corporation as any other organization: "With the subsumation of industrial sociology under organization theory, the distinctiveness of the profit-seeking capitalist enterprise is lost" (1979: 5). However, as early as 1932 Berle and Means pointed towards the coming of age, and the coming age, of the corporation:

> The rise of the modern corporation has brought a concentration of economic power which can compete on equal terms with the modern state.... The future may see the economic organism, now typified by the corporation, not only on an equal plane with the state, but possibly even superseding it as the dominant form of social organization. The law of corporations, accordingly, might well be considered as a potential constitutional law for the new economic state, while business practice is increasingly assuming the aspect of economic statesmanship. (1991: 313)

These corporations are today glorified as the beacons of modernization and the civilization project, and concomitantly demonized as the major force behind the destruction of our planet in the ecological, social, and moral senses. For example, transnational corporations are "held accountable for the imminent demise of the nation-state" (Comaroff and Comaroff 2000: 319) and the corollaries thus implied. Good and evil in ample supply are projected onto the image of these mega-organizations. This moral duality is illustrated to the point on the front cover of Bakan's book *The Corporation* (2004): outlined in red to signify power, the classic image of the suit-clad businessman with a briefcase is drawn on a white background and supplemented by both the devil's pointed tail and a halo above his business hat. Corporations are symbols of both human cultural success and failure, of creation and destruction, of progress and degeneration, of splendor and ugliness. They are branded icons of our own projected good and bad selves. "Global capitalism" is a gigantic moral battleground on which the major actors are transnational corporations, grassroots movements, the politics of state capitalism, and international affairs and civil organizations. Corporations are both a sign and a metaphor for the antinomies—captured in a concrete jurisprudential but nevertheless elusive form—of the celebrated and denounced "global condition" of "late" or "reflexive" modernity. In short, they are a fundamental focal point from which the social and moral universe of man in most of his images, from social and economic man to *Homo faber* (man the maker) and *Homo ludens* (the playing man), may be unfolded through most of its manifestations—the magnificent, the quixotic, the abysmal.

The ethnographic material here has been gathered and generated through an ethnographic extended case study (Burawoy 1998, 2009; Evans and Handelman 2006) of managing practices in a set of new international investment projects in the Norwegian-based "global" company Hydro, a leading actor in the light metals industry. The guiding research focus has been to investigate managing practices (as exemplary of knowledge work), particularly related to investment projects (and subsequently realized production plants) that are conducted and operating in various forms across different cultural boundaries (national, organizational, epistemic), so as to identify characteristics of these practices and the projects within which they occur.[2] The goal of this focus has more generally been to give a close-up view of transnational industrial corporate endeavors in a "globalized" economy, and to analyze holistically aspects of economic and cultural development of late modern society. The research was conducted in a mode of explorative discovering and investigation of expanding relational entanglements, leading finally to the present anthropological portrait of globalized capitalism in crisis. The managing of industrial investment projects is, I suggest, an ideal empirical point of departure for such an ambition, because the investment project can be regarded as the main mechanism and motor of capitalist societies' processes of wealth *creation*. Furthermore, these investment projects are all in one way or another situated at connected crossroads of the globalized economy. As will be substantiated below, I propose that the Hydro investment projects that are examined here arguably represent a concrete "totality," or assemblage, of advanced capitalism itself and as such instantiate a microcosm of global capitalism.

The cultural analysis focuses on a set of key dimensions, all derived from what I have found to be core managing practices in the Hydro investment projects. In addition to the transnational or global flavor of these investment projects, their most obvious defining traits are arguably their high intensity in three main dimensions, each designated by a key investigative concept: money,[3] knowledge, and technology. The study "aims for the jugular," seeking to describe and penetrate as thoroughly as possible the central issues and aspects that pertain to managing these investment projects: what these managers are doing and are trying to achieve professionally, and what it means both more broadly and deeply. To this end I outline some of the main contexts, constraints, and implications of their activities. That these projects are highly knowledge-intensive, in terms of both of what we may label research-based and practice-based knowledge, and also intensive with respect to money capital and to technology is uncontroversial. What these combined intensities constitute, are constrained by, mean, and imply as they unfold in real life in complex and multilevel ways, is the goal of investigation in the present work. Thus these "intensities" also constitute important analytical and organizational dimensions of the book. While Part I explicitly outlines key issues related to the concepts of *knowledge* and managing (managing is seen as knowledge work par excellence), it further runs like a theme throughout the entire text. Part I revolves to a large extent around investigations of concepts and enactments of *technology*, and Part II targets directly the realms of *economy*, money capital and finance.

Exploring a domain of formal corporate organization so critically defined by knowledge, technology, and money, we are immediately projected into the conceptual space of *instrumental rationality*. As anthropology often is seen as "traditionally" being engaged in exploring forms of rationality in non-Western and small-scale societies associated with "premodernity," here the focus is on forms of rationality in the midst of "modern capitalism" itself. I concur with Wilk and Cliggett that rationality should be the subject, not the assumption, of economic rationality (2007: 194), wherever it is studied. Similarly, seeing—as Heidegger (1977) does—technology as a form of human instrumental activity, the subject rather than the assumption of instrumentality leads the investigation to question assumptions of these forms of rationality that are more or less taken for granted. One of the arguments unfolded in the present book is that the forms of rationality at "the centers" of modern capitalism must be qualitatively differentiated, and that these centers are constituted by what I call "mixed regimes of rationality" rather than by one homogeneous and hegemonic form that in turn is colonizing all others.

The study is, finally, a cultural analysis in the sense that it recurrently discusses key distinctions and differentiations as well as unifying relations between culture and nature. In the orthodox view, culture, not least through what we conceptualize as "technology," aims at the "mastery" or "interpretation" of nature (Wagner 1981: 67). As discussed below, issues of rationality and human nature are at the forefront of various perspectives and debates in economic anthropology. Through questioning "technology" and "economy," idioms of the culture/nature constitution will be enacted and conceptions of rationality itself challenged.

Investment Projects and the Reproduction of Relations

A core tenet of the present study is the notion that the endurance, or persistence, of the capitalist corporative form is only apparent and cannot be taken for granted. Like any other enduring pattern of social relations it has to be continually created, that is, reproduced. And once the question of reproduction is posed one needs to *go beyond* the organizational boundary and examine the wider interrelationships that guarantee its reproduction (Burawoy 1979). From the point of departure in the set of Hydro international investment projects, the book "extends out of the field" and provides an analysis of contemporary global capitalism as it is now engulfed in, paraphrasing Max Gluckman, a total context of crisis. Bruce Kapferer, in his assessment of the contribution of Max Gluckman, identifies a rediscovery of the value of Gluckman's perspective among some contemporary scholars "at what appears to be a new period of crisis in world history, one of globalization and neo-imperialism" (2006: 123). From the analysis of events of managerial practices in investment projects, the analysis extends out to include the broader historical situation and contextual structures in which the events described are positioned, occasioned, and endowed with additional significance.

The main proposition of the book is that the efforts involved in transforming Hydro into a "financialized" corporation represent a significant signal of our age of global capitalism and its development. These transformative efforts instantiates the age of the "high-finance hegemony" of millennial capitalism—with the "financialization of society" and the corollaries of spiraling wealth and poverty alike as corollaries. Unfolding the life of Hydro investment projects, the core case story of the book is the production of the contemporary financialized "productive system of relations" itself. This means examining, for example, how firms add value to their extractive and manufacturing capabilities by commodifying abstract notions of value, and not least how value *assessment, appreciation,* and *origination* have moved to center stage of productive relations and their so-called "value creating" activities.

The general argument of the financialization of the global economy is, in a nutshell, as follows (Arrighi 1994; Duménil and Levy 2004; Epstein 2005). Similar to some significant historical precedents, the power balance between industrial capital and finance capital shifted dramatically in the global economy starting in the 1970s. During the 1980s, 1990s, and 2000s the upper hand of finance got stronger and stronger. This was a response to the structural crisis constituted by a deepening stagnation, or stagflation, of the economic system since the 1970s (Foster and Magdoff 2009). From the 1970s on, profit rates in capitalist economies declined and growth rates in the global economy slowed down. As a result, more and more investments poured into pure financial business, the finance economy grew radically, and the process combined with other factors to culminate in what is now widely considered a "culture of neoliberalism" (Comaroff and Comaroff 2001) or a "neoliberal culture complex" of global reach (Hannerz 2007). I argue that what has emerged is a *globalized culture complex of neoliberal financialization*—the historically unprecedented lever-age and expansion of finance capital, including the accumulation of mas-sive debt and the radical redistribution of income and wealth that it has actively promoted (Harvey 2005; Reinhart and Rogoff 2009). Not only was capital captivated by the allure of finance, but in a complex spectacle the social relations of capitalism were culturally remade as well.

Financialization might in one sense be seen as a major capitalist re-sponse to a crisis in the social relationships of Fordism, along with other important socialities on which industrial capitalism has been founded (Hardt and Negri 2009: 289). Finance was supposed to save both capital-ism and society from the structural crisis, and in some ways it did—but only for a while, and with a vengeance. One of the biggest real surprises of the financial crisis of 2008 was that it seemed to have come as a surprise to so many (cf. Stiglitz 2010: 1). At least, it has been heavily promoted as a "total surprise for everybody" by people in power.

A brief overview of the facts of financialization paints a telling picture. Estimates from the International Monetary Fund (IMF) indicate that global financial assets rose from US $12 trillion in 1980 to $241 trillion in 2007 (IMF 2009a). Trading in foreign currencies alone amounted by the end of the century to $1.5 trillion a day, "a sum equivalent to more than the *annual* Gross National Product of the UK (Fulcher 2004: 94). The emergence of the Eurodollar, or Eurocurrency, market in the 1960s is the single most important factor in this picture (Arrighi 1994; Dickens 2005). By 2004 this market alone amounted to transactions of US $1.9 trillion a day (BIS 2004). According to Manuel Castells, international investment of a mostly speculative nature increased by a factor of nearly 200 from 1970 to 1997 (Fulcher 2004: 94). Likewise, global cross-border capital flows more than doubled in just the short period from 2002 to 2007 (Blankenburg and Palma 2009: 531). By 1990 "money managers had increased their control of US corporate equities from 8 percent in 1950 to 60 percent.... Similarly, pension funds had extended their share of total business equities from less than 1 percent to just short of 39 per-cent" (ibid.).

Taking into account the astronomical rise in the financial derivatives market, the magnitude of financialization becomes even more pronounced. The total value of financial derivatives globally was probably only a few million dollars in 1970. It subsequently grew to about $100 million in 1980, $100 billion by 1990, and $100 trillion by 2000 (LiPuma and Lee 2004: 74). By June 2008 the estimated volume of derivatives outstanding (notional value of all over-the-counter derivatives, excluding derivatives traded on public exchanges) had reached a staggering $684 trillion (BIS 2009).[4] Historian Niall Ferguson concludes that "Planet Finance is beginning to dwarf Planet Earth," and that we are living in a time defined by the ascent of "man the banker" (2008: 4–5). Given that the derivatives market alone has grown to about eleven times the size of global GDP, and about forty times the size of US GDP, this proposition seems warranted.

The outbreak of global financial crisis had the result, as estimated by Alan Greenspan among others, of total global equity loss in the range of US $40 trillion, about two-thirds of world GDP (Greenspan 2009; Robbins 2009), from just 2007 to 2009. More significantly, the impact was not confined to the financial sector. The IMF predicted in April 2009 a decline in world economic activity of 1.1 percent, and 3.4 percent for the advanced economies in 2009 (IMF 2009b). In September 2009 the European Central Bank predicted that GDP would fall by 4.1 percent in 2009. The International Labour Organization estimated that unemployment worldwide rose to 30–50 million people from 2007 to 2009, and that more than 200 million people were pushed into poverty (Blankenburg and Palma 2009: 532). This, added to the outcomes of more than thirty years of neoliberal financialization, indicates that global patterns of economic inequality now have reached levels unprecedented in modern times (Hart 2002; Blim 2005; UNDP 2005).

At Hydro, the shift to finance did not kick in hard until 1999, when it made a broad-based turn to shareholder value and finance (Lie 2005). With this move Hydro adapted to the major change in US-led global capitalism, a fundamental shift that by 1990 had dominantly installed the idea that the corporation's absolute focus should be on shareholder maximization (Ho 2009). The shareholder value movement was pivotal in effectively ending the almost century-long tensional coexistence between two visions of capitalism, one that perceived the corporation as a social entity with broader social and stakeholder responsibilities, and one that saw the corporation as purely financial property. In effect, the shareholder value revolution prepared the way for "dismantling the corporation in the name of the shareholder" (ibid.: 176), ultimately to the benefit of Wall Street and the global finance capital communities—a benefit, however, that came with the dubious prize of contributing to sinking the global economy.

The severe constraints finance capital imposed on Hydro investment projects and the industrial corporation's activities and culture more generally did not, however, stop it from highly successfully surfing the global wave of financialization (Røyrvik 2008a). From 1999 to 2007—that is, in eight years—the market value and stock price of Hydro, a solid 100-year-old industrial company, increased by 638 percent,[5] a figure that demands explanation. Then, with the onset of the finance crisis, the stock price and market value of Hydro plummeted. As an industrial corporation, Hydro was increasingly in an ambivalent position, resisting the financialization of the economy even as it adapted imaginatively to the overall global economic context in which it operates, a context that might be described as a fundamental "financial takeover." The full unleashing of the finance crisis on 15 September 2008 with the bankruptcy of Lehman Brothers, the largest bankruptcy in world history with its $613 billion in debt, proved the point to the public at large.

In the first instance I am thus concerned with the managing practices that were more or less directly involved in bringing about the new industrially based, technologically advanced production projects and plants in Hydro. Moreover, what I have been particularly preoccupied with is the emergence, the bringing forth, of these facilities. Particular attention is devoted to the *early phases* of the projects, and the early phases of the materialized plants. The focal point of early phases further implies a focus on immaterial symbol work, concept work, idea work—on design and integration work, and on the social formation of ideas and abstract instruments. These early aspects of project work are described in Hydro project language as "value creation." (The later phase of "executing" projects, that is, building the physical plant itself, is called "value control.") Thus I am particularly interested in describing and revealing the practices and conceptualizations that constitute the notion of *value creation*.

The bringing forth of projects and plants is a fragile process of great complexity and depth, contingent upon a multitude of cultural dimensions, and it may be further enabled or may break down at various junctions of the process. It may also be brought forth unsuccessfully, that is, it becomes and materially instantiates a production facility, but it does not live up to the ideals of its "creators" and thus fails to embody its purpose(s). I find that these purposes are embedded in societal functions and are morally legitimized in much broader terms than "business as usual" or "pure profit making." Through the "native concept" of value creation, related practices, and appropriate theories, I am thus also trying at a further remove to unravel and describe some of the key practices and conceptualizations pertaining to what I will argue is the reproduction of relations of societal wealth creation, and by implication relations of inequality, under capitalism as a contemporary "world system."[6]

The primary guiding research questions have thus been: What are these managing practices in investment projects? What do they make and what do they signify? What do they produce, how are they constrained, and arguably even more significantly, what do they reproduce? At the first instance, the people and the enactments involved in projects produce ideas, concepts, communicative interactions, designs, drawings, contracts. These are again abstract anticipations of techno-economically advanced capitalist industrial production plants. Therefore they are significantly also anticipations of producing profits. As will be conveyed, these projects provide particular circumstances in which a political and moral universe is reproduced. Investment projects are thus vehicles for the reproduction of relations on several interconnected levels:

1. Projects as vehicles for the reproduction of relations that produce new projects.
2. Projects as vehicles for the reproduction of the particular corporate organizational form (projects are one of the main devices through which a corporation is sustained and grows, that is, the way it secures its continuing existence).
3. Projects as reproduction of the capitalist corporation as a vehicle for the reproduction of capitalist economic and social relations.

Finally, in the investigated projects the book finds an alternative trajectory to the presently dominating ethos of a contemporary "financialized" capitalist economy; thus:

4. Projects as the reproduction of another and partly alternative variant of capitalist relations of cultural reproduction.

Production Capital and Finance Capital

Having studied investment projects for establishing new production facilities around the world, I acknowledge that the three most pronounced characteristics of the Hydro investment projects—i.e., the combination of their money capital, technology, and knowledge intensiveness—are also at the core of the dynamics of capitalism's own genesis and reproduction. From the vantage point of surveying a cluster of such investment projects, much of the whole complex of capitalist relations comes into view. It provides a strong impetus to study in real time the transhistorical, but changing, interrelationship between the sphere of production, in this case particularly industrial production, and the flow of money.

A common distinction in theories of capitalism is that between "production capital" and "finance capital." In historically changing configurations, these main forms of capitalist activities have interacted both symbiotically and parasitically (Reinert and Daastøl 1998). Following Perez (2002), the purpose of finance capital is to make money from money and thus to serve as agents for reallocating and redistributing wealth. By contrast, the term "production capital," again following Perez, "embodies the motives and behaviors of those agents who generate *new* wealth by producing goods or performing services" (2002: 71, italics in original).

Furthermore, as for example Hart (2000) reports, writers from Aristotle to Polanyi have identified two distinct orientations to the market. Marx called the first one the "simple commodity circuit" (CMC), where commodities are sold for money to buy what one wants. This conception developed into variants of merchant trading. The second one he called the "capitalist commodity circuit," which starts with money and has the aim of realizing more money, expressed in the general formula for capital, MCM' (where M is money, C is Commodity, and M' is surplus value or profit). Simplifying vastly more complex issues, we might distinguish in Marxian terminology between two broad types of MCM' by calling the first the "finance capital" variant (MM'), and the second the "productive capital" variant (MCM'), although both are derived from the latter.[7] Significantly, the distinct *industrial* capital element of the capitalist commodity circuit was, according to Marx, not so much the mechanization and the factories as the penetration of money capital into production.

As will be described, the continuity and changing relations that constitute these historical dynamics of capitalist relationships are highly relevant to the present study. In contemporary economic flows, finance capital has overwhelmingly gained the upper hand in these relationships, and since the millennium Hydro, although still employing the industrial capitalist formula of MCM', has been strongly influenced by the global wave of financialization. However, it is ambiguously situated because it is simultaneously offering a form of resistance to the overall financialization trend in the global economy. The ambition in the present work is thus to go beyond theories of management and organization and reestablish concrete, particular historical action, context, and circumstance. If successful, we become able to question and possibly shatter the appearance of naturalness or inevitability in the present order of things, both in terms of the corporate form and in the present globally integrated capitalist social and economic "system."

At a further remove, the present book is an effort to provide an in-depth description and analysis of some of the central contemporary capitalist practices of producing societal wealth and affluence. I find a basic premise of this in the adoption of the general Schumpeterian and Chandlerian notion that large nonfinancial corporations operating in oligopolistic markets have been the main source of capital investment, technological change, and productivity growth for most of the twentieth century in the capitalist economies, at least in the US (Crotty 2005: 78). In this perspective the current case proves exemplary, as the focal point of empirical investigation is the creation and realization of advanced industrial investment projects that are ambiguously situated at the contemporary crossroads of industrial and financial capitalism in a globalized economic world. As such, capitalism(s) is anthropologically analyzed not from the periphery, but from actions and activities at the center(s). However, analyzing the creation of wealth is, by implication, also a study of the reproduction of relations of economic inequality. By examining the present condition of capitalism, the study at hand may shed some illuminating light on the institutionalization of asymmetrical relations of inequality in contemporary capitalist social relations.

The analysis of these processes is comprehensive, in the sense that it seeks to understand phenomena on several interconnected levels of analysis, reflecting the differentially constituted "reality status" of the phenomena. Rather than being framed as a problem that the analysis embraces different levels ("micro," "meso," "macro"), I see it as a strength of the extended case approach and the holistic ambition of anthropology. By following the "object"—the flows of people, knowledge, and money through managing in investment projects—the various levels are not seen as ontologically distinct entities but as "assembled" dimensions along which the social field is unfolded. The study thus seeks to disclose economic and ideological, epistemological and ontological aspects of the emergent movement of these investment projects.

The present study cannot therefore, easily be classed under any of the sub-labels commonly used to categorize anthropological or social science research in these realms. It rather bears affinity to what Czarniawska has labeled "creole researchers, hybrid disciplines and pidgin writing" (2003) and as such is a transdisciplinary effort. In its approach to theory in the ethnographic research process it follows Van Maanen's simple statement: "No overarching theory required" (2011: 222). Yet it advocates a holistic ambition. Edelman and Haugerud complain about the fragmented discourses in anthropology of modernity, development, and globalization, where "culture is on proud display while historical political economy and economic and financial globalization is largely absent" (2005: 1). In this light the present project is but one small effort to remedy this situation.

In doing so it necessarily also tries to answer their call: "Rather than encourage continued separations of these analytical tracks, we need new intellectual hybrids: adventurous combinations of culture, economy, discourse, power, institutions and history" (ibid.). With anthropology's historical legacy in its "respect for the existing" (Sørhaug 2004: 19, my translation), of "actually occurring realities," as constituted through a web of "reflexive relationality" that is not demarcated by any disciplinary boundaries, anthropology might itself be seen as a transdisciplinary discipline. Indeed, it may offer an arena for a dialogical and reflexive "new unity of science," as proposed for example by anthropologist Reidar Grønhaug (2001).

This new unity, however, should avoid what Grønhaug calls the *confla-tions* of much so-called post-modern writing, "where the unlimited diversity of human phenomena is squeezed into an apparently homogeneous sausage..." (ibid.: 65, my translation). Grønhaug suggests that we rather honor phenomenological diversity while unifying difference with differentiated connections and synergies. In a somewhat similar vein, Brian Morris notes that "anthropology surely needs to go beyond the tired dichotomy of textualism ... versus positivism (phenomenalism) and embrace a truly materialist ontology, a critical realist perspective, and a dialectical (relational) epistemology" (2007: 28). This would, according to Morris, enable a continuation of what Maurice Bloch described as the "dual heritage" of anthropology, "combining interpretative understanding and social science" (ibid.).

Indeed, the present work is not constrained by the social sciences, but is to some degree informed by the natural sciences and the arts and humanities alike. Grønhaug (2001) argues that anthropology must reinvent the dialogue between the humanities and the natural sciences that was vitally alive before a codified demarcation between them was firmly established in the latter part of the nineteenth century. Grønhaug proposes to reach back to Weber's insistence on combining meaning and explanation, that is, on adjoining the hermeneutical and phenomenological interpretative with causative, explaining sociology.

Likewise, the present description utilizes a varied template of writing styles. All three of the types of ethnographic "tales" outlined by Van Maanen (1988)—the *realist*, the *confessional* and the *impressionist* tale—are used. Although economic anthropology, organizational anthropology, industrial anthropology (or sociology), business anthropology, "global anthropology," and organization and management studies all are designations that are relevant here, and literature from all these streams is indeed built upon, the following study has ambitions to transcend or go beyond such demarcating categories. It is a cultural analysis of contemporary forms of globalized political economy, and as such it is tackling Hart and Ortiz's assertion (2008) that with the financial crisis, it is time for anthropology to yet again engage with political economy.

Contextualizing the Study within Hydro

A major empirical foundation linking the "micro flows" in investment projects to the larger body of the Hydro corporation is a significant observation made by Lie in one of the volumes of the "history of Hydro" (2005). Historically, from the 1970s through the 1990s, Hydro could not be characterized adequately as an "operational culture," in the sense of a continuous focus on the daily operations and consecutive control of economic performance in each business unit. Rather to the contrary, several of the chapters in the "history of Hydro" emphasize the company's capacity "to carry out really big, complex investment projects as one of its foremost qualities" (ibid.: 434, my trans.).[8] The comprehensively written history of the company thus testifies that a key defining characteristic of the corporation has been in the widest possible sense its "project-oriented organization" (ibid.: 435, my trans.). My own empirical material supports this contention. Taking this observation seriously leaves the present study, with its focus on "investment project flows" in Hydro, to investigate the arguably core practices that have been constituting categories of company "identity" and other cultural formations, at least in the recent decades.

My intimate relationship with Hydro commenced with a collaborative research project in 2001, conducted through the research foundation SINTEF. The first SINTEF project collaboration with Hydro, as well as the subsequent ones, was exploratory in design but revolved around the simple yet subtle and intriguing fact that whereas one investment project may be accomplished successfully, the next can fail, and so on and so forth. While Hydro has a well-known reputation as a company with strong project expertise and a solid historical track record, smaller and larger failures, as judged by corporate actors, also occur here. And although comprehensive systems and procedures related to "project management"[9] are in place, history documents that quite considerable complexity and unpredictability nevertheless remains in project endeavors. Investment projects are an inherently complex affair, reflecting along several dimensions what Juarrero has labeled "complex dynamics of action" (1999).

To contextualize my own research in Hydro I want to give as briefly as possible a simple formal overview of Hydro as a corporation.[10] Hydro was formed in 1905 by the "holy trinity" of the *entrepreneurialism* of Sam Eyde, the *scientific genius* of Kristian Birkeland, possibly the most scientifically gifted person Norway has seen and one of the greatest scientists ever, and the *financial brilliance* and muscle of Sweden's Wallenberg family. First established as a fertilizer production company, it moved later into magnesium, power, aluminum, oil and gas, and some smaller areas. In recent decades its main organization has been in the three divisions "agri" (fertilizers), aluminum, and oil and gas. By 2007 it had divested both its agri and oil and gas divisions, and moved forward as a dedicated company focusing on aluminum, the light metal worth more than gold in the mid nineteenth century and now branded by Hydro as the "metal for the future." Its magnesium activities were also sold or closed down by 2007. Interestingly, in the 1960s it was magnesium that was branded as the "metal for the future," and also "the sleeping beauty" (Andersen and Yttri 1997). Once faith was lost in the beauty, the slogan was adopted and used for aluminum instead.

Hydro is presently one of the few companies in the world with a continuous and viable hundred-year history, and it was one of the key "industrial locomotives" in the Norwegian modernization processes. By 2007 some key figures of Hydro were the following: 25,000 employees, of whom only 7,000 were located in Norway; operations in more than thirty countries; annual turnover above NOK 100 billion and market capitalization (stock exchange value) of NOK 99 billion.[11] By April 2010 the number of employees had fallen to 19,000 and market capitalization to NOK 55 billion.[12]

For understanding the impact and role of the large corporations, both domestically and internationally, Hydro's self-description as the world's third-largest "integrated aluminium company" provides a clue. In the evolutionary history of the corporation, development has tended toward increasing internal control over key processes to reduce risk. A central strategy has been to integrate the whole of the "value chain" in aluminum production within formal corporate boundaries, from upstream extraction of bauxite and alumina, to energy production and primary production of aluminum, to midstream casthouse products and alloys, to downstream fabricated products. The business is highly knowledge- and capital-intensive, as well as competitive. It is a common misperception to regard only "downstream" (in the value chain) types of activities as the only ones that are research- and knowledge-based. Both upstream and, not least, "midstream" activities in smelter and casthouse activities have been intensely driven by research, and more broadly, knowledge. Dedicated research and development activities occupy approximately 500 people and annually $85 million within Hydro alone.[13] As documented by several academic publications, the midstream activities are indeed heavily research-intensive (Wulff 1992; Øye and Ryum 1997; Sand et al. 2005; Karlsen 2008). Interestingly, although the vast majority of production, sales, and employees are located outside of Norway, both top management and income tax payments are concentrated in Norway.

An additional important characteristic is that among the top 200 managers in Hydro Aluminium only 16 percent were women in 2010. The figure for top 50 managers was 21 percent.[14] Managing in Hydro is to a large extent a "man's world" (Røyrvik 2008a).

The investment projects I am investigating in the present work have been international Hydro collaborative efforts with the aim of establishing production facilities in both midstream and downstream business, in

Table 1. Distribution of Hydro Activities and Characteristics

	Norway	Europe	Rest of world	Women
Employees	6.019	12.719	3.896	19%
Management top 50	87%	13% non-norwegians		19%
Management top 200	65%	35% non-norwegians		17%
Production:*				
Primary	1019	438	342	
Remelt	135	585	380	
Products	220	1530		
Total	1374	3275		
Tot. rec. injuries (TRI)	3.8			
Sick leave	3.4%			
Income tax	1.002	481	335	
Revenue	88.643			
Investments	9.012			
Greenhouse gas em.	4.1			

All figures for 2008, except * for 2006. Production in thousand tonnes; TRI per million working hours; income tax, revenue and investments in NOK million; greenhouse gas emissions measured by million tonnes CO_2e.
Source: Hydro Annual Report 2008 and Hydro members.

Spain, China, and Qatar. The global flavor of the projects is illustrated by the fact that the Qatar project team included more than 100 persons working from their "home base" in more than ten different countries.

Organization of the Book

From the research focus of investigating managing actions in relation to a set of Hydro international investment projects, the problem complex, as outlined above, is unfolded along two main analytical organizing pillars, each comprising one part of the book, indicated by a key investigative construct: "Technology" (Part I) and "Economy" (Part II). The perspective advocates a holistic approach, and the main pillars are interconnected in numerous ways. Each pillar contains elements of the other and they are as such mutually constituted, but at the same time each of the major aspects of the problem complex is elevated and highlighted in this analytical framing. As indicated above and further elaborated below, these main parts are inspired by both *political economy* and *cultural economics* perspectives.

In Part I of the book, "Construction and Cultures of Creation," the main focus is descriptions and analysis questioning "technology" in relation to management of projects. The first chapter situates the work in relevant academic streams and discussions in theory and method. It outlines the main tensions between varying perspectives and practices of what constitutes value and how "it" is constructed, hence an outline of "cultures of creation."

Seen as an anthropological issue, the research focus on *managing practices in international investment projects for industrial production in a capitalist nonfinancial corporation* has many literature streams "leading up to it." While few, if any, target the subject matter directly, the chapter gives a brief overview of relevant literature concerning some of the major academic debates. This theoretical dialogue is important because the volume is cast as an ethnographic extended case study and is thus both theoretically and empirically driven. Relevant issues in economic anthropology as well as organizational and industrial anthropology are covered, alongside discussion of key concerns in managing, modernity, and forms of rationality. A brief outline of the research design and methodological considerations is presented, leading up to a description of the approach of the *ethnographic extended case method* that inspired the study. Significantly, it utilizes participant observation to locate everyday life in its "extralocal" and historical context.

In Chapter 2, "Managing in the Middle Kingdom," the question of technology is addressed directly, and the "instruments" used in interpreting and mastering both nature and the culture related to investment projects are discussed. The questioning of technology is addressed by empirically describing the managing involved in bringing forth a set of three Hydro investment projects in China. I analyze the understanding and disputes surrounding the role of "technology" in a broad definition of the term and discuss, in light of this, the "nature of technology"—as both technology of production and technology of enchantment (Gell 1988)—in terms of its implications in projects and in Hydro at large. The move from technology to the commodification and commercialization of culture is analyzed, as is the way it implies a move in management from idioms of engineering to idioms of finance.

In Chapter 3, "Presencing Projects," some of the main themes from the foregoing chapter are continued. I outline some of the mechanisms and idioms of what I call the *social reality of construction* in the field of managing to bring forth industrial projects in Hydro. Here "technologies" of project genesis are in focus. Some of the key instruments and constructs identified are "process structuring," "concentration and projection," and "intersubjective intentionality." Through these phenomena the projects' "coming into being," their balancing on the "edge of oblivion," and their emergence to presence(ing), realization, and robustness are understood in terms of fundamental processes related to enabling an ethos of collective creation and coherence to unfold. The fragility of projects is highlighted by the universally "tragic" track record of large investment projects historically, cross-sector–wise, and cross-culturally. Worldwide, a successful large project is more the exception than the rule. While Hydro at large is identified as being constituted by a "project culture," its project results are also convincing, and Hydro is considered "top of the class" in terms of managing projects. The differences and relationships between its abstract "project management models" and the practices of management are scrutinized, and the objectification and commoditization of relational, contextual, and transcendental aspects of project work is thematized. Projects are revealed to be foundationally characterized by their *potentialities*, and the metaphor of the "imagination bank" is used to describe this reality.

In Part II, "High Finance and Contemporary Crisis Capitalism," the point of departure for the investigation of management in investment projects is questions related directly to finance and money—issues of economy. Here the financialization of Hydro and its management practices comes more directly into view. In Chapter 4, "The Turn to Enchantment," the investment projects are exposed from the angle of financing and practices conventionally associated with "economy." The chapter analyzes the financial constraints within which the Hydro investment projects are embedded and partly constituted. It describes a set of practices and cultural transformations in both project work and the corporation in general that in sum signifies the strong "turn to finance" that has emerged since the millennium shift. Still positioned strongly as "production capitalist," Hydro's management practices have to a considerable extent adapted to the logic of the finance economy, for example through notions like value-based management, the importance of shareholder value, and the adoption of finance control mechanisms throughout the company. Also highly significant, the introduction of the main project management methodology by the name of Capital Value Process (CVP) instantiates the change.

In Chapter 5, "Wagging the Dog," the analysis from the previous chapters continues in the "macro" direction. Here, Hydro's turn to finance is further investigated, and the wider constraints that are constitutive of this shift are identified. This discussion reveals a set of tensions that is generalized to the conditions of the integrated globalized capitalist economic system as a whole, as it is instantiated in contemporary forms of neoliberal financialization. Hydro's movement from production to value creation to value appreciation is identified, and Hydro's positioning in relation to constraints and changes in the Norwegian form of "democratic capitalism" is discussed. This broader movement is symptomatic of an overall "reenchantment" of the whole capitalist economic and social "world system" of relations, and signifies moreover the contemporary crisis of fundamental scope and depth. Illustrated by Hydro's ambiguous positioning in the contemporary global economy, the hegemony of the finance economy is now akin to the tail that is wagging the productive economy dog.

Chapter 6, "Money Manager Capitalism and Reverse Redistribution," presents and analyzes two further major bodies of empirical material indicative of Hydro's "turn to finance." First, its stock options compensation program and the loud critical debate it instigated in the Norwegian popular media are discussed. The options debate illustrates the moral economy also at work at the "core of capitalism." Secondly, Hydro's investment-related financial risk management strategies are presented, whereby the disjunction between the productive and the financial economy is illustrated. Generally, an interconnected double shift has occurred: while capitalism changed its locus from production to finance, management moved from engineering to "money managers." The chapter paints an overall picture of how the wealth redistribution of currently dominating finance capital has a parasitic effect on the wealth generation processes of production capital, and how wealth is radically and reversely redistributed *upward* in the system, thus contradicting the distributive power mandate as identified by, for example, both Marcel Mauss and Karl Polanyi. The total effect creates devastating economic inequalities and reconstitutes (finance) elite class and power. The discussion moves on to depict consequences in terms of global stratification and patterns of inequality, as well as the acute dire straits of the current crisis in the capitalist system—possibly the most dramatic in the entire history of capitalism.

In the final, third part of the book, "In Good Company?" I summarize and expand upon the main threads, synergic points, and continuing questions of the present work. The broad issues of management, modernity, and capitalism as they relate to morality, globalization, and economic development are outlined, the current state of the deep crisis in capitalism is fleshed out, and anticipations about the future are given. Chapter 7, "Directors and Directions of Creation," first reprises and reviews the major foregoing issues. It is proposed that, in order to fight poverty and enable broader economic development, the democratization and dissemination of the productive, real wealth powers of capitalism that enable the creation of a higher economic horizon must proliferate. Homogeneous notions of "managing rationality" are questioned, and in terms of "qualifying capitalism" the need for conceptual differentiation of economic spheres also within capitalism is substantiated. Not only has managing itself been differentially legitimated both historically and cross-culturally in the contemporary scene, but capitalist economic activities more generally differ qualitatively in terms of their real wealth–creating potential and moral underpinnings. Thus capitalist corporations *are* different, and they can be normatively assessed differently. Not only is there a difference between financial and nonfinancial corporations, each linked with two radically different processes of historical capitalism, but there are also huge differentiations in both the external relationships and the inside workings of these two broad categories. At Hydro, tensions arose when a particular democratic and personal participatory, technocratic managing tradition was partially substituted with an emerging financially based and what I label "accountocratic" tradition. The turn to financial management and financialization is described as a trait of the whole globalized economy, which has emerged as "money manager capitalism."

In the final chapter, "Managing in a Total Context of Crisis," I conclude by positioning Hydro's management practices in terms of some alleged universal features of precapitalist economies. These are the different "transactional orders" in economies, which in turn are justified by quite oppositional moral values and idioms. Finding that the notion of transactional orders applies also to the capitalist system, I position Hydro in the "medium range view," where it is in one sense ambiguously situated within different orders. The moral philosophical debate over the inception of capitalism, the corporate form, and the establishment of the institution of management is invoked to cast a new light upon the contemporary predicament. Substantial qualifications of both management and capitalism are also proposed, indicated in the conception of "mixed regimes of rationality." The chapter discusses the state and gravity of the current global economic collapse, and reflects on the possibility of future new modes of global political economy and cultural forms, potentially rising like a phoenix from the ashes of the crisis. To that effect, I again call forth the notion of the common weal—of a "tragedy or triumph of the commons."

Notes

1. Fieldwork interview, 9 May 2007.
2. Most prominently the national boundaries crossed are related to the Norwegian heritage and top managerial and ownership control of Hydro in relation to projects, the Hydro organization at large, and Hydro as a "global company" in globalized world. *Organizational* boundaries refer mostly to internal divisions, sub-units, and organizations within Hydro, while *epistemic* boundaries relate mostly to the "engineer versus economist" relation.
3. Or "money capital," using Marx's terminology. Conceptions of "money" and "capital" may lead to various forms of confusion. In common usage among the people in this study, the two terms are frequently interchanged. When they use the term "capital"

in meanings other than "money capital," usually another term is put in front of it, as in "human capital" or "social capital." Referring to phenomena included in "productive capital" in Marx's terminology, they use concepts like "technology," "competence," "human resources," and "knowledge."

4. Although difficult to estimate, the exact number BIS gives for June 2008 is $683.726 billion, which decreased to $591.963 billion by December 2008. The by far largest volumes of derivatives contracts were interest rate contracts, particularly interest rate swaps, amounting to $458 and $419 trillion for June and December 2008 (BIS 2009).

5. The figure compares the market value of Hydro as a conglomerate comprising three main divisions (Oil and Energy, Aluminium, and Agri) in 1999, with the combined market value of these three divisions as divested into three separate companies in 2007.

6. As such the study also touches upon the field of "anthropology of development and globalization" (Edelman and Haugerud 2005).

7. Of what is here lumped together as "finance" (MM') variants, we might note that Marx distinguished between two broad types; "trade capital" (again comprising "commodity trade capital" and "money trade capital") and "interest bearing capital." It would possibly be fruitful to outline a more rigid scheme describing the various pre- and noncapitalist and capitalist commodity and money circuits based on the letters M and C. The following proposition is made by economic anthropologist and philosopher of science Stein E. Johansen (personal communication), where the A's designate pre- or noncapitalist forms of production and exchange, and the B's capitalist commodity circuits:

A1 CMC   Simple commodity circuit
A2 MCM   Simple money circuit (simple merchant commodity trade)
A2 MM(m)   Simple direct money circuit (simple merchant money trade)
A3 MM(r)   Simple conflated money circuit (simple rent from credit)
B MCM'   Universal capital circuit
B1 MCM'(p) Complex primary money circuit (capital production)
B2 MCM'(c) Complex secondary money circuit (merchant commodity capital trade)
B2 MM'(m)   Complex direct money circuit (merchant money capital trade)
B3 MM'(r)   Complex conflated money circuit (capital rent from credit)

8. *The History of Hydro* comprises three volumes; see Lie (2005), Andersen (2005) and Johannessen et al. (2005).

9. There is by now a quite extensive academic literature on "project management." However, this tradition has evolved from "operations analysis," with overly positivistic emphasis on rationalistic control mechanisms and simplistic assumptions about complexity and communicative interaction in social networks. For a critical review see for example Cicmil and Hodgson (2006). As analytical or conceptual resources this literature's relevance for my study is limited, and a review is not embarked upon here. To the extent necessary, this body of work is invoked when brought forward by direct reference in the empirical material.

10. All of it, and more, is available at www.hydro.com. Some of their own presentations are utilized here.

11. Hydro, "Investor Presentation," July 2007.

12. Hydro, "Investor Presentation," April 2010.

13. Trygve B. Svendsen, Plant Manager Sunndal, Norway, Capital Markets Day Presentation, 5 September 2007.

14. Hydro Annual Report 2010.

Part I

Construction and Cultures of Creation

Chapter 1

SITUATING
"GLOBAL CORPORATE MANAGEMENT"

... there are always, in any society, conflicts between symbolic
powers that aim at imposing the vision of legitimate divisions...
—Pierre Bourdieu, "Social Space and Symbolic Power"

Follow your nose wherever it leads you.
—Max Gluckman, "The Extended Case"[1]

But fools with tools are still fools...
—Norman O. Brown, *Apocalypse and/or Metamorphosis*

The current phase of the cultural history of capitalism seems to provide
particularly favorable conditions for studying the ambiguities and dilemmas, the creations and destructions of capitalism, and the multiplicities
and complexities of "a" capitalism turned planetary. One of the primary
characteristics of contemporary capitalist societies is the thriving development and excess multiplication of organizations. The "modern world"
is "a society of organizations," and arguably chief among them is the corporation—a key capitalist institution since the invention and widespread
establishment of the "limited liability joint-stock company," incorporated
as a "legal person," in the latter half of the nineteenth century (Micklethwait and Wooldridge 2003; Bakan 2004). As Berle and Means con-
templated in 1932, the development and multiplication of what they

called the "quasi-public corporation," so as to differentiate it from the private company "proper," caused a revolution in socioeconomic organization. The most radical invention was the "separation of ownership from control," in that it "produces a condition where the interests of owner and of ultimate manager may, and often do, diverge, and where many of the checks which formerly operated to limit the use of power disappear" (1991: 7). Writing from the premises of neoclassical economic theory's assumptions about individual ownership and private property, Berle and Means correctly identified the emergence of something qualitatively new: "In creating these new relationships, the quasi-public corporation may fairly be said to work a revolution. It has destroyed the unity we commonly call property.... Thereby the corporation has changed the nature of profit-seeking enterprise" (ibid.). In separating owners from control, the neoclassically perceived "holy" unity was broken, and managers were created as a new and previously unknown consequence of the invention of the modern corporation. Below I discuss more thoroughly the neoclassical foundations and tensions of the corporation, and of management.

Corporate management has by now become a key institution in modern societies, and while Peter Drucker, arguably the most influential thinker on management theory and practice, expressed ample reasons for studying modern organizational management thoroughly half a century ago, there is still no tradition of anthropological management research. Drucker wrote:

> The emergence of management as an essential, a distinct and a leading institution is a pivotal event in social history. Rarely, if ever, has a new basic institution, a new leading group, emerged as fast as has management since the turn of the century. Rarely in human history has a new institution proven indispensable so quickly; and even less often has a new institution arrived with so little opposition, so little disturbance, so little controversy. (1954: 3)

The inception of management can be traced to the American discourse among engineers in the US in the years from 1880 to 1932 (Shenhav 1999), the latter year being the date when Berle and Means announced the "managerial revolution" (1991; cf. Dalton 1959; Mintzberg 1973). Shenhav exposes the "process by which managerial rationality crystallized to become the unquestioned pacemaker of the modern social order" while playing a critical role in "diffusing repertoires of instrumental rationality worldwide" (1999: 2). A study of corporate management is thus a study of key aspects of modernization and modern forms of rationality. And while there is indeed ethnography of formal organizations and corporations, and a rich variety of occupational ethnographies, there are but a few comprehensive ethnographies specifically focusing on corporate management, where Watson (1994) and possibly Jackall (1989) serve as examples.

Although anthropological efforts to discuss managing, for example in relation to "meaning" (Gowler and Legge 1983) and "magic" (Cleverley 1971), have ensued, and Sørhaug (2004) addresses managing in the knowledge economy in terms of his concise concept of "mangementality," none of these are based on in-depth ethnographic investigation. Thus Linstead notes: "There is no extensive tradition of sociological participant observation in *management* research" (1997: 96). The ethnographically based collection of essays in Dubinskas (1988) touches upon issues of managing by way of studying technologically advanced organizations, but only marginally, and the focus is on time or temporality in organizing. Ho's in-depth discussion of managerialism in relation to financial work is an exception in this overall picture (2009). In particular, few if any ethnographies have been especially focused on "global corporate management." And ethnography is in great demand in management and organizational research, importantly as an alternative to the increasing convergence, especially in American journals, on a positivistic "factor analytic" version of grounded theory that "commonly reduces large amounts of qualitative data into meaningful 'factors' that are theoretically derived from the data but can also be generalized to other similar contexts" (The Editors 2011: 198).

There are thus ample reasons for ethnographically based anthropological contributions to the study of corporate managing in the globalized economy. As such, this volume is also a contribution to an anthropology of contemporary *expert* and professional *elites*, a study that is, according to Holmes and Marcus, long deferred and awaited, and that "by this time is belated" (2005: 248). While discussing the study of management more thoroughly below, I will ground the present study also in a dialogue with the other contingent theoretical fields in which an anthropology of global corporate management is situated. In addition to the emergence and dominance of management itself, I discuss most notably economic anthropology and the neoclassical economic theories and neoliberal premises within which both contemporary corporate management and global economic relations are dominantly constituted. Finally I will briefly outline the research approach and perspective.

Hydro's Ambiguous Position

During the unfolding of my research process, increasingly I came to realize that Hydro Aluminium[2] proved to be an exemplary corporate context for illuminating some of the most basic ambiguities, asymmetries, and complexities of the developmental processes and contemporary predicament of economic globalization. Hydro illustrates a vast range of the tensions and paradoxes of the world economic canvas. Its history reflects the complex transformations of the industrial society into the so-called "knowledge society": Hydro is presently viewed both as a "traditionally industrial" and a "knowledge firm," with a leg in both the "old" and the "new" economy. Hydro furthermore manifests the tensions between the national and the supranational, because it is a flagship national company of Norway and at the same time a multinational or "global" company with a presence in more than thirty countries. Hydro may also educationally illustrate some of the basic mechanisms by which asymmetries and inequalities of contemporary economic life on the global scale came about and are reproduced and expanded. Just as the massive circulation and accumulation of money worldwide is in fact concentrated mainly in a few rich countries, so are the bulk of Hydro's activities.

In the wake of the establishment of the modern Norwegian state by the end of the nineteenth century, Hydro was conceived and quickly developed the role of a major locomotive in the Norwegian industrialization process, and subsequently the welfare state. Hydro has arguably been the single most important industrial company in Norwegian history. And quite contrary to the economic structures and processes that enabled Norway's transition out of poverty, the rules Hydro must play by today are prescribed by the hegemony of a financialized economic order that is ideologically legitimated by neoliberalism or neoliberalization (see below and Part II). This climate is upheld by what "pro-globalizer" Bhagwati (2004) has labeled the "Wall Street–Treasury complex," including the Washington institutions of the IMF and the World Bank. Whatever complex processes "globalization" is a shorthand designation for, what is historically remarkable in the present situation, as Edelman and Haugerud note, "is the celebration of a particular form of globalization—economic neoliberalism" (2005: 23). Over the last thirty years or so the neoliberalized playbook has accelerated the devastating global economic inequalities (see below and Chapter 6).

Hydro, also in its capacity as being partly state-owned, is a formidable exploratory example and thinking device in making sense of the complex and historically changing relationships between the state and interstate system on the one hand and the market economy on the other, which in different configurations have constituted the various capitalisms that so profoundly shape the contemporary globalized world order. Although partly state-owned, Hydro might also be seen to exemplify bourgeois society (economy), as demarcated to include both the family and the private sphere on the one hand, and on the other the democratic state (politics), in Hegel's trilateral differentiation.

Hydro's status in the contemporary capitalist mode of production is certainly ambiguous, not only because the Norwegian state owns 34.26 percent of the company (as of 2011), but also because of its uneasy positioning in a cultural and economic matrix increasingly defined by finance and consumerism. As will be discussed at length, while Hydro's "production capitalism" is increasingly defined in terms set by a financialized economic order, it cannot ultimately feel at home in the stereotypical idioms of "consumer culture" (Douglas and Isherwood 1996; Miller 1997a). As noted by Comaroff and Comaroff: "As consumption became the moving spirit of the late twentieth century, so there was a concomitant eclipse of production; an eclipse, at least, of its *perceived* salience for the wealth of nations" (2001: 4, italics in original).[3] Hydro, as a knowledge-based, industrial corporation that does not produce directly for consumer markets, is to some extent, and differently so, positioned in a tensional relationship with both "cultures of finance" and "consumer culture."

The context of the present study, the "production" of corporate capitalist investment projects, also highlights some of the shortcomings of much of economic anthropology. A major problem lies in its almost exclusive focus on barter, exchange, and transactions, and on consumption, at the expense of production in various forms, not least "knowledge-based" production.[4] As Reidar Grønhaug notes: "In terms of economy… contemporary anthropologists have by and large abdicated the task, with the exception of some studies on consumption and identity" (2001: 66, my trans.). Industrial production has, however, received its fair share of attention in industrial sociology and anthropology, often with a Marxist outlook. The approach in the present work also draws to some extent upon Marxist notions of capital. However, for all their differences, Marxist theory and classical (and to some extent neoclassical) economic theories share one basic fundamental premise: the labor theory of value.[5] As Reinert argues, production, knowledge, and invention were lost in the economic theory of Adam Smith, because he reduced both production and trade to "labor hours." David Ricardo, following Smith in this respect, created an "even more abstract theory of 'labor'—a concept devoid of any qualities—as the measuring rod for value" (Reinert 2007: 41). Because the proper interpretation of Marx theory of value, as Harvey notes, "is a matter of great contention" (2006: 35), I shall here just note that although significant differences exist among Marxist and liberal labor theories of value, their common premise on variants of the labor theory of value overshadows some other important possibilities.

The present analysis thus illustrates the "predicament of production" in this climate, and as Reinert notes, "It is in the sphere of production that the best arguments both against and for globalization are to be found" (2004: 75, my trans.). Hydro still keeps the "banner" of knowledge-based production high, in the midst of an economic and cultural context of consumer and finance pressures and expansions, and its investment projects epitomize its ambiguous positioning at the crossroads of production and finance capitalism. Choosing to gloss over many of the "great contentions" in these debates, an overall focus on qualitatively void labor hour accounting consequentially reduces and conflates the modern economic sphere of activities because it downplays notions of human creative powers, imagination, knowledge, and wisdom—of the "human spirit," as stressed in, for example, Germany's historical school of economics and its engineering tradition. This latter domain is vividly described by Goethe's term *Willenskraft* and Nietzsche's *Geist und Willenskapital*, man's "wit and will" (Reinert and Reinert 2006).

Some of these notions, including those of *Schöpfungskraft* and *Schöpfungslust* (the power, desire and joy of creation), akin to possibly more familiar constructs like *Homo faber* and *Homo ludens*, man the maker and player, were continuing ideas in the German economic and philosophical tradition. Articulated by thinkers like Henri Bergson, Hannah Arendt, and Max Frisch, *Homo faber* refers to humans as controlling the environment through tools. Henri Bergson referred to it in his *Creative Evolution* as defining intelligence in its original sense: as the "faculty of manufacturing artificial objects, especially tools to make tools, and of indefinitely varying the manufacture" (2007 [1907]: 153–154). *Homo faber* identifies "man as the tool-making animal," but it also indicates "the working man," who is confronted and completed by *Homo ludens*, the "playing man" concerned with joy, humor, and leisure. *Homo faber* is also related to the concept of *deus faber*, God the creator or the "making God." In this sense we can also recognize the notion of man the creator, *Homo creator*, who like God may create and bring new things into the world, that emerged during the Renaissance (Larsen 2009). The power to create is related to both the joy and pain of the process of creation. A notion captured by the old Hindu conceptions of creation and destruction and introduced to nineteenth-century European discourse as "creative destruction" by Nietzsche, it was brought into economics by Werner Sombart and subsequently made famous by Schumpeter (Reinert and Reinert 2006).

These ideas, perceived as major, spiritually based "productive powers" that create innovations and fundamentally different types of economic activities, are reflected in Schumpeter's twentieth-century notion of the "entrepreneur" (1982 [1939], 2008 [1942]), with different types of consequences in turn for bourgeois society, and for economic and social life. Schumpeter's entrepreneur, whom he sees as the most vital force in capital formation, is not a risk-taking speculator but an innovator driven by the joy of creation, the drive to introduce the new. Indeed, Schumpeter foresaw the "obsolescence of capital's entrepreneurial function and its replacement by a mechanized, routine form of economic progress dictated by management rationality and the faceless gray suits that populate boardrooms" (Hardt and Negri 2009: 297). And if it loses its innovative and entrepreneurial power, capital cannot survive for long either, according to Schumpeter: "We have seen that the function of entrepreneurs is to reform or revolutionize the pattern of production by exploiting an invention or … an untried technological possibility…. It consists in getting things done…. This social function is already losing importance" (Schumpeter 1942: 132). Should this function be lost, the vitality of capitalist evolution vanishes and capital undermines itself, and by implication also the middle class (bourgeois) upon which capitalism rests.

Schumpeter's prediction has proved correct, judging by the current crisis. At the core of the crisis is the failure, since the 1970s, to invest profits in innovative and productive real wealth–generating activities, and the choice to instead pour investments into more or less pure financial speculation, concomitantly "innovating" radically in this latter realm. This failure might to a large extent be attributed to a decline in the entrepreneurial function in society, a decline that has eroded the capacities for creating opportunities for productive investments and realizing innovations. Schumpeter's true innovating entrepreneurs were to a large extent substituted or transformed either into mechanized "managerial" administrators and/or "money managers," and creative financial speculators (see Part II).

Changing Configurations of Value

In the development toward a more immaterial "knowledge economy," Tian Sørhaug notices a shift or a drift with respect to economic ontology (2004: 278). The constitution of what economic objects "are" has changed. His argument is that the dominating capital objects now are abstract. He tries to capture the shift through the metaphorical contrast between a machine and the *invention* of the machine. A similar contrast is found in the relationship of the product and the *concept* of the product. The invention and the concept are moving to center stage, and can be perceived as the presence of a relation. As project work in Hydro to a large extent is idea and "concept work," some of these ontological considerations will be elaborated in Chapter 3. Some of these insights have been in circulation at least since the Renaissance, but arguably there is something particular in the current relationship between the abstract and physical objects. Regarding the eclipse of production, Grant argues that if we apply a "knowledge theory of the firm" perspective, the importance of production is not lost, being still "the most important and complex means of value creation" (Grant 1996: 111). I argue, however, that in the financialized economy, creation of anticipations of value and value "origination" seem to have become the dominant form of production.

As will be shown later, we are seeing a move from "productive value creation" to expectation-based "value appreciation." In the anticipatory game of value appreciation, the machine and the product, and the knowledge about the machine and the product, we might add, are only indirectly value-creating. The ontological realm of the physical object is, as Sørhaug notes, primarily an excuse for value appreciation, which is in a sense the value creation of the abstract objects (2004). We have seen the same dynamics also in earlier historical periods of capitalism, when "high finance" emerged and dominated extensively, moving from symbiosis to parasitism in its relationship to productive capital (Arrighi 1994; Reinhart and Rogoff 2009; Appendix).

Nevertheless, certain specialties seem to characterize the contemporary constitution of the relation because of the need to differentiate between qualitatively different types of both physical and abstract objects. The relationship constituted in the contemporary financialized economy of abstract value appreciation has arguably reached a stage of appreciating expectation values *between* abstract objects, evolving beyond, and to a large extent released from, the relations with the physical objects—even positing itself as a space beyond the power of representation. The explosion in the financial derivatives economy is in this respect exemplary, having grown, as noted in the introduction, from probably only a few million dollars in 1970 to about $600 trillion in 2007. Meanwhile the GDP of all the countries in the world combined is only about 60 trillion dollars (BIS 2009), and growth in GDP has been steadily *declining* over the last thirty years or so (Maddison 2001; Harvey 2005). The move to abstract economic objects was more a transformation than a drift.

Investment Projects as "Global Assemblages"

In the continuation of two of the most important "ideal types" of capitalism—production and finance capitalism—Hydro furthermore illustrates the struggle between two fundamentally different corpuses of economic theories and economic history of thought: exchange theories (the "standard canon" of mainstream economics), and knowledge- and production-based theories, which economist Erik S. Reinert and others have labeled "the other canon" (Reinert 2007).[6] A key feature of the other canon is that creating wealth and welfare is seen as *activity-specific*. That some countries "get rich" is to a large extent the result of their engagement in certain economic activities rather than others. Following the credo that economic activities in modern capitalism are *qualitatively* different, one of the main points in the other canon is that activities yielding high potential for wealth creation are those that create, emulate, and absorb new knowledge and technology (ideas, inventions, innovations). The conditions that bring forth such activities have been known since the Renaissance and the heyday of the Italian city-states from which capitalism emerged.

Simplified, the core tenet is that wealth is created in synergistic clusters of activities with a complex division of labor, displaying increasing returns and continuous and innovative mechanization. These activities are generally found in manufacturing, enabled by the machine process and advances in organizing. Thus some knowledge is more valuable, in terms of its capacity for wealth creation, than other knowledge; consequently, if a state or nation is to prosper it is in its interest to create and protect such knowledge. This valuable knowledge emanates from the mind and souls of people. This concept is described above in terms such as *Willenskraft, Geist und Willenskapital*, man's "wit and will," and *Schöpfungskraft and Schöpfungslust* (the power, desire, and joy of creation), and not taking these into consideration would deprive any theory of understanding the processes by which humanity's material condition is reproduced and increased—that is, the processes of wealth creation and economic growth (Reinert 1997: 250). The emphasis here is on understanding the importance of both the "common weal" and the imaginative creational powers of individuals. Notable thinkers and traditions of the other canon include Giovanni Botero and Antonia Serra from the late sixteenth and early seventeenth century, to Friedrich List, from German cameralism and antiphysiocracy to the German historical school, to Thorstein Veblen and the institutional school in one direction, and to Schumpeter and evolutionary economics in another. Thinkers as diverse as Marx and Keynes, Kaldor, Minsky, Myrdal, Penrose, and Polanyi have also presented elements of this alternative canon.[7]

These two idealized theoretical trajectories, or canons, reflect different worldviews that have governed economic policies and practices of capitalism and globalization since the emergence of capitalism and the interstate system in the fifteenth and sixteenth centuries.[8] By extensively studying the management of projects to establish new factories as cross-cultural "global assemblages," I have been studying the basic processes that have enabled modern capitalism to flourish and made some states wealthy. Today, Holmes and Marcus contend (2005), as the political economy of the nation-state is effaced by transnational forces, the overarching interpretive challenge for the ethnographer is to gain access to the practices of expert subjects, through which their knowledge work, society, and economy are re-created, and new formations of political economy emerge. Moreover, as Edelman and Haugerud note: "The seismic economic and political changes associated with neoliberal globalization coincided with anthropology's turn away from macro-narratives, grand theory, and realist ethnography" (2005: 17). By studying the processes of bringing forth "projects for industrial production" (for realization in Norway, Spain, China, and Qatar) ethnographically, I intend to provide both a somewhat detailed picture and an outline of critical differentials in the workings of capitalism in the contemporary neoliberal financialized moment of the renewed era of globalization since the 1970s.

As Hannerz notes, anthropologists should be "wary of terms which come into fashion and where the border between analytical scrutiny and political cliché threatens to become blurred" (2007: 2). He continues, however, to conclude in the same vein as my realizations: "Yet it seems undeniable that in the last couple of decades or so we have seen the emergence of a major, more or less worldwide set of ideas and practices which I would describe as a neoliberal culture complex" (ibid.). The recurring buzzwords characterizing this culture complex are, according to Hannerz, *accountability, transparency, privatization, quality control, branding, auditing, excellence,* and *ranking.* As will be illustrated and exemplified throughout the following text, this worldwide culture complex is a most relevant historical and macro-contextual background of the present empirical investigation. Moreover, the culture complex is felt in everyday lives throughout the world. The field sites and "fieldflows" that I have investigated have thus revealed the possibility of an analysis of some of the processes at the core of the emergence of contemporary forms of the more or less worldwide neoliberal capitalist culture complex. This possibility arose because the types of projects under investigation are characterized by a particular "global quality," in the sense specified by Collier and Ong describing the term "global assemblages": "They are abstractable, mobile, and dynamic, moving across and reconstituting 'society,' 'culture,' and 'economy'" (2005: 4). These projects embody a specific global form in the contemporary, and as such they can be described as instantiating a particular form of node, or abstracted materialization, in the flows of the global.

Framed through the recently popular concept of *assemblages* (Marcus and Saka 2006), my ethnographically investigated projects can also be described thus: "As global forms are articulated in specific situations—or territorialized in *assemblages*—they define new material, collective, and discursive relationships" (Collier and Ong 2005: 4). In recent cultural analysis "assemblage" has provided a "structure-like" anti-structural surrogate concept enabling researchers to "speak of emergence, heterogeneity, the decentered and the ephemeral in nonetheless ordered social life" (Marcus and Saka 2006: 101). Following Latour (2005), the "sociality" in these relationships is not seen as some sort of essential quality that can be discovered or measured, but rather means something connected or "assembled." Likewise, in his moves to trace the social, the first move consists in "localizing the global," in the sense of realizing that there is no "global" but a chain of connected localities: "No place can be said to be bigger than any other place, but some can be said to benefit from far safer connections with many more places than others" (ibid.: 176). The second move in tracing the social is to recognize that the local is never confined to one place, and thus to redistribute the local, in a sense to "globalize the local." The third move then becomes to recognize what seems to be both global and local consists of, and is the product of, many connected times and places.

A question that remains is what reproduces and changes the stability of the connections, what lifts the social into hierarchies above the "flatland." Study in a formal, corporate context brings some of the answers to these questions into focus: the processes of standardization, formalization and classification. Adhering to the argument of Collier and Ong, the empirically investigated investment projects constitute forms of global assemblages and are thus sites for the "formation and reformation of what we will call … *anthropological problems*. They are domains in which the forms and values of individual and collective existence are problematized or at stake, in the sense that they are subject to technological, political, and ethical reflection and intervention" (2005: 4). Thus, these investment projects for industrial production, brought forth by Hydro as both localizing the global and globalizing the local "all over the world," are in this book framed as a form of global assemblages that poses anthropological problems for investigation. And the tensions inherent in the concept of global assemblages should be emphasized because they are also key to my concern with investment projects on the "global scale": "global implies broadly encompassing, seamless, and mobile; assemblage implies heterogeneous, contingent, unstable, partial, and situated" (ibid.: 12).

Hydro is an integrated light metals company. That is, it covers the entire value chain in the light metals industry, from upstream alumina mining at the one end, through a variety of midstream products for industrial and construction use, to providing key parts in consumer goods at the other (downstream) end. This is interesting because Hydro businesses thus cover the range from what are now commonly categorized as highly "resource-based" economic activities, to highly "knowledge-based" activities. The advanced services Hydro delivers may also be included in the latter category. This situation offers a possibility for studying how qualitatively different economic activities are constituted under radically different constraints and premises, and how they create a variety of effects. For example, the economic "laws" of diminishing versus increasing returns (Arthur 1994), as inherent to qualitatively different types of economic activities, have an impact on economic inequality, wealth generation, and asymmetric accumulation and distribution, among other things. Hydro activities are exemplary "increasing returns" economic activities, situated both in the process industry and in advanced manufacturing. These activities have created and absorbed both new knowledge and new technologies (i.e., innovations and inventions) and huge amounts of productive capital investments for over a century, constantly generating real wage increases, something that testifies to the activities' huge potential in wealth creation. Before proceeding, it is worthwhile to revisit the anthropology of economic activities and discuss some notes on organizations and global industry.

Economic Anthropology Revisited

A study of corporate management in a global industrial firm like Hydro is positioned in a reflexive dialogue with economic anthropology and the anthropological study of organizations, business, and industry. During the last decade or two we have witnessed a substantive renaissance in the fields of industrial, organizational, and business anthropology—the anthropology of formal, purposeful organizations. It is conceptualized as a rebirth because anthropology was one of the prominent disciplinary founders of organization studies on the whole, proving especially significant in forming the Human Relations school, which was seriously launched in Chicago from World War I into the 1930s, spurred among other efforts most notably by the famous Hawthorne studies (Baba 1986; Schwartzman 1993; Jordan 2003). Industrial "factory studies" were conducted quite early on in the history of anthropology (see Gouldner 1954, and arguably Jaques 1951); furthermore it was anthropologists who established the first academic journal in organizational behavior (*Human Organization*), and the social anthropologist W. F. Whyte, a student of Radcliffe-Brown, who wrote the first textbook in the same field (1969).

"Organization theory" did not emerge until the 1950s, when it entered the discourse as a blend of theory of management/administration,

Human Relations, and systems theory (Jacques 1996). In turn systems theory merged with organization sociology and organization psychology during the 1960s (Czarniawska 2003: 432). Yet since the earliest days and until quite recently, the fields of anthropology and organization studies were drifting apart and have had very little to do with each other, at least when considering *organizations* as the unit of analysis (Czarniawska-Joerges 1992). A recently emerging trend, both with regard to theory and in some ethnographic studies, of putting anthropology and organization studies "back together" is noted by several authors (Bate 1997; Linstead 1997), but it is still too early to draw definite conclusions in this respect. As mentioned earlier, however, the approach in the present work depicts managing actions in the investment projects of the Hydro corporation as the starting point for an analysis of the reproduction of relations at several interconnected levels. While the unit of practical observation is the managing actions in investment projects in the Hydro corporation, this does not limit the units of analysis. Rather than depicting the projects and the corporation as restricting the units of analysis, the present work utilizes them as the empirical context from which both broader and deeper issues are investigated.

The anthropology of "global industry" is captured by Rothstein and Blim (1992), who present a research program that in a globalized world might supplant industrial sociology. Drawing on the anthropological legacy from the early factory studies, and studies that even before the 1930s had linked industrialization, local communities, and the wider society (e.g., Lynd and Lynd 1959 [1929]; Warner and Low 1947), they argue that the world has become a "global factory," in the sense that industrial production for the world market has spread to every continent and most regions worldwide. I share some of their propositions on the conjunctures of global capitalist production in the late twentieth century. First, "the global factory" must be seen as emerging within the context of an expanding and increasingly combined and uneven world capitalist economic growth; and secondly, in line with what I referred to in the Introduction as the Schumpeter-Chandlerian doctrine, manufacturing and industry must be considered the main growth engine in contemporary capitalism.

Economic anthropology is summarily divided into three broad bodies of theories and knowledge: (1) neoclassical microeconomics, or utilitarianism for short, (2) political economy (including Marxist *critique* of political economy), and (3) moral or cultural economics (Wilk and Cliggett 2007). These three broad bodies reflect moreover different basic views of rationality or faces of human nature: the selfish, social, and moral being (ibid.: 190). Notably, in this classification "the other canon" of uneven economic development (Reinert 2007),[9] of a spiritually inspired *Homo faber*, or Homo Creator, driven by knowledge and the joy of creation, has more or less disappeared from view. In addition to the "other canon" I will draw insights from all of these three traditions, in line with Wilk and Cliggett's invitation:

> [A] better way to think about the three models is to recognize that in practice we are always mixing them, shuffling through to find the one that best fits, or combining them on an ad hoc and case-by-case basis. In practice, most anthropologists make hybrid models by combining bits and pieces of middle-level theory, rules of thumb, and their own experiences. (2007: 184)

From the starting point in the empirical material and the focus on the *genesis* of investment projects, that is the origin and mode of formation of such projects, I have, contrary to most economic anthropologists (Gudeman 2008), found that utilitarist neoclassical microeconomics is of lesser constructive relevance. The critical reasons for this choice are more thoroughly described below, and thus I have in the present work to a large extent "substituted" neoclassical perspectives with insights from the "other canon" tradition. On the other hand, I draw extensively on the theoretical perspectives in various streams of both political economy (and its critique), and moral and cultural economics.

Indeed, as argued by Edelman and Haugerud (2005: 30), the specialization and atomization of social sciences and the humanities in the twentieth century were accompanied by a growing division between approaches to social change based on economics and politics on the one hand, and those based on cultural values and beliefs on the other. In line with the transdisciplinary, hybrid, and not least, integrative ambition of the present work, I seek here to bring aspects of these diverging streams of thought together. I interpret "the other canon" of economics also with an eye to linking insights from political economy, cultural economy, and aspects of microeconomics. While the political economy influence in the present work is obvious, the influence of "cultural economics" is possibly less clear. While differentiating these "social" (political economy) and "moral" (cultural economy) theoretical perspectives is sometimes difficult, as noted above, a key is their different approaches to rationality and human nature. The latter approach tends to focus "on the moral meanings of work, money, obligations, and other forms of exchange" (Wilk and Cliggett 2007: 120). Thinkers from Weber and Malinowski to Sahlins and Geertz argue that economic behavior is deeply embedded and constituted in cultural beliefs. Although universal human needs are often recognized, as with Malinowski, the forms these needs attain are seen to be culturally variable. In various ways this tradition relativizes rationality itself, depicting it as a social or cultural "product." This relativization has several implications, for example on the one hand a ranking and evaluation of cultures according to "levels of rationality," or on the other hand, a postmodern perspectivism that perceives morality and values as culturally relative symbolic systems of signs.

Whatever their differences, many writers in this tradition think "that the symbolic aspect of cultural order is the most basic and that this is why it is revealed most clearly through the study of primitive economic systems" (Wilk and Cliggett 2007: 143). There are several recent examples of this kind of research in modern economic contexts, works that are also heavily influenced by political economy, for example Hart's (2000), Bell's (2004), and Blim's (2005) work on wealth, money, and inequality in contemporary capitalism. In the investigation of aspects of economic life, moral issues are never far away, and in the present study the "cultural" approach to economics is focused, by the subject matter of industrial investment projects, on the management of industrial and financial production and thus on the creation and distribution of wealth on various levels and in different modes—and therefore on the moral and cultural corollaries thus implied.[10]

More generally due to the hegemony of neoclassical economic theory, and the ideological triumph of neoliberalism the last quarter century, as discussed below, production as the central tenet of modern economic activity seems to have been largely forgotten. Even in China, the new "workshop of the world," the subsumption of production under consumption has come a long way both as an economic ideology and as a social value (Ngai 2003). "In short, all across the political spectrum production as the core of human economic activity was lost" (Reinert 2007: 69). Below this transformation is chronicled by briefly tracing the historical emergence and trajectory of management. In doing so it becomes apparent that a significant shift has occurred in the legitimating idioms of managing, and by implication modernity.

"Managing Man"

This is not the place for an extensive review of the history of management. Relevant for the purpose here, however, is first to note that "scientific management," understood as Taylorism influenced by the Human Relations school, originated in *engineering* (Shenhav 1999; Czarniawska 2003). The roots of corporate management are thus to be found in the discipline of engineering and in the practices of engineers, "those great despised figures of culture and history," as Latour writes (1996: 24). The origin of management in engineering is significant in a company like Hydro, which traditionally defines itself as an "engineering culture" (cf. Kunda 1993). Its approach to managing is informed by Hydro's tight research relationship throughout its history with the former NTH—the Norwegian Academy of Technology, now merged with the social and human sciences into NTNU, the Norwegian University of Science and Technology—where many of its managers have been educated (Hård et al. 1997; Andersen 2005; Johannessen et al. 2005; Lie 2005). Here terminology is of the essence. In Norwegian this academy was formerly called Norges Tekniske Høgskole (NTH); the present-day NTNU is Norges Teknisk-Naturvitenskapelige Universitet. The key thing to notice is the use of the concept *Teknisk*, which translates into "technology" in English. However, a direct translation of "technology" in Norwegian would be *teknologi*, not *teknisk*; thus the choice of *teknisk* is significant.

NTH, established in 1911, was formed on a German model emerging out of a discourse on *"die Technik"* in the second half of the nineteenth century. As outlined by Schatzberg, *die Technik* "referred to the practical arts as a whole, and especially those associated with engineers and modern industry" (2006: 487). This conception hinges upon the nineteenth-century understanding of technology, as outlined for example by Jacob Bigelow in 1829, as the "principles, processes, and nomenclatures of the more conspicuous arts, particularly those which involve applications of science, and which may be considered useful" (ibid.: 491). Throughout the nineteenth century the term "technology" remained secondary, harking back to Bacon and the project for a natural history of the arts, later realized with Diderot and the *Encyclopédie*. The shift in the meaning of "technology" did not occur until the entry to the twentieth century. As will be shown, the practices of managing projects in Hydro that center around notions of "technology" still have a strong affinity to pre–twentieth century concepts and associations related to *teknisk, teknikk*, to *die technik*, to the modern Latin term *technologia*, and even back to the meanings embodied in the Greek etymology of *Tekhne* and its relationship to the Aristotelian concepts of Poiesis, Praxis, and Theoria (see Part I).

Moreover, as the present description unfolds, it will illuminate how the practice and values of managing in recent years, both in Hydro and more generally in the capitalist economy, have shifted and transformed their legitimating basis from a marriage between technology and engineering to economics and finance. Along the way the focus of technologies and invention was refashioned to form abstract and complex financial "products" that proved instrumental in dismantling the global economy. We have witnessed the large-scale emergence of a "money manager capitalism" that has ultimately benefited the financial strata of societies. I argue, however, that today a hybrid engineering/financial legitimating basis for managing still prevails in Hydro. Considering the tensions this shift implies, it reflects Thorstein Veblen's early (1904) distinction between productive and beneficial industrial institutions on the one hand, embodying such things as workmanship, the machine process, and technological knowledge, and pecuniary and parasitic institutions on the other: a distinction between industry and business in Veblen's terms. Drawing heavily on the German discourse and the German historical school of economics, Thorstein Veblen was the first American scholar to make "technology" a key concept in a social theory. Inspired by the way he developed the term into a sophisticated concept for a critique of capitalism, I will treat it as such in the present study. Rather than conflating the whole of the "industrial arts" into concepts of technology as a deterministic form of "applied science," a widespread misconception today, and like the managing practices conducted in Hydro investment projects testify, I will rather treat the concept in an open-ended "polysemic" notion subject to inquiry (see Part I).

Hydro's historical heritage and positioning in the "engineering managing" tradition requires a few more words. Management based in engineering was canonized by Taylor's (1911) principles of scientific management, and in tracing the genesis of management to engineering, Shenhav (1999) has shown how management later differentiated itself from engineering, and how the key managing concepts of systematization and standardization, productivity and efficiency—hallmarks of disseminating instrumental rationality—were translated from the "technical" field to the operations of the whole organization. In such a light we might appreciate that managing, as an "autonomous" activity and domain of social reality, grew out of the modernization processes' proclivity to abstract, classify, and "autonomize" ontological qualities. While obviously formed by both the US and the German traditions of engineering management, on the other hand Hydro is also characterized by the sociotechnical tradition (e.g., Trist 1981) that co-constituted the Human Relations school of organizational thought, with its practical goal of turning adversarial behavior in the organization into productive collaboration (Whyte 1984; Lysgaard 1961; Baba 1986). However, for different reasons, as of the mid 1960s an explicit resistance or alternative to both the US-based Taylorism and the British human relations thinking emerged in Hydro (Johannessen et al. 2005). This had fundamentally to do with a managerial view of technology and industry stressing the collaborative efforts of workers and management to "get to the core of the issues" in production.

As indicated above, in an anthropological study of industrial investment projects the concept of "technology" is obviously central. In all of its various definitions it is easy to overlook the fact that it can be seen both as the study of the object and as an object of study. Some of the wider implications of "technology" are indicated by Pfaffenberger in his argument against the "standard view" of technology:

> the sociotechnical system concept puts forward a universal conception of human technological activity, in which complex social structures, non-verbal activity systems, advanced linguistic communication, the ritual coordination of labor, advanced artifact manufacture, the linkage of phe-nomenally diverse social and nonsocial actors, and the social use of diverse artifacts are all recognized as part of a single complex that is simultaneously adaptive and expressive. (1992: 513)

In his genealogy of the concept of technology, Schatzberg (2006) found that the emerging discipline of anthropology devoted a lot of attention to the study of material culture among "primitive" peoples. From 1882 on-ward, the prominent Anthropological Society of Washington, founded in 1879, specified four main sections: technology, somatology, ethology, and philology. One of the founders of the society, John Wesley Powell, pro-claimed that "the science of the arts is technology," and technology was referred to as a field study within anthropology. But it was not until after 1940 that technology held a significant place in English-language anthro-pology, and by then it referred to material culture itself, not the study of material culture. As such it had by now acquired the present-day com-mon meaning of technology as "the methods and material equipment of the practical arts" (Schatzberg 2006: 490) (Part I of this volume provides a more in-depth questioning of both its wider and deeper meanings).

In the contemporary focus upon competence and knowledge, rather than on "the technology in itself," as one Hydro division president put it, Hydro's management reaches back to areas of concern that earlier lay within the concept of technology but are circumscribed by present us-age. In *The Century Dictionary*, published in New York in 1911, technol-ogy was defined as "the science or systematic knowledge of the industrial arts and crafts, as in textile manufacture, metallurgy, etc." (ibid.). In Hydro project work, the skills or arts "surrounding" or enabling techno-logical processes are of huge concern, but since "technology" presently is mostly perceived as the "thing itself"—as the object—Hydro often employs phrases like "the technology in itself" to make clear that some-thing more or other is being spoken of. This indirectly reaches back to mean-ings with affinity to the *technik*, *technologia*, and *tekhne* of earlier days. Draw-ing on the emerging field of "anthropology of science and technology" (for a short overview, see Hess 2008), especially in Part I of the book, notions of nature and culture are questioned from the perspective of technology.

As noted above, in the present work technology is perceived, both by collaborators and the author, as both an object of study and a study of the object. And as we will see more clearly in Part I, "object" in these senses includes vast realms of both the natural and cultural landscape.

Managing Rationality and Modern Globality

Given that the formal context of the present study is managing practices within the corporate organizational form, we are immediately propelled into discourses on rationality, and indeed, "instrumental rationality." From Kant to Weber, Habermas, and Giddens, to name a few, these debates of modernization are obviously huge discourses. At the core stands the differentiation of the value spheres. Simplified, this is the differentiation into different realms of life: the good, the true and the beautiful. A monumental basis for these debates is Kant's influential *Critique* trilogy: of pure reason (objective science); of practical reason (morals); and of judgment (aesthetic judgment and art). The anthropologist Tord Larsen, in his essay "The Global Conversation" (2009), argues that the modernization processes emerged with the constitution of a fundamental "package" of abstractions, which subsequently has been exported globally as the *intercommunicative* infrastructural basis that makes cross-cultural commensurability possible. This "package" includes the ideas of the *abstract autonomous self*; of *abstract value* (modern money, which enables comparison of values from different value spheres in so-called "premodern" societies, e.g., cattle, food, and land); *abstract time and work* (enabling, e.g., the distinction between working hours and leisure time—which, one might add, by implication makes the unemployed also lack leisure time); and *abstract place and space* (e.g. length units, straight angles, and mathematical calculations that render possible the measurement of all particular spaces).

Larsen argues that these homogenizations, including that of the individual, value, time, work, and space, were a locally produced medium of communication that now provides the basis upon which a global modernity is possible. Indeed, he proposes that modernity might be defined as the medium making "globality," or globalization, possible (2009: 267–68). Communication is also, of course, fundamental in Habermas's definition of rationality. Rationality, according to Habermas (1984), is basically a social construct, because rationality is developed, exchanged, and evaluated reciprocally between actors and audiences. In fact, rationality and sociality, seen as requirements of justification expressively conveyed in social interaction, are immanent to such a degree that the rationality theme is constitutive of sociality itself, "as social practices distinct self-logic" (Vetlesen 2006: 202, my trans.). The minimum requirement of rationality, following Habermas's discussion of "reason and the rationalization of society," is that it be criticizable and justifiable communicative action. And this form of social practice is particularly characteristic of modern societies (ibid.).

Framed in light of this discussion, what is under investigation in the present work, as a subject of inquiry, are the practices of managing investment projects as, heuristically for now, conceived of as practices of "instrumental rationality." I conclude not so much either by confirming or criticizing a notion of an all-encompassing system that colonizes the lifeworld. Rather, from an investigation of an allegedly source domain of these colonizing processes—from the midst of the purported "cognitive-instrumental value sphere" of the contemporary globalized capitalist economy, as it were—I argue that the particular example examined here shows that knowledge claims are validated by an entangled corpus of value legitimations. The notion of the "system" as a homogeneous and hegemonically colonizing conceptualization seems to be too undifferentiated, and I argue that rather than (only) colonizing the lifeworld, the source domain itself is differentially constituted on value claims drawing extensively from the other value domains as well, the moral and the aesthetic-expressive—in sum constituting what I call "mixed regimes of rationality" (see Chapter 8).

The Neoliberal Triumph and Tragedy

The broader ideological context in which capitalist enterprises need to operate in the contemporary situation of economic globalization is, as noted above, neoliberalism, or better, neoliberalization or a neoliberal culture complex. I will refer to neoliberalization as the practical realizations of the neoliberal ideological program. That neoliberalism, in a reifying expression, is the "ideology of our time" and has been so the last decades, is fairly well documented by now. A working definition of the term might be adopted from David Harvey:

> Neoliberalism is … a theory of political economic practices that proposes that human well-being can best be advanced by liberating individual entrepreneurial freedoms and skills within an institutional framework characterized by strong private property rights, free markets and free trade. The role of the state is to create and preserve an institutional framework appropriate to such practices.… Furthermore, if markets do not exist (in areas such as land, water, education, health care, social security, or environmental pol-

lution) then they must be created, by state action if necessary. But beyond these tasks the state should not venture. (2005: 2)

Neoliberalism's intellectual origins, especially in terms of neoclassical economic theory, has until recently been poorly understood. Thanks to a series of recent publications, we now have the knowledge necessary to assess the origins of neoliberalism and unfold many of its meanings and implications.[11]

"Neoliberalism," although ambivalent along several dimensions, is the common term now used to describe the transformations capitalism has undergone since the turning points of the 1970s and 1980s in response to the "structural crisis" in the capitalist system of the 1970s. The answer to the crisis was the emergence of a more or less global "neoliberal society," which, as noted in the introduction, has since constituted a "culture of neoliberalism" (Comaroff and Comaroff 2001), or a "neoliberal culture complex" of global reach (Hannerz 2007). As will described in Part II, a defining feature of the neoliberal order has been the restoration of power to a particular form of capitalist class, often mistakenly euphemized as "market powers": what broadly can be described as "finance." Here "finance" means not only the financial sector of the economy, but the "complex of upper capitalist classes, whose property materializes in the holding of securities (stock shares, bonds, Treasury Bills, etc.), and financial institutions (central banks, banks, funds, etc.)" (Duménil and Lévy 2004: 16). As will be extensively documented later, the response to the structural crisis of deepening stagnation, or "stagflation," of the economic system in the 1970s, was "neoliberal financialization"—the historically unprecedented leverage of finance capital and the accumulation of debt and economic inequality that it actively promoted.

Following extensive documentation of the research on neoliberalism (e.g., Harvey 2005; Klein 2007), I concur that the present predicament is indeed one of globalization, but possibly more importantly, a neoliberal financialized globalization. Recently also a few anthropological analyses have ventured to describe and understand finance capitalism. These include broader reflections on culture and "millennial capitalism" (Comaroff and Comaroff 2000) and "culture and finance capital" (Jameson 1997); attempts at locally situating finance capitalism in key Wall Street agencies (Ho 2005, 2009; Tett 2009); discussions of the "failure of economic knowledge" in Japanese financial markets (Hirokazu and Riles 2005); and analysis of finance traders' activities, and of how the sweeping digitalization of financial exchanges and trading has transformed "economic cultures and the craft of speculation" (Zaloom 2003, 2006). Relevant issues from these works will be introduced as the analysis unfolds and the discussion of neoliberalization and financialization picks up in Part II of the book. Meanwhile, the legitimation of neoliberalism in neoclassical, utilitarian, economic theory is discussed next. This is important because of the theoretical dialogue that partly drives the present study and the ideological context of its objects of study—not least because neoclassical assumptions lie at the heart of the modern corporation and the challenges of managerial capitalism.

How Did Economists Get It So Wrong?
The Neoclassical Premises

While economics undoubtedly has been the discipline providing the dominant theoretical perspectives on the functioning, goals, and values of the corporation, mainstream economics in turn has been dominated by the neoclassical tradition. And as Ho explains, the most obvious problem with neoclassical theory is that it clashes with "any understanding of the firm as a social organization" (2009: 172). The first reason is that the premises of neoclassical theory, that is, its particular capitalist ideology and worldview, rest on the notion taken from Adam Smith, that individual self-interest through the invisible hand of market forces creates the best outcome for society at large; and secondly, neoclassical theory allows the presence of only two entities, the *individual owner* (entrepreneur) and *private property* (ibid.) As will be discussed later in relation to the turn to finance and shareholder value in Hydro, the global wave of shareholder value from the 1980s can be seen as "the culmination and most effective demonstration of neoclassical values in the history of American business ... [and] part of a long line of neoclassically inspired worldviews attempting to collapse and treat the corporation as single profit-maximizing individual in the market" (ibid.: 173). As we will see later, this did not sit perfectly well with the Hydro tradition and contexts of operating, and Hydro and its managers thus ran into several problems in their turn to shareholder value and found themselves to be ambiguously positioned with respect to this new paradigm.

Neoclassical economics has recently received strong criticism. When Gudeman states that "[m]ost economic anthropologists employ concepts from neoclassical economics to interpret their data" (2008: 173), this critique becomes vital also for economic anthropology. A critical academic debate related to the philosophical premises, theoretical constructs, and methodological practices of modern economic theory has emerged, gaining new impetus from the financial crisis. It is reevaluating some of the basic premises of neoclassical theory, for example its focus on laws of equilibrium (Hausman 1994). In these debates the mainstream field of economics is criticized for inappropriate and abstract models that in sum signify that economics to a large extent has abandoned its aim of being an empirical science of human behavior, and by now rather resembles a branch of mathematics. Its predictive failures also position economics as a peculiar science (ibid.). A case in point was provided by the OECD as late as in their *Economic Outlook* of May 2007, in which an editorial by Jean Philippe Cotis notes that "the current economic situation is in many ways better than what we have experienced in years." Lawson identifies the most fundamental problem as "emphasis on mathematical deductivist modelling *per se*" (2009: 760, italics in original). Lawson argues that such models at best can provide only limited insight into economics or any other aspect of social reality, because such models presuppose a view of reality as atomistically isolated. Social reality, he argues, is composed of phenomena that are far from isolated, constant, or atomistic. This view echoes my own later outline of the "social reality of construction" (Chapter 3).

The critiques of mainstream economics for being out of touch with reality are exemplified by six winners of the so-called Nobel Prize in Economics: "economics has become increasingly an arcane branch of mathematics rather than dealing with real economic problems" (Milton Friedman); "[Economics as taught] in America's graduate schools ... bears testimony to a triumph of ideology over science" (Joseph Stiglitz); "Existing economics is a theoretical [meaning mathematical] system which floats in the air and which bears little relation to what happens in the real world" (Ronald Coase); "Page after page of professional economic journals are filled with mathematical formulas.... Year after year economic theorists continue to produce scores of mathematical models and to explore in great detail their formal properties; and the econometricians fit algebraic functions of all possible shapes to essentially the same sets of data" (Wassily Leontief); "Today if you ask a mainstream economist a question about almost any aspect of economic life, the response will be: suppose we model that situation and see what happens ... modern mainstream economics consists of little else but examples of this process" (Robert Solow).

These quotes were assembled by the Post-Autistic Economics Network, which publishes the online journal *Real-World Economics Review*.[12] Launched in the summer of 2000, it now comprises thousands of professional economists from a range of countries. The movement, under the banner of "sanity, humanity and science," advocates for the reform of economics education and research in the following ways, relevant to the discussions in economic anthropology: to broaden the definition of "economic man" to include not only the self-interested, autonomous rational optimizer, to recognize the importance of culture, to consider history, to advocate a new theory of knowledge, to ground theoretical claims in empirical findings, to expand the set of methods, and to facilitate interdisciplinary dialogue.

Since the dramatic onset of the financial crisis in late 2008, some of these insights have now also entered mainstream economic debates through some instances of honest self-reflective soul-searching. One of the main proponents of this mainstream self-critique is Paul Krugman. In a series of essays in the *New York Times*, Krugman seeks to wrestle the bull by its horns. For example in his piece "How Did Economists Get It So Wrong?" Krugman writes: "As I see it, the economics profession went astray because economists, as a group, mistook beauty, clad in impressive-looking mathematics, for truth … economists fell back in love with the old, idealized vision of an economy in which rational individuals interact in perfect markets, this time gussied up with fancy equations" (2009: MM36). Economists romanticized and idealized both the rational actor and the perfectness of the market. Along the whole spectrum of mainstream economics, from monetarism and other neoclassical schools to New Keynsianism, argues Krugman, the charms of rational individuals and efficient markets stood strong. The models, also of New Keynsianists like Krugman himself, left no room for big bubbles and banking-system collapses and crises like the contemporary one. In short, throughout the globally dominant economic community an all-out consensus, which now seems quite absurd to most people, prevailed as a hegemonic paradigm, a paradigm that seemed oblivious to what the self-critical Krugman calls "the inconvenient reality that financial markets fall short of perfection, that they are subject to extraordinary delusions and the madness of the crowds" (ibid.).

In reviewing the intellectual history of neoliberalism and neoclassical economics as its academic legitimation, Edward Fullbrook conveys some key insights of contemporary political economy and the processes by which the hegemonic paradigm of economic theorizing came about. In his argument, Western universities both gave rise to neoliberalism and continue to be its primary advocates. Neoliberalism, he states, "out of its distant, bizarre and unworldly origins it has, via the United States Air Force (that is not a misprint), and university economics departments, become the political ideology that today rules the UK, the US and most of the world" (2007: 161). As Fullbrook argues, since the Second World War the United States has increasingly determined the shape of economics worldwide. The primary engineering of this situation is attributed to a large degree to the US Department of Defense, especially its Navy and Air Force. One of his passages is worthy of a lengthy quotation:

Beginning in the late 1950s it lavishly funded university research in mathematical economics. Military planners believed that game theory and linear programming had potential use for national defense. And, although it now seems ridiculous, they held out the same hope for mathematical solutions of "general equilibrium," the theoretical core of neoclassical economics. The really big event, the one that would make neoliberalism the ideology of our time, came in 1965 when RAND, the research and development wing of the US Air Force, created a lavish fellowship program for economics graduate students at the Universities of California, Harvard, Stanford, Yale, Chicago, Columbia and Princeton, and in addition provided postdoctoral funds for those who best fitted the mould. These seven economics departments, along with that of MIT—an institution long regarded by many as a branch of the Pentagon—have subsequently come to dominate economics globally to an astonishing extent. They control the three most prestigious economics journals, in which papers by their staff and PhDs predominate. Of the over 800 economists employed by the World Bank, a majority have been trained at one of the Big Eight. The International Monetary Fund is similarly provided... (2007: 166)

In addition, Fullbrook continues, economics pulled off "one of the greatest public relations coups of all time" (2007: 166) when the Central Bank of Sweden managed to "incorporate" its prize in economics into the body of the proper Nobel Prizes in the eye of the public, and even many economists today believe that what they call the "Nobel Prize for Economics" is in fact a Nobel Prize. Fullbrook contends that the effects of the "Nobel Prize" maneuvering and the RAND program, in combination with economists' self-suggestive imagery of their scientific status as mathematical physicists since the time of emergence of neoclassical economics with Jevons and Walras, "pushed economics over the precipice":

Within a generation the "dismal science" became the autistic science. Its storylines increasingly bore scant relevance to economic reality. More and more pages of economics journals were given over to mathematical symbols that, unlike those of real science journals, have no empirical, real-world referents.... Out of this enforced fantasy world emerged neoliberalism in the real-life political world.... Given that it was impossible to escape its autism without de-formalising and thereby losing its treasured illusion that economists are kissing-cousins of physicists, *why not demand that the real world change so as to conform to the imaginary world of neoclassical economics.* This is how neoliberalism came into being and continues to be." (Ibid., italics in original)

In a similar vein James Carrier outlined that with its great institutional power, abstract neoclassical economics is engaged in "the conscious attempt to make the real world conform to the virtual image" (1998: 2, cf.

Ho 2009: 35). As Karen Ho elaborates, the move to greater abstraction and virtualism is "creating a prescriptive model for reality, a 'virtual reality' that is reductive, dislocating, and divorced from responsible and engaged social relationships" (Ho 2009: 35). In conjunction with the later description of the financialized economic context of the presently investigated investment projects (see Part II), these intellectual and political origins of mainstream (neoclassical) economics are of importance.

In short, the situation of contemporary economic anthropology, and not only in neoclassical theory, is also to a large extent "dismal." For economic anthropology, the discarding of its neoclassical inspirations seems long overdue. In the context of modern economies, the spiritually inspired knowledge- and production-based tradition has largely been lost, and the focus is on investigating "consumption culture" with many assumptions inherited from mainstream microeconomics. Although the image of the animal-like economic man is challenged to some extent by seeing identity formation and active meaning construction enacted also through consumption, and thus in some ways by trying to portray "consumption as creation," it is still the man the consumer that is portrayed. Man the creative, compassionate, and "spiritual" producer with "wit and will" is difficult to detect.

The deep crisis that is currently unfolding is, however, a period of great potentiality and possibility for change. The finance crisis has laid bare the failures of the neoliberal culture complex. Overlooking neoliberalism's theoretical and ideological shortcomings, however, the devastating blow to the paradigm, as will be thoroughly documented in Part II, comes from its incapacity to provide a schema for capitalism to *produce* wealth and deliver economic growth. In this sense, not only did neoliberalism move from triumph to tragedy but, as Hardt and Negri contend, "Neoliberalism was already dead" (2009: 268). Still dominant, but dead. As Harvey (2005) and others document, the main achievement of neoliberalization has been to redistribute wealth and income, rather than to generate it. And this has been conducted primarily through practices of accumulation by the wealthy through dispossession of the poor and the public. The latest inventions to this respect have been the massive bailout packages states around the globe have offered the financial industry at the expense of the public (Reinhart and Rogoff 2009). But then again, in crisis there is also opportunity. Opportunity for change, but also for study.

At least two ethnographies situated in the work practices in finance communities have succeeded in unearthing significant dynamics of the workings of finance capital and its relations to broader aspects of capitalist culture and crisis (Ho 2009; Tett 2009). Moreover, the arguably most successful anthropological works dealing with finance and capitalism, in the sense that they provided valuable contributions on the looming crisis *before the fact*, have been works with broad and also "macro-oriented" theoretical and methodological approaches (e.g. Jameson 1997; Comaroff and Comaroff 2000; LiPuma and Lee 2004; Ho 2005, 2009). In light of such considerations, I was inspired early on to closely link global flows and connections with local case practices, and use theory to guide the ethnographic work; thus the present work was carried out as a variant of the ethnographic extended case study. As outlined briefly below in the close to this chapter, describing this approach is also a means to disclose key epistemological and methodological premises of the study.

Extending Anthropological Discovering

The epistemological and methodological baseline from which the research presented here unfolded was a reconstruction of the ethnographic extended case method to accommodate a contemporary anthropology of "global capitalism." In line with the extended case method, as developed by and around Max Gluckman and the Manchester school, it seeks generalization from analysis of practice in various types of situations and events (Evans and Handelman 2006). And in this perspective generalization and theoretical knowledge might be seen more as emerging out of, and being premised upon, the *particular*, rather than the *typical*. Furthermore, the extended case method is particularly targeted toward disclosing from concrete cases wider contexts and systems of relation that constrain and occasion the case in question. It does so via a holistic approach that "applies reflexive science to ethnography in order to extract the general from the unique, to move from the "micro" to the "macro," and to connect the present to the past in anticipation for the future" (Burawoy 1998: 5). The extended case is in this sense both empirically and theoretically driven and perceives the particularity of subjects and situations investigated as always embedded within and engaged with the larger processes and "forces" of history and great social institutions, which enables a linking of the "micro and macro."

An extended case study is not worried about uniqueness problems or representativity. The possibility of generalization comes along two different but related dimensions. The first is that the extended case study tries to locate as accurately as possible the extralocal "forces" within which the case is situated. That is, it uses qualitative methods to "to locate everyday life in its extralocal and historical context" (Burawoy 1998: 4). The researcher extends out of the field and embeds situated social processes in the wider array of social structures and forces. To the extent that these extralocal contingencies and constraints are accurately described, these forces obviously also have major impacts on cases other than the one ethnographically explored in the given case. Extending outward, in time and space alike, from a particular case enables research to move up close, better informed, in other cases.

The second dimension through which the extended case method achieves generalizability, or objectivity, is in its relationship to theory. In the extended case ethnographers thematize our participation in the worlds we study: "We keep ourselves steady by rooting ourselves in theory that guides our dialogue with participants" (Burawoy 1998: 5). This "dwelling in" theory is at the core of what Burawoy calls a reflexive model of science.

> Premised upon our own participation in the world we study, reflexive science deploys multiple dialogues to reach explanations of empirical phenomena. Reflexive science starts out from dialogue, virtual or real, between observer and participants, embeds such dialogue within a second dialogue between local processes and extralocal forces that in turn can only be comprehended through a third, expanding dialogue with theory itself. (Ibid.)

Objectivity is not reached by various positivist procedures to "map the world," and unlike, for example, "grounded theory," it is achieved by the growth of knowledge. Inspired by Kuhn, Popper, and Lakatos, Burawoy perceives this growth of knowledge to be "the imaginative and parsimonious reconstruction of theory to accommodate anomalies" (1998: 5). Thus, in extending the anthropological process of discovering, we extend from observer to the participant, extend observations over space and time, extend out from process to "force," and not least, extend theory (cf. Burawoy 2009).

Such an approach to ethnographic investigation might contribute to reinscribing the fundamental difference between anthropology and ethnography, as voiced for example by Timothy Ingold (2007). He draws on Radcliffe-Brown's distinction between ethnography as an ideographic practice of describing particularities, and anthropology as a nomothetic science searching for general insights, laws, and generalizations. Arguing for the reinvention of an anthropology with room for philosophy—an "outdoor philosophy"—ontological reflection should be brought back into the anthropological enterprise. Then anthropology could be recast as a study *with*, not *of*, and could be perceived as a way of both knowing and being. Furthermore, in grounding knowing in being, anthropology might be seen as educating our perception of the world. As such, argues Ingold, theory and method come together as both art and craft in a way that opens up rather than closes, and anthropology is framed as a "sideways glance." In this perspective ethnography, as differentiated from anthropology, must be freed from its conceptualization as "method." In relation to the doing of an anthropology with others, ethnography then becomes a form of writing descriptions of the things that happen in the "field." In such a sense the ethnographic extended case method might be extended to both differentiate and integrate ethnography and anthropology in a constructive way.

The cultural analysis of investment projects, the global corporation, and related multifaceted flows of capital, values, and materiality seems particularly well situated to be anthropologically analyzed from such an angle. Especially in the contemporary crisis in capitalism, an approach inspired by Manchester school extended case studies, with Gluckman's strong emphasis on the concept of a *total context of crisis*, is appropriate. As Bruce Kapferer notes in his assessment of the contribution of Max Gluckman:

> For Gluckman, the term "situation" refers to a total context of crisis, not just contradictory and conflicting processes but a particular tension or turning, a point of potentiality and infinite possibility. This conception of the situation as crisis demands an understanding that micro dynamics are always integral within macro forces, and that these larger processes must be attended to if anthropological explanation and understanding are to achieve any kind of adequacy. (2006: 122)

A specific element that I apply for a contemporary and renewed approach to these issues is *scale* as an object of analysis. As noted by Tsing (2002) the perception and construction of scale itself might be turned into an object of analysis. By tracing the specificities of scale related to a particular domain, in this case the global capitalist flows, we became able to analyze phenomena as interrelated on various levels. I move between smaller and larger scales, utilizing statistical measures and, for example, construction of large-scale value appreciation measures of financial economy as an object of analysis.

Another element utilized here is the following of *concrete trajectories and associations*, both in the internal creation of investment projects and in their wider connections. Here particular engagements, links, and close encounters are investigated by, for example, looking for "social processes sparked by coalitions, dialogues, missed messages, and oppositional refusals" (Tsing 2002: 474). The concreteness of "movements" is an object of study, meaning both social mobilizations in which new identities and interests are formed, and travels from one place to another through which place-transcending interactions occur. These two senses of movement work together in remaking geographies and scales. Tracing them concretely, with a focus on particular "routes of travel" (Clifford 1997), is advocated in such a perspective and might offer more insight into global complexity.

Tracing the connections, my empirical "field" as an extended case is constituted both as multisited and multitemporal. As such "the ethnographic trilogy" is challenged—that of the sole researcher spending prolonged time in continuous fieldwork in one discrete geographical location (Trouillot 2003: 125). My fieldwork was conducted in ten main geographical locations, and although I have had a collaborative research relationship with Hydro in varying degrees and different projects for nearly ten years, I have been "in and out of the field"[12] constantly, so each "continuous batch" of "localized" fieldwork has hardly been in the extent of two weeks. However, the particularities of time and place in my fieldwork have become more and more common in anthropology in recent years. Related to the fieldwork basis of the present work, I provide elsewhere (2008a) an extensive, reflexive self-examination on methodological aspects of participating and collaborating in the fields we study.

Although there is a well-established body of ethnographic research from complex capitalist societies and their localities, such as workplaces, neighborhoods, hospitals, jails, and bars, to a large extent these may not be seen as innovative. Done in a bounded setting in the most conventional way, such a study, as Marcus notes,

> isolates parts for holistic treatment, but leaves direct perspectives on total social systems to other kinds of specialists. In so doing, it evades the challenge of how ethnographic research, through the study of particular subjects, can account for or describe whole systems of societal organization. (1983: 30)

Anthropologists now do multisited and multitemporal fieldwork, but the terms have been in use for only the last twenty years, advocated especially by George Marcus (1986) and Marcus and Fischer (1986), and proliferated especially at Stockholm University since the middle of the 1990s (Hannerz 1998, 2003). Furthermore, in the "networked society" (Castells 2000) of jet planes, Internet, omnipresent and mobile telecommunications, real-time electronically integrated global financial markets, transnational companies, and global media, it is quite obvious that localities are extended in space, and that movement and cultural flow are at the crux of the matter (Appadurai 1996). Although major perspectives on globalization have entered the mainstream of the anthropological discourse,[14] the conceptualization of the geographically located field still stands strong. My multisited field could be seen in light of Appadurai's (ibid.) notion of translocalities, Hannerz's (2003) reflections about the translocal field, and also Auge's (1995) ideas about a field of "non-places" in an anthropology of supermodernity.

The holism I seek to describe through investigating such a field of "corporate managing" is akin to Marcus's exploration of elite "dynasties"

(1983). Like notions of dynasty, ideals and ideas of managing exist across a variety of contexts and settings, transcending time and space while still allowing periodic stability, particular manifestations, and relations connecting locales. In "imagining the whole" of anthropological object construction, Marcus notes, "Spatially uprooted, mobile cultural phenomena like 'dynasty,' then are what ethnography needs to explore to fully conceptualize new ways of thinking about contemporary conditions" (1998: 54). As noted above, I regard the field of projects and their managing as global assemblages: at once emergent, decentered, ephemeral, and fundamentally characterized by movement, while nonetheless exhibiting orderliness and structuredness in quite an extreme sense. As an analytical conceptualization of my research field in terms of both space and time, I thus choose to follow the movements and *flows* of managers and their actions, ideas, and knowledge, "technology," and money capital related to bringing forth projects. The spatial field is not bounded by the particular localities of the sites of the emerging plant, but rather the "fieldflows" involved in the bringing forth of the projects. The empirical "fieldflows" are presented schematically below (Figure 1).

Figure 1. A sketch of the sites and connections constituting the main "fieldflows" of people, concepts, knowledge, capital, and technology involved in the emergence of the Hydro investment projects and plants investigated, indicating also the "extending out" of the field from "micro" to "macro."

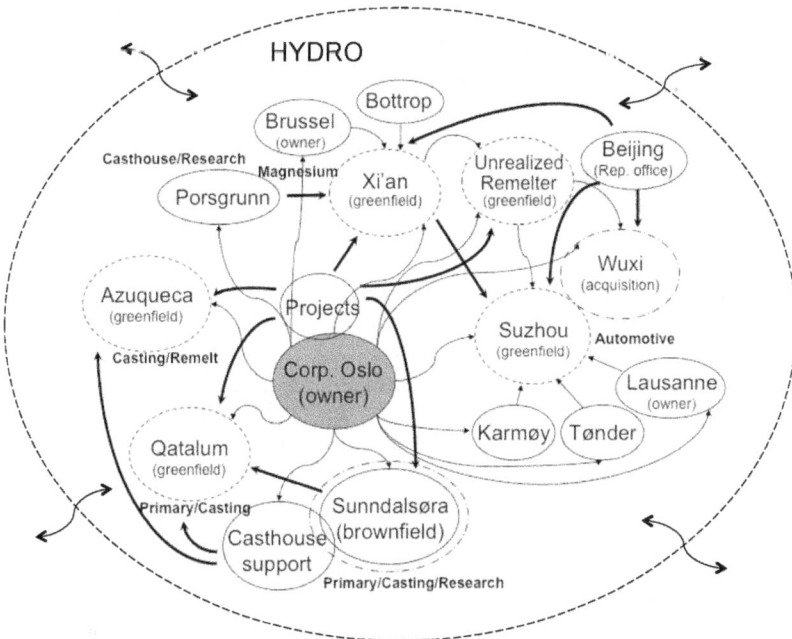

All in all I talked formally and informally to well above two hundred people in the Hydro organization and conducted interviews with about 115 of them (including people outside of Hydro), several times over with many. I visited ten of their geographical locations: the corporate headquarters, a division headquarters (including sales and marketing), seven project and subsequent production facilities (including visits to research centers at two of them), and one representative office (Table 2).

Below I present a brief schematic overview of the major forms and categories of empirical data on which the study is based, seen in relation to the research design and analytical framework (see Table 3). Inspired by Barth's investigative approach to an "anthropology of knowledge" (1975, 2002), the following short list is at the same time a template of the main modes whereby managing actions are instantiated, expressed, and enacted, with their "instruments and encasements," as a bringing forth of projects. Both language-based and non–language based idioms and codes are included, as are conceptual dimensions of time and space, and arenas and materialities of communicative action. Through all of this the managing actions in projects and the knowledge tradition(s) are expressed (historical and statistical data are omitted here; see Table 3 below).

1) Language-based idioms
   I) Verbal communication
      a) Informal face-to-face talk (in "quiet rooms," hallways, cafeterias) open space offices, on the shop floor, at project dinners, and other areas)
      b) Face-to-face and telephone interviews
      c) Official external presentations
      d) Official internal presentations
      e) Internal meetings
      f) Project work meetings
      g) Virtual meetings (phone, teleconferencing)

Table 2. Overview of Main Fieldwork Sites and Methods of Data Gathering

Organizational unit	Location	Number of interviewees	Participant observation	Non-particip observation	Manager meetings	Open documents	Confidential documents	E-mail exchanges
Corporate headquarters	Norway	15	X	X	X	X	X	X
Project/Production 1	China	19	X	X	X	X	X	X
Project/Production 2	China	6	X	X	X			X
Project/Production 3	China	12	X	X		X	X	X
Project/Production 4	Spain	15	X	X	X	X	X	X
Project/Production 5	Norway	6		X		X		X
Research Centre	Norway	5				X	X	X
Subcontractors	China	7	X					X
Representative office	China	8	X				X	X
Industrial zones	China	5	X			X		
Official representatives	Europe	5	X			X		X
Other global management	China	12	X			X		X
Total		115						

II) Written and multimedia communications
    a) Corporate textual information, internal and external
    b) Pictures and official presentations
    c) Project reports and presentations
    d) Project models and templates
    e) Plant design drawings
    f) Internet presentations: text, pictures, movies, "live casts"
    g) Intranet presentations: text, pictures, movies, intranet cafés
    h) Project-related e-mails
    i) Project- and corporate-related flow charts, tables, and numbers
    j) Public media discourses (i.e., newspapers, televised debates)
    k) Hydro consultancy reports

2) Non-language idioms
    I) Objects (public/secret, like project design models) and acts (like taboos and celebrations in projects, and the centennial celebration)
    II) Clothing (suits and worksuits, protective equipment)
    III) Body language

3) Dimensions of space, time, and occasion
    I) Ordering of experience in time (i.e., scheduling of meetings, phases, projects; jetlag, etc.)
    II) Ordering of experience in space (project and plant locationing, buildings, traveling)
    III) Degree of space-time "distancing" in communications (i.e., from face-to-face to dispersed and virtual communications, synchronous and asynchronous)

4) Organization of persons and audiences
    I) Titles and roles (i.e., hierarchical, occupational, and epistemic)
    II) Categorizations according to the salary and compensation system
    III) Gender (male/female)
    IV) Egalitarian/hierarchic (participation and steering, i.e., project steering committees)
    V) Assembling, and breakdowns in size and diversity, of project and work groups
    VI) Internal jurisprudential groupings (i.e., governance structures and unions)
    VII) Various scenes for "mass communication" (public, e.g., Capital Markets Day, parts of the centennial celebration; and internal, e.g. seminars, centennial celebrations).

A brief note on the use of language during fieldwork might at this point be appropriate. The official language in Hydro is English. This means that all official documents, including various documentations in project work, are to be written in English. This does not mean that verbal and written local languages are not used. In the verbal domain, the practical rule of thumb seems to be that whenever there is someone present who does not speak the "local" language, English is used. In terms of project work this is often the case. Thus I spoke to all non-Norwegian managers in English. When talking individually or in groups with only Norwegians present, Norwegian was used. This echoes the internal Hydro practices as well.

In terms of written exchanges, one project manager, for instance, expressed frustration that he sometimes received e-mails from Norwegians in Norwegian. This meant he could not easily forward them to include non-Norwegians in further exchanges. He tried to set an example by replying to e-mails only in English. Thus "informally" there are some translation issues for a Norwegian-based "global" company. This was evident not least in China. In recruiting managers it was a requirement to speak English, which in practice proved a challenge; however, those who spoke little English when hired quickly learned, so even here the use of an interpreter was seldom needed. Where quotes appear in the text they have thus either been assembled directly in English or translated from Norwegian. When there is something difficult to translate or express in English, I have included the original Norwegian phrasing.

As outlined above, the research focus in the present study is on investigating *managing practices* in a set of new international investment projects in Hydro. The research challenge has been to understand Hydro's managing practices (as exemplary of knowledge work), particularly as they relate to their international investment projects. The managing and the investment projects in question cut across different cultural boundaries (national, organizational, epistemic), and the research task has been in the first instance to identify characteristics of these practices, and the project-specific and corporate contexts within which they occur and are occasioned. In the second instance the research task has been to situate these managing practices and their project and corporate contexts in the wider network of globalized capitalist relations within which they are co-created. This approach enables more generally a close-up view of industrial corporate endeavors in a globalized economy, and a holistic analysis of central aspects of economic and cultural development in contemporary late-modern society. Also noted earlier, the problem space of the book has been broken down and organized around two main research pillars, each indicated by a key construct and each thematically organized as the two main "substantial" parts of the book: Technology (Part I) and Economy

(Part II). Both political economy and cultural economics perspectives inspire both parts. Key constructs of the two pillars are represented as in the figure below, an outline of the research design that highlights the main research themes and main bodies of ethnographic data, as well as historical and statistical data, while linking these with the major bodies of theories that are invoked and discussed in the book.

Table 3. Outline of the research design, emphasizing the research focus on managing actions in a set of Hydro's international investment projects (IIPs).

Research themes	Main corpus of ethnographic data	Historical and statistical data	Main bodies of theory	Thematic organizing pillar
•Managing projects as knowledge practices of dissemination and transformation •Technology of production and enchantment (projects as "industrial arts") •Technology as instrumental rationality and causality (culture as instrument) •Idioms of "managing culture" cross-culturally	•(A) Participant and non-participant observation of managing actions in relation to the IIP's studied (see figure 1) •(B) Document studies of the above projects (e.g. minutes of meetings, experience reports, e-mails and a managers diary) (see table 3) •(C) Interviews with managers and other IIP relevant people	•Hydro history •Technology history •Moral legitimation of capitalism historically •Management tradition	•Anthropology of technology •Science and technology studies •Philosophy of technology •New science and ontology (quantum physics and the new epistemology of entanglement and undividedness)	"Technology" (PART I)
•Managing projects as economic and societal "value creation" •Projects and Hydro activities as knowledge and production capitalism •Projects and Hydro activities as constrained by "globalized financialization"	•A, B, C (see above) •The Norwegian public debate on the Hydro stock options case •Managing project and corporate financial risk: discussions and annual reporting	•Hydro and Norwegian history •Hydro finance figures •Historical capitalism •Globalized finance capitalisms data •Global economic inequalities data	•Economic anthropology •Critical political economy •"The Other Canon" economics •Moral and cultural economics	"Economy" (PART II)

Research focus: Managing in IIP's

Notes

1. Gluckman, quoted in Handelman (2008: 94).
2. During my fieldwork period Hydro divested two of its three main business divisions. The fertilizer business became the Agri corporation, and its oil and energy division merged with Statoil to form StatoilHydro. Hydro continued in 2007 as a dedicated aluminum company. Throughout my research I have been solely working with the division Aluminium.
3. For an ethnographic effort to analyze contemporary capitalism from the consumption angle, see for example Miller (1997b).
4. See for example the updated textbook in economic anthropology provided by Wilk and Cliggett (2007), which lacks the entry "knowledge" in its index.
5. Obviously a key characteristic of the neoclassical turn was its move away from the labor theories of value, and through the "marginalist revolution" it came rather to be focused on marginal utility ("utility maximization" rather than "profit maximization") where labor is taken into account as a "factor of production." In neoclassical economics and the neoclassical synthesis—that is, modern mainstream economics—the focus shifted to perfect market competition, supply and demand concerns, general equilibrium theory, individual wants and needs, etc. Nonetheless, among others Jevons, one of the founders of neoclassical economics, considered his marginal analysis consistent with the labor theory of value. His proposition was that equilibrium marginal utility equaled marginal labor value. A critique of mainstream neoclassical economics is provided below.
6. For publications and bibliographies documenting and extending the "other canon" tradition, see http://www.othercanon.org/ (accessed 19 April 2010).
7. For a figure summarizing the "family tree" of "other canon" economics history, see: http://www.othercanon.org/papers/tree.html (accessed 20 April 2010).
8. For a concise introduction to the "other canon" tradition, including a long table that summarizes and contrasts the "standard canon" with the "other canon," see: "The Other Canon: The History of Renaissance Economics. Its Role as an Immaterial and Production-based Canon in the History of Economic Thought and in the History of Economic Policy," draft version by Erik S. Reinert and Arno M. Daastøl, to be found at http://www.othercanon.org/papers/index.html (accessed 19 April 2010). A final version of this essay, with a modified summarizing table, is published in Reinert (2004), and a similar table is also found in Reinert (2007).
9. See note 6.
10. My own position on some of the basic assumptions touched upon here is that knowledge beyond culture is indeed possible. On the question whether morality and values beyond culture is possible, I prefer to be agnostic while nevertheless fostering an intuitive inclination that it is.
11. See for example Comaroff and Comaroff (2000, 2001); Duménil and Lévy (2004); Harvey (2005); Epstein (2005); Edelman and Haugerud (2005); Fullbrook (2007); Klein (2007).
12. See http://www.paecon.net/ (accessed 1 December 2007).
13. Again evoking the notion, heralded in many anthropological conceptualizations, that culture resides in discrete geographical places.
14. See for example Featherstone (1990); Jameson and Miyoshi (1998); Appadurai (2001); Eriksen (2003).

Chapter 2

MANAGING IN THE MIDDLE KINGDOM
Three Investment Projects in China

[Engineers] ... those great despised figures of
culture and history ... they're novelists.
—Bruno Latour, *Aramis, or the Love of Technology*

Logic is a poor model of cause and effect.
—Gregory Bateson, *Mind and Nature*

Human knowledge and human power meet in one....
Nature to be commanded must be obeyed...
—Francis Bacon, *Novum Organum*

"Last year, I think we had eight days when we actually could see the sun."
The driver behind the wheel of the brand-new General Motors car twists
and turns through the mind-boggling traffic in Xi'an, Shaanxi province
of the People's Republic of China, one of the world's most polluted cities.
He drives with authority, not aggressively but with confidence and concentration—something highly appreciated by us passengers. He passes the
many creatively constructed vehicles inhabiting the roads, from walking-
carts and bicycle-tractors to massive trucks spewing black exhaust. The
general manager of Hydro's new magnesium alloy plant, located at the
fringes of the city, peers out of the car window at the people and traffic
outside amidst all-encompassing smog—a visualization of the characteristic smell he is already long familiar with.

Outside, old people are doing their morning line gymnastics, tai chi, beneath voluminous interchanges, each in different ways aesthetically beautiful in its lines and movements, but quite a contrast. A great number of people are walking, bicycling, or driving to work. Shops are opening; sweepers clean the streets, standing in the middle of the road seemingly without fear of death, not looking up, hardly noticing the cars—our car— rushing by at high speed. Almost every time you watch traffic through a car window you anticipate an accident. "I think I see a serious, possibly lethal, accident about once a week," the manager says, somehow reading my thoughts.

> Safety at the plant is a big issue, I'll tell you. I don't drive here myself, no chance. In Shanghai or Beijing I'll do it. Here, no way. But you know, even here it is somewhat civilized. When traveling around to find the location for our plant, we went to Ningxia, virtually on the border to Inner Mongolia, Elkem has a plant up there. Our first day we saw people driving around with "pigs and carts," and when we came across a dead guy just lying there along the street—people didn't seem to take any notice—we had second thoughts. Xi'an was more or less the farthest from the east coast it was possible to go, I guess. And here we are also close to our suppliers, and the infrastructure is good. It is a fascinating adventure.

Earlier, the project manager and chief technical advisor on the Xi'an investment project had talked about some of the trials and tribulations. On a cold day in February 2001, for example, local farmers with shovels, crowbars, levers, and small machines worked side by side with big bulldozers from a subcontractor to prepare the site for the new Hydro magnesium alloy plant.[1] The farmers' work consisted mostly of backfilling land and blending soil and lime. The farmers themselves had coerced the subcontractor, and thus Hydro, into this collaboration by physically shutting off the site for any work until they could partake in paid work in the preparation of the site themselves.

A bit earlier the new venture had hit upon challenges of a more historical character. In December 2000, the site had turned into an archeological excavation that, from the project scheduling point of view, represented a delay in the planned progress of the project.[2] From a cultural-historical point of view, the discovery was both astonishing and somewhat anticipated. Cultural relics from the Early Western Han Dynasty (206 B.C.– A.D. 24) were unearthed with the aid of local archeologists. Among other things discovered and brought to a museum was a special bronze "Fang," believed to be a ritual object to be used to offer sacrifices to Gods or to the ancestors. As one of the Hydro project members dryly noted: "You cannot dig a small hole in the ground in this area without stumbling upon cultural treasures of inconceivable dimensions."

Named after this dynasty, the large majority of contemporary Chinese see themselves as "Han Chinese." The Han dynasty succeeded the short-lived but highly significant Qin dynasty (221 B.C.–206 B.C.), which, under the ruthless rule of Qin Shi Huang Di, literally meaning "the first emperor," is recognized to have united China under one dynastic rule and given us the present name "China." The Qin dynasty thus historically marks the transition from Ancient China to Imperial China, with the capitol located in Xianyang (a few kilometers northwest of present day Xi'an). Nearby in Lintong county, a site where a group of peasants stumbled upon some pottery in 1974 became the possibly most significant archeological excavation of the twentieth century, listed on UNESCO's world cultural heritages list in 1987—the uncovering of the Terracotta Warriors and Horses, near the mausoleum of Emperor Qin.

A one-third–sized replica of the "Fang" relic excavated from the magnesium plant site in contemporary Republican China is today used by Hydro as a beautiful company gift with historical significance. For Hydro, the localization in Xi'an of their first wholly owned light-metal plant in the People's Republic of China had a radically more contemporary justification. In the last decade or so, the metals industry has faced an emerging revolution as China enters the market at high speed. In 1990 China produced 5,000 tonnes of raw magnesium (of a world total of 260,000 tonnes). In 2006 China produced 526,000 tonnes alone (of a world total now of 726,000 tonnes).[3] About a third of Western raw magnesium producers have been shut down as a result. The Chinese formula for outcompeting advanced Western producers has been a low-tech, labor-intensive, heavily polluting production process called the Pidgeon process, developed by the Canadian researcher Lloyd Montgomery Pidgeon in the 1940s. As the Hydro executive responsible for Asia stated concerning the Xi'an investment, "We had to enter China or exit the business." As it turned out, they did both: first they entered China, and in a few years they exited the business.

However, do Emperor Qin and these millennial sweeps have anything to do with the establishment of a contemporary magnesium alloy factory in China, apart from the somewhat spurious link that the plant was located firmly on historical grounds of considerable depth? Arguably, the success of the whole unification of China was owed to the most extensive, radical, effective, consequential, and ruthless acts of standardization known to mankind. If this is so, we might appreciate that the abstraction and standardization processes of modernization, including the management revolution itself, have an ancient precursor in the practices of Emperor Qin. He reorganized society completely,[4] and with "demonic energy" he was "phenomenally successful" (Morton and Lewis 2004: 47).

All people were brought under direct control of a centralized government (their former allegiance to individual landowning lords was discontinued), and uniform laws and taxation were enforced regardless of former state boundaries throughout China.

Unconcerned with earlier traditions, the emperor proceeded to standardize weights and measures and to adopt a unitary system of money (a single coinage). The written script was also standardized in form, and to further enable trading and transport throughout the vast empire the track width between the wheels of carts was standardized. As Morton and Lewis (ibid.) explain, this was not a minor matter, as the carts wore ruts into the friable loess soil of northern China's roads to an extent that forced goods to be transferred between vehicles at the borders of the former states. Another of Emperor Qin's major feats was the redefinition of pitch standards for musical instruments. Although practically inclined, he somewhat ironically died quite young due to overexertion trying to secure an elixir of immortality.

Most of these standardizations were embarked upon in the same year, and all were decisive means of securing economic, political, and social integration in the unified empire, a unification that has continued for more than 2,000 years since his death in 210 B.C. The continuation can be seen, for example, in the bureaucracy and in the whole future Chinese conception of law. The tasks of the latter have, according to Morton and Lewis, in short divided citizens into the good and the bad, keeping the peace and strengthening the power of the state. Authority was built upon systems of punishment and reward. It was, however ironically, the unpopularity caused by this emperor's excessive policies of standardization that effectively brought an end to the Qin dynasty, and that has marked emperor Qin as a ruthless tyrant in Chinese history. One "achievement" not easily forgotten in China was accomplished when, in 213 B.C., he ordered all books (except those on the practical subjects of agriculture, divination, and medicine) to be burned, and all scholars who disobeyed to be executed. On Mount Langye, near the east coast of Shandong, one of the many stone stelae he erected on sacred mountain peaks reads:

> Everywhere under vast heaven
> He [Qin Shihuang] unifies the minds and integrates the wills.
> Vessels and implements have their identical measures,
> One uniformly writes the refined characters. (Kern 2000: 27)[5]

As will be illustrated throughout this chapter's descriptive analysis, managing the start-up project of a new magnesium alloy plant within a self-designated "global company" requires an impressive apparatus of standardization and formalization devices, or techniques and technologies, not completely dissimilar in their fundamentals—though in terms of brute force far less ruthless than the approach Emperor Qin pursued. The standardization and classification apparatus in the case of investment projects for establishing a new corporate venture seeks to produce particular but differential forms of both objectivity and subjectivity: creative and knowledgeable "human reseources," ingenious and precise tools and technologies, high quality and globally consistent products, uniform ways of working, coherence of values, predictability of operations, stability of organization, safety in all practices, universal respect for life, responsible individuals, and motivated employees (and the list is not meant to be exhaustive).

These are both instrumental and expressive efforts of commensurating cultural forms in the company, concurrently with its globalization process. Significantly for Bruno Latour, "technology is society made durable" (1991), and what makes the "global" assemblages of connections *stable*, what holds them together, is the obvious role of standardization, formalization, and classification of various kinds (Latour 2005). But as we shall convey, they are in effect not only standards for homogenizing processes of correspondence and unification, but also means for diversification and transformation in a global context.

Technology, Art, and Truth

The present exposition is informed by various traditions of sociotechnical theory (Emery and Thorsrud 1976; Herbst 1976; Trist 1981; Bijker et al. 1987; Czarniawska-Joerges 1998), and especially Latour's ontological position that "[t]here has never been such a thing as a pure 'thing' or a pure 'human'" (1993: 138). That is, technical and social systems are seen as constituted in processes of co-occasioning. On this premise, and because the focus here is on the deeper relationships between technology and management, the presentation is first and foremost inspired by the profound questioning of technology provided by Heidegger (1977), who raises a number of epistemological and ontological issues of high relevance to modern industrial management through reflections on the "nature" or "essence" of technology. Heidegger argues that definitions of technology, commonly perceived as a human activity (the anthropological definition) and as a means to an end (the instrumental definition), belong together. The whole complex of human activities involved in positing ends and procuring and utilizing the means to them "belong[s] to what technology is" (ibid.: 4). Thus, he considers technology itself a contrivance, in Latin an *instrumentum*.

A similar definition of technology is reached by Gell, who sees technology as "those forms of social relationships which make it socially necessary to produce, distribute and consume goods and services using 'technical' processes" (1988: 6), and "the ingenious pursuit of difficult-to-obtain objectives by roundabout means" (ibid.: 7). With an outlook similar to much of the sociotechnical perspective, Gell provides a classificatory scheme of human technological abilities in which he differentiates between three main forms. First is the "technology of production," defined as "comprising technology as it has been conventionally understood, i.e. roundabout ways of securing the 'stuff' we think we need; food, shelter, clothing, manufactures of all kind" (ibid.). In this form of technology he also includes the production of signs, that is, communication. The second type is the "technology of reproduction"; included under this heading is most of what is understood in anthropology as "kinship." The third form of technology he calls the "technology of enchantment," which is seen as the "psychological weapons which human beings use to exert control over the thoughts and actions of other human beings" (ibid.). Gell considers this form of technology to be the most sophisticated that we possess, and includes in it "all those technical strategies, especially art, music, dances, rhetoric, gifts, etc., which human beings employ in order to secure the acquiescence of other people in their intentions and projects" (ibid.).[6]

In my own investigation here I consider "technology" in these wide and inclusive meanings of the term, and include some of Heidegger's premises as well as both the first and the third forms of technology as defined by Gell, leaving out the second because issues of kinship are arguably of marginal relevance to our case. In the following I investigate how both the technology of production and the technology of enchantment or signification are enacted in managing actions for interpreting and mastering nature, and not least *culture*, for the purposeful goal of creating and realizing projects for industrial production. Thus, extensive space is devoted to cultural descriptions.

Instrumentality and Causality

These broader meanings of technology are all linked to aspects of "bringing about" something: creating, controlling, enrolling, and strategizing. Technology is thus intimately linked, as noted earlier, to the domain of instrumental rationality. For Heidegger, the instrumental definition of technology does not tell us what technology *is*, and consequently technology cannot be understood without understanding instrumentality itself. He argues that in the realm where means and ends belong, wherever instrumentality reigns, there reign causes and effects, that is, causality. To understand instrumentality requires thus a more in-depth scrutiny of causality. In Heidegger's words, "What technology is, when represented as a means, discloses itself when we trace instrumentality back to fourfold causality" (1977: 6). The four causes he reckons with are (1) the *causa materialis*, the particular material or matter involved (in our case information and communication technologies (ICT), tools, drawings, construction tools and materials, etc.); (2) the *causa formalis*, the form or the shape the material attains (in our case design basis and templates, "uniform" sites and plants, etc.); (3) the *causa finalis*, the end context of use (in our case a plant in full production with proper qualities and standards and competent organization); and finally (4) the *causa efficiens*, which brings about the effect, that is, the finished material with its form in relation to some context (in our case the managers, experts, and other participants' actions in project work).

Discussing what causes are, and their relationships, Heidegger sees the causes as being *co-responsible* for the outcome. There are four ways, according to Heidegger, that are interlinked in being responsible—not in either the moralistic or the purely effectual way, but responsible for bringing something forth into appearance, in *presencing* (*An-wesen*). These are four ways of unison *occasioning* that bring forth that which is not yet present into presencing and appearance. Heidegger designates the bringing-forth by the Greek concept of "Poiesis" from antiquity; Poiesis "comes to pass only insofar as something concealed comes into unconcealment" (1977: 11). Heidegger's view hinges upon the antique Greek trilateral differentiation between Praxis, Theoria, and Poiesis. As the lowest, most profane level in a moral hierarchy of activities, Poiesis, or "*tekhne*," comprised the whole realm of artificial creation, thus including both of what in the modern meanings are separated as fine arts on the one hand, and (industrial) production on the other (Øfsti 1999). Heidegger understands this "poietic" bringing forth as a form of revealing where technology, art, and truth come together, summarizing his questioning of technology at one juncture the following way:

> What has the essence of technology to do with revealing? The answer: everything. For every bringing-forth is grounded in revealing. Bringing-forth, indeed, gathers within itself the four modes of occasioning—causality—and rules them throughout. Within its domain belong ends and means, belongs instrumentality. Instrumentality is considered to be the fundamental characteristic of technology. If we inquire, step by step, into what technology, represented as means, actually is, then we shall arrive at revealing. The possibility of all productive manufacturing lies in revealing. Technology is therefore no mere means. Technology is a way of revealing.... It is the realm of revealing, i.e., of truth. (1977: 12)

It is as revealing, not as manufacturing, argues Heidegger, that poiesis or "*tekhne*" is a bringing-forth. While Heidegger, through an investigation of technology, comes to see technology and art as intimately related and the same, Gell also comes to the same conclusion, but rather via the investigation of art (1998). Yet, Heidegger sees the particular nature or essence of *modern* technology, which he labels "Enframing," as distinct, as "the way in which the real reveals itself as standing-reserve" (1977: 23). The bringing forth, the revealing of truth in modern technology, is a "challenging-forth," a "setting-upon" and "setting-in-place," an ordering of the real as a "standing-reserve." And modern technology is intimately linked to the rise of modern "exact science," especially physics, because the revealing in modern technology concerns above all nature as the chief storehouse of the standing energy reserve.

Such considerations are strongly present in Hydro's sphere of project and corporate activities. Hydro was founded on the taming of waterfalls' energy powers, to apply them as wanted from their "storehouse" in nature as a standing reserve. Aluminum activities are also heavily based upon the extraction and managing of nature's "energy reserves." Furthermore, aluminum products are branded by Hydro as "energy banks." For example, in Hydro's 2009 information brochure "Climate Matters: Our Approach to Addressing Climate Change," it is written beneath the heading "Investing in an 'Energy Bank'" that "[p]roducing aluminium from recycled metal requires just 5 percent of the energy used to produce aluminium initially, effectively turning it into an 'energy bank,' storing the energy for pay back each time it is reused."[7] In one of their corporate feature stories, titled "Good Past the Last Drop," we find a similar statement: "Aluminium is a virtual energy bank."[8] The "energy bank" is a metaphor that vividly illustrates Heidegger's point. Modern sciences are a prerequisite for modern technology, pursuing and "entrapping" nature as a "calculable coherence of forces." Few have captured the image of entrapping the energies of nature better than Kristian Birkeland, arguably the most gifted scientist in Norwegian history, whose technologies (fertilizers), which produced food out of "thin air," provided the knowledge basis for Hydro's establishment in 1905. As we shall see, it is not only "nature," seen as some "outer physical category," that is interpreted and mastered in contemporary Hydro managing. Culture is likewise turned into an object of mastery and management.

In light of this theoretical and philosophical outline, the questions that linger have to deal with what kinds of technologies of production and enchantment are utilized, and what modes and kinds of revealing are at play in our empirical context in the project work. How is management constituted by "managing technology"? And what is revealed of management itself, and thus what kind of truths might happen here? To be able to start answering these questions, we have to look more in detail at the ethnographic material at hand. The material will seek to display some of the immediate aspects related to the anthropological definition of technology in the present context, that is, technology as human activity. At a further remove, unfolding the consequences of the anthropological definition of technology as human activity provides us with a rich basis upon which to further investigate the instrumental definition of technology, and arguably also a more ontological definition and thus a basis on which to explore truths related to "managing technology" both in particular and in general. In the words of Heidegger, we cannot directly observe the "essence" of technology, nor of modern technology of Enframing, and therefore we must instead disclose some of the "managing technology practices", the efforts of standardizing and categorizing, and the strategies of production and enchantment performed in the "technological" activities of the social actors. As with technology itself, we need to approach the subject by "roundabout means," in a combination of empirical description and analysis as well as philosophical investigation. As such, it is an example of anthropology conceptualized as what Tim Ingold calls "outdoor philosophy," of philosophical reflections in the real world (Ingold 2007).

Counterfeiting and Strategic Secrecy

The Hydro magnesium start-up project, for the establishment of the plant, chose not to implement cutting-edge technology in the new venture. Although Hydro deploys possibly the most advanced technology in the magnesium industry, it chose for the Xi'an plant a "medium tech" standard that was operative at the Herøya plant in Norway in the 1980s. One of the main reasons for this was the fear of being imitated by competitors. As one technical supervisor on the project noted: "Of course there was a fear that our technology would be imitated when entering China. You have to expect that in a couple of years your neighbors have the same equipment. That was the reason we refrained from bringing our [cutting-edge] black boxes in—they would disappear."

Indeed, the fear proved to be well founded. Due to lower production costs and proximity to the Hydro production plant (whose location was chosen for ease of maintenance, amongst other reasons), Hydro chose to source almost all technology from suppliers who were geographically located as close as possible to the new plant. Soon after the Chinese technology supplier had produced the Hydro proprietary casting belt technology for the Xi'an plant, it offered the same technology on the open market—complete with pictures of Hydro staff at work in the plant. Other Hydro plants in China also had major experiences of counterfeiting, and stories and cases from global companies in China experiencing the same abound, for example in the automotive industry (Li 2004). However, for the most part Hydro managers[9] and technical advisors did not express the fears that would emanate from a naïve technology replication and knowledge imitation model. As one of the presidents of Hydro Aluminium noted: "Our competitive advantage does not lie in technology per se. Everybody, including competitors, is free to buy the same or similar technology, as they may feel like. It is the competencies of our employees and the way they together utilize the possibilities offered by the technology which award us competitive advantage." The president displays a sophisticated model of the relationships between technology, practice, knowledge, and good results. Indeed, the head of the largest division within Hydro, the executive who had advocated the Xi'an investment in the first place, also voiced the case for technological transfers as development aid to China, for the principal good of helping develop China into a modern industrialized country.

The apparent tension, implied in these two quotes, of counterfeiting vs. technological transfer "aid" manifested itself in the views of organizational members other than the top-level management just noted, as an overall necessity for strategic secrecy. Most of the executives and major and mid-level managers involved to a larger or lesser extent in the Xi'an start-up mentioned the necessity of keeping "competitive knowledge" as secret as possible. Against this position another view was thriving, conceptualized in the local Xi'an start-up organization as critical for a successful start-up. This other view stressed local organizational learning and building of individual and collective competencies. That is, on the one hand, some of the higher-level managers were trying to keep as few people as possible informed concerning critical knowledge that affected competitive advantage—for instance, temperatures in casting procedures. On the other hand, concern for the great difficulties involved in getting the local plant to operate at the necessary levels of quality, Health, Environment and Safety (HES) standards, and management practices was a driving force keeping information flows and knowledge exchanges as open as possible.

The end result in the Xi'an plant was that all relevant information was openly accessible to more or less all employees—including procedure manuals, specifications of "critical knowledge," and research results and reports from the research center in Norway. Thus, in the local operational plant management perspective, the need for local organizational learning and knowledge development was seen as more imperative than the perceived strategic management need for knowledge secrecy. As some strands of the knowledge management literature suggest,[10] this victory of the "epistemology of openness" over the "epistemology of secrecy" may not have posed an acute "danger" to long-term Hydro operations because there is, as the president eloquently noted, much more to "knowledge imitation" than duplicating black box technology and the replication of written-down "best practices."

The GM Relay

Management resources are perceived throughout the company as pivotal to a successful investment project and start-up of a new plant. But in what ways is success measured and assessed? On the most easily understood level, a successful start-up is achieved if the project is completed according to the planned schedule, within the appointed budget, at the right level of quality and safety, and with as little damage to health and environment as possible. A completed project means a plant that is up and running with a local workforce only, producing high-quality metal at uniform Hydro global standards, made with technology, processes, and procedures at the same health, safety, and environmental levels, and based on the same basic values when it comes to respect for life and the work ethic. Next, of course, things get a bit trickier. The people responsible for enabling and instilling these standards are the management. At a light-metal plant, especially in a perceived culturally alien context, the general manager—the GM—was seen as the most critical resource securing the long-term success of the new plant.

The notion of staffing a new plant solely with a locally based workforce stands strong within Hydro top management, and also, arguably, throughout the whole organization. Thus, contrary to all the advice in any best-selling literature on "how to do business in China," Hydro chose to try to find a Chinese GM to run the plant from "day one." Thus, when the start-up project had set up the plant, and withdrawn to some extent, the responsibility for operations was in the hands of the Chinese GM. He was hired during the project period, and it was the Hydro chief representative (with international experience and education, and of Chinese origin) located in Beijing and the Hydro expatriate with the most experience in China who organized the first major appointments for the new plant. As the chief rep recalls: "We appointed the General Manager, but after a few months we felt he was not good enough. Then we thought about what we should do. So I left myself for Xi'an to become the General Manager."

But what had happened? They had sought him by searching advertisements on websites, and through headhunters. They got quite a few candidates, and as the chief rep continued,

> this guy had working experience, with a MNC [multinational corporation], and other companies, spoke English, had an MBA from England, and wanted to go to Xi'an, not so many want to do that, so my feeling was that he probably would be OK as a GM. But for the human being you never know. Especially, when he was there, he didn't have enough experience as being GM in China, it is a very tough job, you have to handle so many things at the same time. He did not have the ability to handle the people issue, also he was not so capable to set up all the systems there. After a few months we felt things were messy there.

The expatriate chief technical advisor assigned to the start-up project from its inception to its end, who had many years of experience both as a production manager and with Hydro's magnesium research center, explained:

> We wanted a Chinese with experience from multinationals, who had lived in the West and who spoke fluently English. We got that. The problem was that he soon started build his own little empire here. You know, this Chinese personal type of management style where you are a high-and-mighty "small emperor" with unquestionable power. So he started to hire a lot of people, many drivers, many secretaries, spending a lot of money on useless things. Of course, we couldn't go on with that in Hydro.

Thus, the chief rep went to Xi'an to become the second GM. She was a senior executive Chinese, with a PhD in organizational behavior from England and a lot of experience with multinational companies operating in China. It was not easy for her to go to Xi'an, having a sick mother at home in Beijing who was finally convinced to follow along to Xi'an. Also, she noted: "I had never been GM, but I had done much on human resource, also business development, I even have a technological background, I have a degree in material, metal science, a MBA in Europe on joint ventures in China." She had worked, among others, with the large chemical company ICI set up in Shanghai, very successfully, she said, and "ICI have more stronger management focus than do Hydro. So it was a good chance for me to see how we could do it."

Once in Xi'an, she told people that she worked with two hands: "I have to sort out all the day-to-day issues, there so many people coming with so many things, but on the other hand, I wanted to build a strong management system, so that in the future all things will not depend on single persons. We can then use the system to achieve good work. China is not used to this, they are people related not system related." She thus set forth to implement safety standards—Hydro management principles and rhetoric are fiercely concerned with safety—and to make management systems for all the different departments of the plant. She felt that other Hydro managers and technical advisors, indeed the "Hydro culture," did not address these management systems seriously enough. Providing a corollary of this impression, several of the Norwegian managers in the project disliked what they saw as an overemphasis on management "systems" from the Chinese side. To this the Chinese GM replied that the expat Hydro people had to understand Chinese culture and realize the need for "systems." She was also responsible for making internal Hydro communications and presentation material, for example, stating Hydro's status as a Fortune 500 company, and its leading positions in the different businesses it engaged in. This proved important in attracting competent employees and retaining highly valued "resources."

However, soon the new GM, the project, and the plant all faced problems. "She did not know how to treat people," one of the project expatriates noted, alluding to the way he felt she ordered people around. Her perceived weakness in delegating, noted humorously also by herself, in addition to her lack of production experience, but also her family issues, played a part in clearing the way for the third GM. He was picked, according to the executive responsible for hiring him, "because he was *not* a team player." This could be seen as a somewhat audacious remark in light of Hydro management principles and rhetoric, where managers are conceptualized, by definition as it were, as team players. But the statement of this as the main principle for hiring the new GM had a deeper meaning: there had to be some exceptional legitimation for this unorthodox approach. The reason given was the need for "enforcing by acceptable means" Hydro standards at the Xi'an plant. The plant had several problems in these early days, both regarding safety standards of working procedures (use of protective equipment, and following Hydro established "best practices" in other areas), and concerning the quality of the metal. From an executive management perspective, the local organization had to reach acceptable levels quickly. If it did not, it would be shut down in the near future. The organization "had to be disciplined."

At Hydro, the issues of force and explicit means of punishment may be considered as very sensitive. The company "culture" is allegedly built upon values of openness, cooperation, respect for people's own judgment and expertise, low hierarchies and close relationships between management and workers, and to a great extent on self-management. Thus, hiring a Canadian *non*–team player with many years of management experience within Hydro to go to China to get the local organization "to level" with all "acceptable" means was almost a bit obscene. He introduced punishments, such as one day or one week without pay, for employees who repeatedly failed to comply with safety rules. He got all safety equipment to comply with Hydro standards, and he did not compromise at all on the safety issue. "They have to be told everything," he said concerning his local organization. "If there is a broken light bulb in someone's office, they do not change it. If the cleaner's broom is broken, she will not ask for a new one, if the receptionist is freezing like hell because it is winter and no one has told her that she can close the door, she will not close the door, and the same thing in the production. If there is an SO_2 leakage, no one takes action. You have to repeat and repeat and repeat."

Discussing these issues, one of the former expat GMs of Hydro's Wuxi plant said they had had many of the same experiences there, including that the former Chinese GM there had been a "Confucian pater familias" of the company. Soon the safety issue was "solved" in Xi'an, meaning it reached an acceptable level in the eyes of the GM and corporate management. Among the Chinese managers he was looked upon as a competent boss, although especially the HES manager thought he should take more time to explain the reasons behind all the strict procedures. Nevertheless, throughout 2004 the plant still struggled to achieve the right quality standards for products sold to fastidious Asian customers, especially the Japanese. One reason was the relatively little technical experience of the GM; for this reason the plant was on Hydro's internal list of its own "nonperforming companies" when the GM moved to another assignment after his contract ended. The head of the Hydro magnesium business humorously noted that it was a big contrast for the GM to move from Xi'an, which had no proper labor union, to a plant in Belgium where "they go to strike if they find no sugar on the table!" Meanwhile, at the Xi'an plant, if things did not improve fast the plant was to be shut down. Hydro could afford that: it was a relatively small investment, and one of the main reasons for establishing it in the first place was to learn about the Chinese market. It was never intended to be a "cash cow."

In 2004, the expatriate technical advisor, who had participated in the project from day one, accepted the job of GM. Having gained experience, the executives now felt that it was still too early to try with a new Chinese GM. The plant had to be a good performer, in the sense of producing high-quality metal in safe ways, and be making money before that could happen. The new GM's full attention was directed at producing high-quality products. A production man to his fingertips, he was not so much interested in either financial issues or management systems. He was a civil engineer of European origin who had acquired a lot of his work experience from the Norwegian Herøya research centre and community in Hydro, arguably characterized by some of the historically most pronounced participative and nonhierarchical work relations within the company. He continuously tried to enable this tradition and related practices at the Xi'an plant. With a multitude of other factors also playing a part, the result was nevertheless that by the end of 2005 the magnesium alloys produced by the Xi'an plant were the best quality in the world, better than any of their historically confident sister plants and better than any of their competitors. The plant was even doing a highly significant and high-status development project, in collaboration with the Herøya research centre, for a major customer in the automotive industry.

The transfer of management practices for handling technology, people, "systems," culture, and politics from Hydro's home bases to its new corporate venture in China was far from a linear, one-way, straightforward issue. Different knowledge traditions, sources of power, styles of authority, and perceptions of good leadership were instantiated at different junctures and intersections, and in a multitude of contested constellations.

The Mercedes and the Carriage

From being a fresh effort in uncharted territories with not-too-high expectations of success—indeed, even considered a calculated loss in the service of gaining learning in a new market—the new venture in Xi'an emerged like a dark horse in its fourth year. Already halfway depreciated by corporate management, the plant managed to manifest itself at the top of the list of high-performing magnesium plants. Other than the succession of GMs, what other factors played a major part in the transformation? After some of the initial lessons in China were learned, the point of departure, as perceived by the management involved, was not too optimistic: the challenges to success in China seemed gargantuan.

As noted above, during the start-up process it soon was conveyed by the project and start-up management team that knowing how to replicate pieces of equipment from Western Hydro plants was still a long way from replicating the quality of the end product, the process, and procedural standards expected of Hydro in China as elsewhere. It became obvious to the expatriates involved that it is not easy to replicate competencies that consist in tacit know-how, knowledge that is situated (context-dependent) and relational. And in magnesium plants, compared to other light metals works, these types of knowing have proved even more significant and critical, as the last GM stated. Such knowledge issues are closely related to the more elusive concept of culture. Without elaborating superfluously on the subtleties entailed in the concept of culture and its relation to "technology" and knowledge processes (see Chapter 1), it is simply recognized that the Hydro informants perceived the importance of these depths and linkages, and tried to interpret and "master" them. For example, one Hydro expatriate manager in China stated:

> It is quite a complex evolution behind Hydro's development in China, and it says something about learning in Hydro ... obviously too few have had anything to do with the wisdom and mystique of the East. That Chinese culture is quite different from European or Norwegian. We often talk about how it is difficult to understand Italians from say Norwegians, but after all we share the same culture. We have that common Christian ethic foundation, but the Chinese don't. They have a culture that is based on the boss deciding and the emperor being right no matter how wrong it might be. The last emperor was Mao, you know. He could just conjure up anything and people just had to bow down to it, and that is really the Confucian tradition playing its part. It influences the common culture pretty strongly. This means that whatever the boss says, it is ok, and even if it is illegal one has to do it. You don't protest against it. That was also true for our well-educated leaders—they had worked in other western companies, but they didn't oppose us, Hydro, as the responsible owner, even on illegalities.

This type of thinking exemplifies the "China-experienced" managers. Hydro expatriates held similar conceptions concerning Chinese practices related to processes like supply chain management, production planning, preventive maintenance, quality control, and spare parts scheduling. A quote from one of the most experienced Hydro managers in China regarding forecasting highlights some of these issues:

> To do quality control you have to have people who are skilled at planning, detailed planning for a streamlined process that can then be verified. But a Chinese doesn't do it that way, a Chinese produces, and then he'll step back to watch what happens. If there is something wrong, he adjusts. After a while he'll somehow get into the right track. The Chinese, they don't know planning at all, totally incapable of thinking "what if." That is one of the reasons that stuff goes wrong. They can't abstract, they think concretely and in a short-term perspective, they are opportunists. It is a culturally conditioned weakness that they don't know how to plan. Chinese culture never had a scientific revolution, to think hypothetical-deductive method doesn't exist in the culture, this has come the last 20 years with education. The younger ones get it, but the older ones don't. The sales manager that we had and generally a smart guy—it was impossible to get him to make a budget. "I don't know anything about next year," he said. "Can't you guess?" I asked; "you know these customers." "No, they haven't told me what they are going to buy next year. All our contracts are for two months." So I had to make the budget assumption. He wasn't able to or didn't want to—it was

against his mode of thinking—which goes "what I don't know anything about, I don't want to know anything about." Full stop. These are some of the cultural challenges you have to relate to, and then you have to adjust your practical management and your practices according to the landscape. Don't think anything about the Chinese that they cannot fulfill. If you are in negotiations and discussions with a Chinese and propose something about the future, then it's always fine. They don't have any conceptions, critical ability to evaluate whether it is a sensible plan or not. If you ask them about something—the implied response was "yes, what do you want to hear?" This is a cultural thing, it has nothing to do with intentions of lying or trying to trick you.

Much of the locally produced Chinese technology made for the Xi'an plant was of poor quality in the eyes of the Hydro technical advisors and managers. For example, several of the machines had old and worn-out parts, such as the straps and the valves. The feedback communication loops required to sort out all such quality issues and bring them to a perceived "Hydro standard" was complex, involving fundamentally conflicting expectations. As one Hydro expatriate jokingly announced: "Chinese don't understand why they should make a Mercedes when they can build horse carriages that function almost as well." Some of these considerations were also reflected in the personal diary entry of Kurt, one of the expat Hydro GMs in China. On 10 June 2005, he wrote beneath the heading "Punishment or Recognition..." the following:

Now after 8 month living and working in China I am on the way to change some of my basic believes. To give people freedom to develop does definitively not work. People's creativity to find out what is expected, or to think that they are paid to work for a certain performance is not strongly developed. This is even a too nice statement. But I think also that it is never the peoples own fault only. It is a surprise to me that even people with a university degree are to be told what is the issue. Discipline is weak and excuses are found for everything quickly. Comprehensive thinking is probably the most strange an animal to them. They always react to what has happened and very seldom I could find proactive measures and actions. Now my people [have] had a long period of training and are not used to produce and perform. We are now in a critical phase where we have to make a mini turn around from not respecting clear rules, bad habits and no time pressure to a performing organization. What surprises me more is the resistance of the labor force and the reasons brought forward as excuses. There is no doubt that we have to take some measures to show the people that we are not only here to joke. From my friends working in other foreign companies I heard that people respond very well to a tough management style. All the recent experience has seeded some doubts in my belief in a motivational management style.

In his last diary entry, on 25 August 2005, he laments some of the same issues:

> My first enthusiasm for the Chinese managers and operators has cooled down significantly, and in a way I am more prepared to do in my home culture. In my way to lead you have to lead through yourself or you relay more on a team. I have chosen the second one because I feared that the first one would not lead to success in the Chinese environment. The issues are always the same, and for my own certainty I have checked with other expat colleagues of foreign enterprises on the situations. Very little own initiatives, little ownership and a tendency to cry instead of facing the problem and look for a solution. I like to admit that it's not a generalization, but we at least, in our company there are probably three to five exceptions from the total 80 [people].

While reading through a draft of this chapter, one of the experienced Hydro expatriate managers in China noted the following in terms of assessing the type of work conducted by the Chinese employees:

> The Chinese are extensively creative, to some extent also innovative, but they do not like to "work to rule." They consequently have some difficulties in combining creativity and systematics. They are ad-hoc oriented, just-do-it, and fix the deviances later if it creates problems. The western tradition exhibits an industrial approach, with "plan-do-check-correct," while the Chinese tradition is more "do-repair-do-repair." A consequence of this, is a problem with the conception of preventive maintenance. The very philosophy is alien. "If it ain't broke don't fix it," works well. Also, relating to the experience of not taking initiative to changing light bulbs and the like; they only do what they are explicitly told to do. "You cannot be punished for something you do not do," I was told by one of my experienced colleagues in Beijing. He had learned that at school in the 1980s. If they are told to "take initiative," they more often do it on more or less random issues, to show they are "taking initiative," rather than doing it in relation to something that fits with an overarching strategy or plan for the year.

A similar concern related to "preventive mainenance" was often expressed also in the Azuqueca project in Spain (discussed in Chapter 3). It seemed, however, that in China the most positive experiences were those of Peter in the Xi'an project, both as a technical advisor and later as GM. He often praised his team and underscored the necessity of not underestimating the local employees and treating people decently. Here are just a few observations he made during our many conversations:

You have to respect them as people. They need no authoritarian leader, but someone with production experience, not only to control. These people are self-reliant and need leaders with consistency in their behavior and approach. Someone who reacts when people take shortcuts, when they compromise on safety, trickeries and so on and so forth. Those people you have to let go. If you can get to those five percent you hit the mark, and everybody at the plant gets happy. I think we have managed that now, more or less. I am not sure the Chinese are that different from us. They must be treated with respect. If you find the right people they have incredibly fast response-times, no limits, they are happy and enthusiastic. It takes very little both to please and disappoint them. And they are excellent in Powerpoint…. [smile] If you don't find the right people, it is frustrating. All in all I have few problems here in comparison to things I have experienced other places.

The importance of cultural "brokerage" was often heavily stressed. The start-up project team included three Chinese members with firsthand knowledge of Hydro "standards" and "ways of working." These "middlemen" seem to have been acutely critical to the accomplishment of the start-up. Regarding two of them, the project manager stated: "They are very competent, very smart and have an extraordinary ability to communicate with people. They are completely honest—maybe sometimes even too honest. One of them participated in an oil-project earlier in Norway. It is very important when we cooperate with foreigners that they understand our project methodology and ways of organizing. Both of them are just great. I have never earlier conducted a two year project were there have been no problems with the relationships." Another expatriate member of the project team stressed the "cultural brokers'" negotiating skills: "He is the friendliest man on earth, but watch him in negotiations with Chinese partners! We could never have done that by ourselves."

Circulating Safety, Dodging Danger

In spring 2005 an employee of a subcontractor fell from a ladder from about two meters above ground and nearly broke his foot. He needed medical treatment and stayed home from work a couple of weeks. The incident caused major havoc in the Hydro magnesium organization. One of the vice-presidents, the head of the Asian operations, flew in immediately, launching the full arsenal of managerial investigations, requiring all the reasons behind the incident, demanding an inside-out examination of all aspects of the accident and exhaustive suggestions for actions to be taken, procedures to be changed, and people to be responsible to ensure such an incident would never happen again. Although the local managers perceived the vice-president as highly competent and experienced in working in China, and generally held him in high regard, to many of them the seriousness of the demonstration was somewhat surprising, given that the incident seemed relatively trivial. One factor explaining his energetic commitment to the situation, outside the extreme focus on safety in general among Hydro managers, could have been an experience early in his career in the magnesium business: he had been the GM of a plant, not owned by Hydro, where a major explosion cost two persons their lives. Even so, safety standards seem to be something of an obsession throughout the whole Hydro organization. In both official and more informal presentations and conversations, safety is especially strongly emphasized. The story repeatedly goes like this, in the words of one start-up advisor: "Before we start talking about quality of the products or economic results, safety should be properly taken care of. That is first priority, first base. Without that in place, nothing else proceeds. With a not satisfactory safety culture we rather shut down the whole business."

Lumped together with the conception of safety are also issues like good housekeeping and good environmental and health-related working conditions, where the latter refers to preventing employees' exposure to, for example, toxic gases (Hydro is arguably known for stressing the S in HES, more than the H and E). Safety is particularly linked to the use of the technological equipment and the handling of hot metal on the shop floor. The everyday use of the hybrid medium-low-high technology on the shop floor in Xi'an can be illustrated by an episode related to procedural and HES issues. At the Xi'an plant, some staff has excellent education; some even come from the top-ranked universities in the whole of China, like Tsinghua—but nonetheless did not meet the expectations of some of the expatriate managers. For example, during a quite serious SO_2 leakage, none of the staff or supervisors reacted. It was not until someone from the international support team came in, smelled it, and reacted immediately that it was discovered—and found to have a maximum level measurement on the SO_2 meter.

I myself, having little experience at a magnesium plant shop floor, smelled a strange "deviation" at once when entering the production hall. Level two was the maximum accepted level, and now it was at ten, but the actual concentration could have been higher since the meter stopped at ten. The workers, foremen, supervisors, and production manager continued as if nothing was wrong. Afterwards the GM informally tried, though it was obviously difficult, to get the supervisors, the maintenance manager, and the production manager to engage in a reflexive and learning type of dialogue. Such a dialogue was the intention of the expatriate GM, who wanted to use the incident as an opportunity for learning rather than retribution. Most of the responses from the local staff and managers, however, were of the "yes, yes," or "yes, we will fix it now" type of reply. Some of these behaviors were interpreted by the expat as these employees' lack of interest in taking responsibility for their own safety and work environment, or lack of ability to do so. The standards of safety and a healthy work environment, with the TRI (total recorded incidents) as the measure making diverse safety situations commensurable, is one of the issues that Hydro's global managers and advisers devote their greatest efforts and resources to circulating uniformly throughout their plants worldwide. A fatal accident in the early phases of the Xi'an start-up would most probably have jeopardized the whole project.

The safety-related experiences in Xi'an were later reinforced in Hydro's new investment project in Suzhou. On 8 April 2005, the entry in the diary of Kurt, newly a Hydro expat GM in China, conveyed the following:

… and the economic value of the life …

The life and its cost is any easy understandable relation. One living in China feels that life seems not be too important. Accidents with a high death toll have a much lower importance in the media than we are used in the western world. The continuous fatalities in the coal mining industry are in the news, but the attention given is rather low. It seems to be the destiny of coal mining workers. On the other hand people do not really care about their life. Otherwise it is unexplainable how people can risk their life driving like hell without respecting any rule, working in risky environments rejecting protection or breaching rules as they would not exist. For us it is easy to foresee that that will lead to short life. But the Chinese are in general not scared about that. I am not sure if this has to do with a stronger collective feeling, giving less weight to the single person. In an interview about life or death of the American girl Terri Schiavo the people [here] expressed that if the cost are to high the best solution is to "disconnect the feeding tubes," no value, no life. It is not a question about ethics or moral, it's a simply relation of cost and benefit. Strange to live in a society with that high potential of "suicide."

In his entry for 22 May, he picks up on the issue of risk and safety, and a practice by the Chinese that he labels the "lifelong and consequent practice of inattention":

It is really remarkable to see how little attention the people pay to things they are exposed to, or even could bring them in dangerous situations. You have the feeling that people if they are driving never look behind to see what's going on, they just see in front of them and act, as they would be alone. As a westerner you should never suppose that the bicycle rider in front of you will not change his direction without giving any sign, or that the truck coming from left having red light will stop at the junction. The same attention people pay at their daily work. If in my factory people are producing customer goods, and if they see that there are only scrap pieces coming from the machine, they would not think that there must be something wrong or they have done something wrong. A friend told me recently that he heard a loud and frequent banging from his workshop; he went there to have a look to see what happens. He saw an operator trying to hit a bolt into a hole, which he could not achieve. The bolt was already bended, but the worker still banged onto the bolt to get it into his hole. The diameter of the hole was to small or the bolt was to thick and instead of finding out what was wrong, the worker did as always … he banged onto the bolt. Especially in our task to work with Chinese people this fact is exhausting for the managers (western), because it requires more and thorough thinking even for simple tasks. The cleaning workers on the street are a very brave species. They face all cars with no fear by paying no attention to any of them. I have asked myself several times the motivation of that consequently practiced way of paying no attention, but could not find the reason. Maybe I will find out one day.

Related to these diary entries is the issue of the training challenges perceived by the start-up management in the Xi'an team as critical for success. The challenges perceived as most severe were related to getting employees to follow procedures and routines. On the one hand the Hydro experts wanted the new staff to learn to follow the routines flawlessly, but on the other hand, they also wanted them to be what Schön (1983) calls "reflexive practitioners," who understand fully what they are doing and can improvise in situations of crisis and breakdowns. As one of the technical expatriate advisors said about the local staff: "they can be very creative in seeking innovative solutions to problems, and you want them to think independently and critically, but you don't want them to be running around doing everything in novel ways!"

Indeed, inventive they were, as exemplified for instance by the maintenance manager, who got a new casting pump to work smoothly in the production by making serious modifications. Another plant in Hydro, with a strong magnesium history, was unable, even when presented with the maintenance manager's drawings, to get the pump to work smoothly in its own production. Nevertheless, some expatriates expressed frustration that the balancing of this double-edged sword sometimes resulted in people not following routines for which they did not understand the rationale, while simultaneously doing things in ad hoc and improvised ways. The continuous stream of suggestions pouring into the plant's "suggestion box" for improvement to HES, coming from the operators, further illustrates the inventiveness of all when put in enabling situations. Fifty suggestions for improvements came in during a period of three months. A Phillips plant in China had a similar box but did not receive any suggestions, until they realized they had put the Chinese sign for "ideas" on the box. "Ideas," the Phillips management realized after a while, are perceived as coming only from the top in China. Once the word was changed to "suggestions," ideas started to appear. When talking about her work and asked about the Phillips case, the HES manager in Xi'an noted, with a somewhat different interpretation, that putting "good ideas" on the box would raise the expectation bar too high to get any ideas from the operators, for they would think that "my idea is not good enough." Thus she had put "suggestions" on the box from the outset.

The Carriage *cum* Mercedes

The final sign of the unexpected positive turnaround at the Xi'an plant—that is, in the eyes of corporate and start-up management—from being a "Chinese carriage" with few if any conceptions about "being a Mercedes" to becoming the number one, top of the line, highest-quality high-safety magnesium producer in the world, came during the summer of 2005, when the plant was given the opportunity to expand its production capacity with a 50 percent increase. The request came to the GM from the head of magnesium Asia: the customers wanted more products from the plant in Xi'an. Since its inception the plant had fought to get the demanding Asian, especially Japanese, customers to accept metal products from their Chinese plant. They had been strongly suspicious of "Chinese quality." Now they preferred "Chinese quality."

In addition to the two production lines already in operation, a third one had to be installed and ramped up. In conjunction with the production stop during this upgrade, Hydro chose also to venture upon a project to replace the whole roof of the plant building. Normally, for a project of such dimensions, the internal Hydro Projects organization would have been involved and running the project. The GM felt, however, that by this point his own personnel had acquired the competence to do the whole upgrade project by themselves. He assigned the maintenance manager to lead the entire project, including the replacement of the roof. It was a daring choice: a person inexperienced with such projects, in China, supervising dozens of unskilled subcontractors, who had little or no experience with safety equipment, crawling in summer temperatures of 50 degrees Celsius up and down the factory walls, balancing high above ground during the tearing down of the old roof and the erecting of the new. If they failed, if serious accidents occurred, or if someone died, severe criticism would pour in from all over Hydro about breaches of standards and procedures. Heads would probably roll. But if they succeeded, the project would prove inexpensive and efficient: it would be a showcase.

The maintenance manager was, however, not only in charge of overseeing the replacement of the roof. No, he also designed it, and even more, he completely redesigned the layout of the whole shop floor in conjunction with the installation of the third production line. A new design for the roof was needed for three reasons: (1) to decrease temperatures on the shop floor by 10 to 20 degrees Celsius (during summer the temperature inside could reach 70 degrees Celsius), (2) to stop the leakage of SO_2 that permeated through to the office wing when the winds outside blew from certain directions, and (3) to mitigate corrosion damage, which had brought the old roof to an unacceptable condition; holes were detected and it was on the verge of falling apart. The changes in the layout of the shop floor were substantial: the location of the cooling and packaging area was exchanged with the metal stock area, the restrooms were moved so that people escaped all the noise and could go outside to smoke (thus smoking became prohibited inside), and several other ingenious changes were effected. A much smoother, more efficient and safe U-turn flow through the production process was the result. Interestingly, this implies that major improvement changes and modifications to the original design made by the world-class engineering consultancy of Hydro Projects (HTP at the time) were carried out locally.

The approach to the upgrade project was circumspect. The maintenance manager, the management team, and the GM collaborated closely to plan and accomplish it together. The main pillars of the approach consisted in comprehensive management, fostering close collaboration in the management team and tight relationships with contractors, and securing a safe working environment through a special focus on the physical facilities. The elements of this approach involved giving all the involved subcontractors proper and thorough HES training, securing access control, follow-up checks, safety guarantees, and a detailed system of fines for breaking safety rules. Training records were kept for all subcontractor employees performing work at the site.

The training consisted of the following major parts: (a) introduction to work tasks, (b) common safety requirements (detailed on different activities), (c) tool risks and requirements, (d) utility cut procedures, and (e) other means, including site check records (plant managers controlling the site), work meetings with subcontractors, utility cut records (predictability of when power was shut on and off, for example), logouts and tagouts (labels attached to switches and buttons telling others not to touch), work permits and work marks (physical signs telling people where to go and where not to go). Care was taken to secure safe facilities, for instance ensuring that all equipment the subcontractors used, like ladders and scaffolding, was solid and unbroken, and making sure the facilities (such as machines and cables) were well protected.

The list of fines imposed on subcontractors for breaking the safety standards is given below. It was made by the maintenance manager and presented in management meetings and to subcontractors on a Powerpoint-slide. It was originally in Chinese, and was verbally translated for me to English by the maintenance manager: not wearing safety glasses (50 RMB), not wearing helmet (50 RMB), not wearing safety shoes (50 RMB), bad scaffolding (100 RMB), bad footing on ladder (50 RMB), not wearing safety belt (50 RMB), do not use working clothes (50 RMB), gas cut bottles not bound (50 RMB), presence in forbidden areas (50 RMB), use of Hydro equipment without permit (100 RMB), do not throw garbage in the right boxes (200 RMB), smoking and drinking in wrong places (100 RMB), do not obey work permit (100 RMB), site is not tidy (30 RMB), the facilities and tools not good enough (50 RMB), and breaking remaining safety rules that were not listed but must be obeyed (30 RMB). The final point on the list reads, "if someone does not obey and change, the person will be sent away."[11] Sent away from the plant, that is.

More than twenty fines were levied in total, most commonly related to the glasses, the bottles, and the safety belt. No one had to be sent away, though in one incident the maintenance manager had to fine a subcontractor who nonetheless refused to change his behavior. The manager got angry but explained later that this was regrettable behavior from his side, and the two of them sat down and talked things through. The end of the story was that the subcontractor became a champion for the safety regime. The final result was outstanding. The project was accomplished without any major hitches. No serious accidents happened, the project was finished ahead of schedule and below the already very low budget, also reaching full capacity ahead of schedule, the ventilation was fixed (no more SO_2 in the offices), and most importantly, the temperature dropped by about fifteen degrees on the shop floor.

Several other signs of the turnaround at the plant were also evident. For one thing, the production and maintenance managers were engaged to help their experienced sister sites in Europe to improve quality on certain alloys and processes in production. The production manager was also sent to a seminar at the corporate headquarters in Europe as one among an exclusive group of the "young and promising managers" of the Hydro global system. Peter the GM had a hard time picking the one candidate he would send, as he himself explained, "it could just the same have been the maintenance manager, the HR manager or the quality manger. I have an excellent team here." Peter praised his team often. "They are extremely capable, the people here. They enjoy much respect in the Hydro system." He laughed one time, saying: "The quality manager is the dream woman of the head of the Asia business." The main continuing challenge in Xi'an was on the market side, and market and sales issues were managed mostly from the headquarters in Europe.

Social Organization and Construction

A vast array of complex issues have been touched upon by the empirical exposition above, and in the following I will reflect a bit further on some of the most significant ones. Hydro is a global company, not least in the sense that it may actually operate throughout the whole world based on managerial decisions. When it chose to venture into China—a realm whose cultural history differed significantly from that of Norway and Europe, the company's home base—the cross-cultural intersections became highlighted in its ambitious efforts to classify and standardize the practices and values of the emerging venture. Take for example the efforts of standardizing and implementing abstract legal systems of "proprietary technology" and "copyright," or allegedly universal notions of safety, quality, management, and organization. In a "mongrel" Western/Chinese cultural context these issues are far from straightforward. As the notable Chinese anthropologist Fei Xiatong (1992),[12] trained by Malinowski and the Russian anthropologist Shirokogoroff, argues with regard to social organization in his comparative anthropology, China is best characterized by "*chaxugeju*"—an untranslatable concept unfamiliar in the West. Chaxugeju, usually translated as "differential mode of association," may be described as the egocentric system of social relations connecting people in multiple ways and at the same time placing different but precisely explicated moral obligations on each person in each particular context.

While Fei Xiatong describes Western societies as being produced through "organizations," much later a slogan made famous by people like Drucker (1993), based upon the notion of the autonomous individual who has legal rights and responsibilities before the state, in China Fei outlines a very different logic. He describes society in China as being produced through the basic concept of "chaxugeju"—not discretely delineated organizations, but overlapping networks of differentially categorized social relations, where the self is not realized through autonomous individuals but through "egocentric-relational" networks. Society is not collectively organized, but centered on the relational networks of each person. The networks are defined by dyadic social relations prescribing ritual conduct, especially personal obligations toward others. The networks have no explicit boundary, and the moral content of actions is constrained by the relationships and contextually determined. Moral conduct is seen as more decided by the situation at hand and the social categories of the present actors, rather than by abstract moral standards that autonomous individuals are to follow beyond time and context.

Not being familiar with Fei Xiatong's work, the most experienced Hydro manager in China found this outline convincing and commented on it: "Ever since my arrival in China I've had exactly the same understanding about fundamental traits in Chinese relationships." Nevertheless, on such a background Hydro and other global companies with "Western-style" abstract conceptions of, for example, health, environment, and safety, of property and copyrights, and of general management principles, arguably made little sense if not exemplified and detailed in concrete situations, relationships, and practices. Take for example the notion of corporate social responsibility. One local manager stated, "When they ask us to report on what we do in corporate social responsibility, it is very difficult to grasp for me, to get the idea of what they want from us."

Noting these differences, it is easy to run the risk of cultural reification in the analysis, especially when Pieke (2005) states that there exists no anthropology in China. This is mainly because it lacks a comparative perspective, and until it acquires one, he argues, we are left with either indigenous stereotypes of Chinese culture or alien, Western anthropological ideas about China. Practices of "managing technology" include, however, efforts of commensurating culture in the cross-cultural encounters happening in Hydro projects. Conceptions of culture and its commodification thus become objects of analysis. Critical self-examination on this matter is nevertheless necessary. How clear, for example, is the concept of corporate social responsibility to anyone?

The situation described above resulted in the expatriate managers' feeling that they had to detail and explicate everything, which in turn was a continuous frustration to Hydro expatriate managers and other "global company managers" with whom I spoke in China. The expat managers' implicit assumption was that general guidelines on the most important matters would suffice, and be appropriate, so that the local people could adapt it to their specific circumstances. Perceptions of the Chinese were, as illustrated earlier, somewhat paradoxical, embracing at the same time the idea that getting them to do something required spoon-feeding them everything in the "recipe" or detailed procedures, and the conviction that they were unpredictable and inventive—metaphorically representing them somewhat as children, or robots with creative imaginations. To these more or less implicitly pejorative and reified cultural perceptions, the Chinese managers themselves would to some degree agree, but possibly not wanting to venture into any argument they often talked about the need for expatriates "to understand Chinese ways, people and culture."

The cultural encounters in investment projects did not, however, cater solely to cultural constructions of the Chinese by the foreign managers. The opposite process was equally evident when local Chinese managers provided cultural interpretations of the foreign managers. The HR manager at one of Hydro's Chinese plants, for example, was in charge of a collaborative effort among the Chinese managers to produce a twenty-page sociocultural analysis aimed at Chinese managers and employees in Hydro. Its networked process of production made the end result quite representative, compared with my own observational data, of the Chinese's perception of Hydro's Norwegian legacy and managerial culture. The report covered such issues as the history of Norway and the Nordic countries, and the national culture and ethnicity of Norway, including socioeconomic data. One subheading concerning Norwegian national culture read: "A shy, distant and reserved people," and the text noted Norwegians' "closeness to nature," the "simple and austere life," egalitarianism, social problems like suicide rates, and nationalism. Norwegian social norms were covered, including "formality," "punctuality," "informal dressing style," their "quick returns on favors," and "telephone use."

Norwegian managerial culture was described with key words like "little hierarchy," "participative style," "efficient goal setting and planning," and as having a "discussion and dialogic based decision making process"; while being "ill at ease with conflicts," Norwegians aim to resolve them in a "civilized manner, having recourse either to the organization or to politics." The leadership style is described as being "involved in his or her team's work," as "non-directive," and as valuing "interactive facilitation, supportive behaviour and personnel development." The style is moreover "often quite apologetic about putting themselves into leadership positions." Furthermore, the communication style is described as "introvert"; emotions are not shown, but they may nevertheless "want to express themselves timely and precisely." Describing the communication culture in Norway, the report states: "In Norway, there is by many people, at least engineers, a profound skepticism toward all forms of shallowness and superficiality. This sometimes gives Norwegians the reputation of not easy to feel at ease in social situations, and lack of sophistication for many visiting foreigners." Memos are written in a "direct" and "non-ambiguous" style. They use informal titles and are "deal focused." While working with Norwegian colleagues it is advisable to be "direct and honest," "make plans before actions," "abid[e] deadlines," "be honestly humble, do not boast," be "patient," "participative," and "punctual," engage little in "small talk in the office," and avoid "topics pertaining to social status."

Reverse Culture Crash

The case has illuminated the significance of investment projects as unique social or cross-cultural encounters. Overdetermined notions about "Chinese culture" or "Hydro culture," from any actor's perspective, might function as a barrier toward constructive communication and interaction in the investment projects. The case illuminated what we might term a "reverse culture crash." The "cultural training" received by expat managers on Chinese culture reified a particular notion of Chinese culture as authoritative, top-down, command-and-control oriented, and radically at odds with traditional Hydro culture. Succeeding in China thus meant managerial practice had to be adapted to this (reified) image of Chinese culture. From the local side, however, many of the local managers and employees wanted to work for Hydro because they had a perception of Hydro that was in tune with Hydro's self-perception as a democratic, collaboratively oriented company. Thus a reverse "culture crash" ensued, contradicting both sides' anticipations and efforts at cultural adaptation and integration.

In the cross-cultural encounters of such investment project occasioning, the Xi'an case moreover illustrates that more open, flexible, and dynamic notions about culture are most fruitful for constructive collaboration and a better result, project-wise. The Wuxi case, on the other hand, illustrates how cultural notions might contribute to the breakdown of new ventures (Røyrvik 2008b). Such cultural encounters might possibly be variously facilitated and enabled through more indirect forms of managing that we might label *managing from behind and below.* The case material indicates that more direct and explicit forms of "cultural management" might rather have counterproductive effects, because their reification of intercommunicative cultural processes and unique cultural encounters can result in distancing, and thus potential stumbling blocks for the investment project.

As an example, the issue of safety—"the dial-tone before we start to talk about anything else," as one manager put it—might be illustrative. General and abstract reasons for performing "safe" (safe as in "Hydro safe") on the shop floor were seen as a challenge by Hydro expats and local arbiters in the first years. The most valued justification for safety in Hydro is "respect for life," a concept that, after a lot of practical cramming, really rang true among the managers and employees in Xi'an. But this morally "noble" ideal was not the only reason for the focus on HES. Experience shows that plants with high levels of HES, housekeeping, and tidiness are also the ones performing best in terms of quality of production and of the metal products. Examining Hydro's recent history confirms our observation. As it turns out, Hydro conducted major turnarounds throughout the company in the area of HES as late as the mid and late 1980s. As one manager described the situation at one of Hydro's most famous production sites: "I remember the first time I visited Herøya, a cold day of January 1986 … I thought he had brought me back to the 19th Century!" (quoted in Lie 2005: 275). The major turnaround at Herøya was preceded by similar major operational changes at Karmøy, and later at many other Hydro sites (Sagafos 2005: 269).

One may thus wonder about why there are no compulsory standard and comprehensive safety courses throughout the contemporary Hydro organization. There are certificates for driving trucks, but none for handling hot metal that under the wrong circumstances can blow up and kill people. Of course there are safety seminars and different safety workshops and tests, but these are mostly performed locally and are thus highly person-dependent. In some respects, we might thus say, safety is treated in an ad hoc manner. The "instrumental reasons"—the realization that a "safety culture" seems to contribute strongly to productivity and the production of high-quality metal—should also add to the question of why a more rigid standardization of safety courses has not been implemented.

The Chinese's conceptions of safety and their approach to their own work environment, perceived as "primitive" by many of the expatriates, need to be qualified with Chinese ideals and knowledge traditions, as emphasized by the Chinese managers. Examples of different conceptualizations were the Chinese's own emphasis upon values of modesty, robustness and not complaining, and endurance of tough work, hardship, and pain. Both the use of and the lack of understanding of the "Chinese ways," as the local Chinese management expressed it, led to a series of different approaches to leadership at the plant, as we have seen. Nevertheless, the local Chinese managers and workers and the Hydro expats found common ground in various basic values related to respecting each other's perspectives, taking each other seriously out of respect for life and health. With a collaborative approach this common ground emerged in work practices and routines as well.

This leads to another major but related theme growing out of the diversity emerging in the hybridizing Chinese/Western project process of erecting new production plants in China: assumptions about, and the performance of, authority. This harks back to our point of departure in investigating technologies of production and enchantment, seen through managing actions as various instrumental and complex causal ways that are *co-responsible* in the purposeful "bringing forth" of projects—creating, controlling, enrolling, and strategizing to interpret and master both nature and culture, so as to realize the goal of a new investment project. Authority is among other things linked with power, creation and "occasioning."

Organizing Authority

In Chinese society, control and power may traditionally be seen as constituted through rituals also prescribed by chaxugeju; that is, order, harmony, and prosperity are achieved through people's loyalty to their social obligations in their network of social relations. The obligations to each category, like son toward father, must be taught and explicated in every detail, and corrections measured out if learning fails. The unit of control is the dyadic relationship, not the autonomous individual "of the West" who is expected to exercise his will and sees authority as based upon the "rule of law." In the latter case the unit of control is the state (with its monopoly on violence to back it up), the constitutional embodiment of the people, the highest form of organization and the only one with mandatory membership, thus the ultimate power container from which everything else may be derived. Somewhat counter-intuitively, in some respects in China the state has always had a much more modest role. As the Chinese saying goes, "heaven is high and the emperor is far away."

When the unit of control is the dyadic relationship, the whole network of the person is implicated when someone does not perform satisfactorily. This was illustrated for instance when the Chinese chief rep, later GM, said that the Chinese are people-related and not system-related. Also illustrative is the fact that at all three of the Hydro plants I studied in China, a network of specific relations among management emerged, contradicting or supplementing the formalized organization and the "chain of command." For example, at one of the plants the HR manager became the node almost all other managers went through to communicate with the expatriate GM. The GM found it odd and difficult at first, but realized it was very effective. In another instance, in the management meetings all of the expatriate GMs felt it was difficult to engage the local managers in an "open reflexive dialogue." The local managers explained that this was not the Chinese way of doing it. To get all their reflections and comments, some of the GMs learned that they had to talk one on one with all of them, or with the central "nodes in the network," after, and also preferably before, the meeting.

Thus we might say that to some degree the means of control is localized in the institutionalized network of egocentric relationships, rather
than in some perceived collective institution or abstract laws and rules
imposed top-down. For example, political institutions in China may be
said to work more "from the inside out." Control is thus a shared responsibility, one in which people monitor each other, a principle we know
Mao utilized to the extreme (Chang and Halliday 2005). In this conception the ideal government should be based on these principles of power
and rule, of "*wuwei*," to do nothing. In principle, if society works well
the need for government will not arise. Where the Western manager, directed by the imperative of action, rules by solving problems, the Chinese
leader should rule by "not having problems" (Sørhaug 2004). It is in this
respect that we must understand the often cited Chinese conception of
authority as "rule of man" (versus the Western "rule of law"), which could
preferably be termed "rule of ritual" (Fei 1992). The challenges contemporary China faces in reforming its jurisprudential system to conform to
the "global standards" of, for example, the WTO illustrate the issue.

At the Xi'an plant several regimes of authority succeeded one another
via the substitutions of the GMs, and several types of authority were and
are exercised side by side. The first Chinese GM was, based on the managerial standards of Hydro executives, probably "too much" characterized
by the logic of "rule of man," noted also by some of the other actors in the
start-up enterprise. Notwithstanding the frequent misconception whereby
the expatriates confused "rule of man" with the Machiavelli-inspired
Western notion of the leader as the independent and cunning "strong
man," in the eyes of the Westerners the first GM built his own "empire"
and left the operation to "solve itself." The second GM's style of authority was part constituted by and part product of her being very knowledgeable about the "Chinese ways." She worked hard and competently to
implement a "system-based" practice at the plant, both because she knew
the need to explicate all kinds of employee obligations and responsibilities in detail, and because she wanted to try to "remedy" the "person-
centeredness" of the Chinese knowledge tradition. She had learned this
system-based approach through work in some of the best-performing
global companies in China, but from another angle she found that it was
also a practice that was quite unusual in the "Hydro managerial culture."

The Hydro style of authority, as it emanates from the Norwegian home
base, has at least since the 1960s been characterized by a participative
management style with plenty of room for delegation within an engineering, development, and project oriented culture focused on production and
technology,[13] but in another sense it is also a "people-centered culture."
In the view of the second Xi'an GM, what had to be addressed was insuf-

ficiency of systematics as it related to the management of all other aspects of erecting and operating a plant in China. Thus, she introduced practices and approaches—"management systems"—new both to the Chinese and the Hydro tradition. Both "sides" had to be adapted, transformed, and reinvented to meet the requirements of the context. Sometimes it created new hybrid cultural forms, and sometimes it reproduced reified cultural conceptions leading to (reverse) cultural crash.

Cultural Encounters

One of the key propositions of global "managerialism," as it originally emerged out of US engineering traditions in the late nineteenth century, was that of "systematization" and "standardization" as social practices and cultural idioms (Shenhav 1999). As we have seen, in the Xi'an case different types of systems focus were advocated from the Chinese and the European, mostly Norwegian, side of the project. While the Norwegian side, comprising to a large extent engineering managers, were mostly concerned with work standards and procedures in production, the Chinese side introduced the better part of the other management systems thinking, systems related to all aspects of running a plant.

The third GM was hired as a "Hydro-man" to enforce by "all acceptable means" a homogeneous Hydro standard of safety. This he executed based on a quite rigid system of punishment and reward, somewhat dissimilar to Hydro practices elsewhere, and more based upon a perceived notion by Hydro executives of how authority had to be executed in China to be effective. A conception of rule, one might say, with historical roots in the legalist philosophy upon which the first Emperor Qin built the unified China. Safety standards were implemented, but as some of the local managers noted, the same result may have become a reality also by other means.

Much of the same form of authority was also, however, exercised by the Chinese maintenance manager when working as a project leader of the upgrade project, at least with respect to his system of punishment. With respect to communication he notably regretted, or at least said he did, the one time he got angry. He did the work alongside Peter, the fourth GM, the man arguably most responsible for the turnaround at the plant, especially the shift to producing world-class quality alloys. Peter had an unwavering belief in the democratic, participatory ways of leading, practices he had learned in the Hydro magnesium plant at Herøya, Norway, the plant with arguably the historically strongest position under such forms of management. The delegation of the upgrade project to the maintenance manager proved his steadfast belief in this model.

Peter was very much appreciated by both managers and other staff at the plant, and many of them emphasized his management style and leader personality as one of the prominent motivations for working for Hydro. As the local quality manager noted: "I want to learn this style. I always wonder how he gets things the way he want while still being so soft." Some senior managers in the Hydro-China managerial network perceived Peter as a somewhat "weak leader," due to his dialogic, participatory style. When his contract ended, the executive responsible for recruiting his successor said that "now I think the plant maybe even runs too well, the people can get too relaxed, so I think after him we need a more strong one again."

Both the main themes analyzed above—forms of social organization and forms of authority—illustrate the ever-present dialectics between person and institution. From the institutional theories arising from social constructivism (e.g., Berger and Luckmann 1966), we know that institutions are social assemblages, patterns of communicative interaction made durable by repetition, symbolic instantiations and material manifestations. However, this notion of assemblage, of an ecology or ensemble of relations in dynamic interaction, and especially related to technology, can be traced back to Marx. David Harvey directs our attention to four crucial lines in a footnote in Marx's *Capital*:[14] "Technology reveals the active relation of man to nature, the direct process of the production of his life, and thereby it also lays bare the process of the production of the social relations of his life, and of the mental conceptions that flow from those relations" (1990: 493). Here Marx dynamically links technology, nature, the reproduction of daily life, social relations, and ideas or mental concepts, and treats the subject, according to Harvey, as a "kind of open assemblage of moments in a process."[15] Moreover, here we get a glimpse of Marx's deeper view of technology as both nondeterministically interrelated and co-constructed, but also of technology as forms of revealing and disclosing, touching our discussion here on several levels.

The imprint of specific persons on the course of events is, of course, strong, but in the case description we have seen how they both mobilize and are mobilized by institutional networks or distributed social "fields." For example, elaborations were made on how the Hydro HES *institution* in many diverse ways was enabled, enforced, and reinvented locally. The institutional "structure" of HES practices was not just "rolled out" or implemented, yet an institutional stability as being "Hydro HES" was reached in a completely unfamiliar environment by newly employed people. Furthermore, we have seen how the HES institution had a spillover effect on production. Before HES was institutionalized, quality of production seemed to be both politically and practically close to impossible.

Likewise, we have seen how the institutionalized forms of authority in Hydro were contested, both from within the organization and from the outside. The particularities of establishing a plant in this cultural and sociotechnical environment produced a multiplicity of perceived constraints, calling for non-institutionalized actions by key actors. The succession of the authority styles of the GMs, for example, may be interpreted as a step-by-step institutionalization of a "Hydro-attractive" (as perceived by managers and employees) power structure, which ultimately proved to be a success. I do not, however, believe this to have been carried out by a long-term rational plan. Rather, as learning was gained, adaptations and changes were made via an "art of the possible" approach by local and expatriate managers calibrating to the best of their abilities the optimal match between available resources, accumulated knowledge, and challenges at hand. And all the while they remained sensitive to enacting both the local and the Hydro "translocal" circumstances that continually regenerate the criteria for what are recognized as valid forms of authority and organizing, of "occasioning" and "bringing about" the desired project and plant goals.

Managing as Revealing

Based on the above expositions, simplified notions of the "standard view" of "management," "technology," and "managing technology," need to be reframed. Having taken in the ethnographic descriptions, we might rather ask questions related to the processes of cultural encounters in managing investment projects. What kinds of cultural forms and modes of epistemologies and ontologies are played out, repeated, maintained, modified, and transformed through the efforts of moving technologies, "best practices," abstract standards, and management styles through various cultural contexts—fixed through the global assemblages of investment projects? We must ask how this translocal network of the people and technological resources that are mobilized in such projects are situated in particular contexts shaped by the flow of a multiplicity of personal histories, knowledge traditions, and sociotechnological regimes. The ambition of straightforward technological transfers and replications, at least in knowledge-intensive operations, proves to be founded in naïve epistemologies. Efforts at standardization and formalization, reassembling the social in project work life, seem also to create its opposite in the same process.

We may consider the rhetoric of different types of management, and translations of management practices, as a combined form of "technology of production and enchantment," the latter described by Gell as "the psychological weapons which human beings use to exert control over the thoughts and actions of other human beings" (1988: 7). For Gell this is the most sophisticated technology we possess, and under its heading he places the technical strategies of art, music, dance, rhetoric, gifts, etc. (ibid.). If these "cultural" standardization technologies in a certain sense are a marriage of the technology of production and the technology of enchantment, then in a form of conceptual time-travel back to the ancient Greek notions of "Poiesis" and *tekhne* we have discussed how differential knowledge traditions including both objects and subjects have been mobilized, bastardized, reshaped, reinvented, and changed in these global flows.

Based on the ethnographic discussion above, we might also reformulate some of the even more fundamental issues related to ontological questions of the "nature" of technology, and arguably also the perspective of management itself as technologies of nature and culture. In our case, what kinds of instrumentality, causality, and modes of revealing (i.e., truth) are we dealing with here in the "managing of technology," and the "technology of managing"? As indicated above, Heidegger differentiates between handicraft technology and modern technology. Modern technology is also revealing, but it is a revealing of another kind. According to Heidegger it is *not* bringing-forth in the sense of "Poiesis," but a challenging, summoning, and "setting-upon," a demanding and provoking kind of revealing. By designating the revealing taking place in modern technology as "Enframing," it can be directly linked to the *managing* actions (and fourfold causation) as outlined in the ethnographic material. As we saw above, the defining characteristics of Enframing are about revealing as ordering, setting-in-place, challenging-forth, of stockpiling energy as standing-reserve, and of unlocking, distributing, and transforming. In these processes "regulating and securing" become chief characteristics (1977: 16).

Here then we can see more about the *nature* of managing from its engineering tradition. Seen as managing modern technology, the nature of managing is very much about Enframing as well. Managers are thus to be seen as revealers in the Enframing sense. In our ethnography we have seen the massive efforts at classifying, formalizing, and standardizing both nature and culture in attempts to interpret and master both. Now we can see that by their nature these managing efforts are forms of bringing about, regulating, and securing the "challenging revealing" (Enframing). Extending the conceptualization of aluminum as an "energy bank," we are now also in position to perceive modern management itself as the constitution of a meta-modality of an energy bank, as a "standing reserve" in the service of processes of "challenging revealing" both nature and culture outside and within itself. Related to human nature, the key characteristic of this meta-modality of management is to unlock, challenge forth, and transform both other and self into modes of wanting to want (to do, think, feel).

The answer to the question about the intimate relation between not only technology, but modern technology and art or "Poesis" hinges in the last instance, however, upon our conceptualization of nature. Different conceptions, or differentially social constructed concepts of nature, guide our conclusion. Heidegger seems to imply some form of a romantic Rousseauist idea of the "good nature" in his distinction between handicraft and modern technology, and to suggest that modern technology's (and management's) setting-upon, ordering, and challenging forth of the standing reserve is a form of revealing that is oppressive and obtrusive toward an inherently "good" nature. Heidegger was thus arguably a pessimist in terms of modern technology. However, taking into account other perspectives of nature—of the Dionysian, unreasoned, and pathological side to nature, conveyed in works like those of de Sade, Freud, or Paglia—other possibilities arise in the assessment of modern technology and its conceptualization as "Poiesis" and art. These general themes are continued in the next chapter. Again through an approach exploring the "technological" side of projects, it will unfold a notion I call "a social reality of construction."

Notes

1. The magnesium business area was a part of Hydro. It was recognized as the leading producer of pure and alloyed magnesium in the world before Hydro exited the business completely in 2007.
2. Many other factors in addition to the farmers' intervention contributed to delays in progress: among other things, the late capital expenditure approval, longer commissioning period, delays in every contract, and insufficient management capabilities.
3. See the International Magnesium Association, http://www.intlmag.org (accessed 23 May 2011), and Chen et al. (2001).
4. The country became divided into forty-eight military districts, each with three officials controlling one another (a civil governor, a military governor, and a direct representative of the central government, a system we recognize also today); all officials were divided into eighteen orders of rank.
5. Referred to in http://www.asianart.com/exhibitions/shandong/9.html (accessed 21 November 2009).
6. See also Gell (1992, 1998).
7. See page 5 of the brochure, accessible at: http://www.hydro.com/upload/3802/Climatebrochure_220109.pdf (accessed 28 November 2009).

8. Hydro corporate feature story "Good Past the Last Drop," posted at hydro.com online 28 August 2007: http://www.hydro.com/templates/NewsArticle.aspx?id=4386&epsl anguage=EN (accessed 28 November 2009).

9. When talking about Hydro managers in the Chinese context they are of three main types: (1) expatriates located in China of whom most are of Western origin, (2) local management, who are mostly of Chinese origin, and (3) corporate management located in Europe, with responsibilities also for the Asian business.

10. E.g., Nonaka and Takeuchi (1995); Easterby-Smith and Lyles (2003); Carlsen et al. (2004).

11. This list seeks to accurately represent its Chinese original in the way the maintenance manager translated the list verbally to me, but some language has been modified marginally to facilitate understanding of the items. Thus quotation marks have not been used.

12. In describing Chinese social organization I rely heavily upon Fei's work because it is widely accepted that in the Chinese context, his work, possibly more than any other, illustrates the power of anthropological field studies, and that, although not concerned with disciplinary boundaries, it also represents perhaps the closest China has come to developing a social and cultural anthropology of its own. For Fei, anthropology stands for a combination of functionalism and holism, firsthand field work and qualitative methods (see Pieke 2005).

13. See the three-volume work documenting the 100 years of Hydro's history from 1905 to 2005 (Andersen 2005; Johannessen et al. 2005; Lie 2005).

14. See David Harvey's lecture on chapter 15 of Marx's *Capital: Volume I*, and his particular focus on footnote 4 of that chapter, online at: http://davidharvey.org/2008/08/marxs-capital-class-08/ (accessed 27 April 2010).

15. Ibid.

Chapter 3

PRESENCING PROJECTS
A Social Reality of Construction

> By definition, a technological project is a fiction.
> —Bruno Latour, *Aramis, or the Love of Technology*

> This is one of those cases where the visible, that which is
> immediately given, hides the invisible which determines it.
> —Pierre Bourdieu, "Social Space and Symbolic Power"

> There can be no doubt that all our knowledge begins with
> experience.... But though all our knowledge begins with
> experience, it does not follow that it all arises out of experience.
> —Immanuel Kant, *Critique of Pure Reason*

> **Project**: ORIGIN late Middle English (in the sense [preliminary
> design, tabulated statement]): from Latin projectum 'something
> prominent,' neuter past participle of proicere 'throw forth,' from
> pro- 'forth' + jacere 'to throw.' Early senses of the verb were
> [plan, devise] and [cause to move forward.]
> —New Oxford American Dictionary

He was bald-headed, vigorous, and warm. Impressive. A man of the sort
you would imagine, without ever having met one, to be a practical, fair,
and effective industrial leader, the one who gets things done. He carried

weight, radiated natural authority. Still quite young for a man in his position, he had led large projects to success. He looked at me, smiling. We were talking about some of the more subtle human aspects related to managing projects and production. Fortunately he was also a storyteller. Outside his spartan, somewhat 1950s-style office, it was a cold day in late autumn, and the steep mountains from where energy was quite literally flowing down in rivers were already partly covered in snow, shimmering visibly in the dark day above the roof of the plant. Now he wanted to tell me an anecdote. "I was talking with Thomas, the foreman at the plant, the other day. Thomas was extraordinarily spirited. And that, I'll tell you, is not particularly common for Thomas. He is a calm, down-to-earth fellow. I'm asking him what the good mood is all about, and Thomas, deeply serious, says: 'Today I found myself a tapper' [a highly critical position handling liquid metal flows]. 'Oh, yeah?' I say, 'How did you find him, then?'" The manager lowered his voice dramatically to underline the point: "And Thomas answers, 'I shook his hand, held it and looked at him for quite some time straight in the eyes, and I *saw* he was a tapper.'"

In this chapter I continue to empirically investigate the "nature" of managing in projects, but here in terms of what I call "the social reality of construction." The argument revolves around my conclusion that the experiential reality in which the participants in project genesis are embedded, along with the operational realities of their work at production plants, is of such a nature that a more seamless and "undivided" reality of becoming is experienced as *pulsating just beneath (or above) the surface.* I find that this "implicate order" (Bohm 1980) indirectly but forcefully informs and underpins their daily work, in many ways in opposition to the common notions that both managing and modernity are constituted by decomposing and objectifying in the name of controlling nature and culture.

The Tragedy of Big Projects

The social life of projects in Hydro provides ample grounds for investigating subtle aspects of the constitution of reality. My own involvement in this realm was spurred, as explained earlier, by the simple yet puzzling questions revolving around why one project is a success, the next is not, and the subsequent one again a success, notwithstanding major efforts to interpret this situation that produced no straightforward answers. In time I learned, through the literature on "mega-projects" (Flyvbjerg et al. 2003), that Hydro could exhibit a comparably quite impressive track record of project accomplishments (without presenting any systematic statistics to back up the claim). Recently, for example, both the largest industrial project in Norway ever, the NOK 66 billion Ormen Lange off-shore gas project managed by Hydro, and the NOK 6 billion new Sunndal aluminum plant, the largest and most advanced in Europe, were completed on time, within budget, and with the required quality.

The "project" has increasingly become the more or less universal way of organizing large portions of work in the globalized industrial production world. It offers flexibility in terms of both differentiation and integration of resources; it is somewhat paradoxically an arena of creativity and innovation as well as control; it evolved as a work form from the development of technology and infrastructure after the Second World War; and as a worldwide phenomenon it was especially driven forward in US defense projects like the Apollo space program. In Norway it evolved especially via shipping and hydropower engineering. The field has been largely dominated by "operations analysis," and "project control" has been the main managerial idiom through the steering objects of the "iron triangle" of time, cost, and quality.

Nevertheless, reviews of the empirical history of project "performance" reveal a fascinating and somewhat disturbing reality (Flyvbjerg et al. 2003). Some spectacular projects with spectacular overruns illustrate a pattern. The Suez Canal project had a cost overrun of 1,900 percent, the Sydney opera house 1,400 percent, the supersonic Concorde airplane 1,100 percent. Looking at some of the large international transport and infrastructure projects, a picture of systematic overexpenditure emerges, for some examples (overrun percentage in parentheses): Boston tunnel project (196), Boston-Washington-New York railway (130), Storebælt railway tunnel, Denmark (110), Shinkansen Joetsu railway tunnel, Japan (100), and the England-France "Chunnel" (85). Public-sector IT projects incur cost overruns averaging 67 percent (ibid.). Some examples from Norway illustrate the same pattern. In the large offshore oil projects cost overruns are the norm rather than the exception: Åsgård by NOK 18.4 billion, Mongstad by NOK 7.2 billion, and most recently Snøhvit with the largest project overrun so far in Norwegian history, by NOK 19 billion. Norwegian construction projects also display a similar pattern (over-run percentage in parenthesis): The National Bank Headquarters (160), the New National Hospital (89), and Romerikporten (50); meanwhile the Gardermoen National Airport provides a contrasting example with a 6 percent cost saving (Kolltveit and Grønhaug 2004).

The "fatal findings" in a historical review of large projects' performance are summarized as follows. Huge overexpenditures have been a stable feature of large projects for sixty years, and this is a global and cross-sector phenomenon. The initiators of projects lie systematically, and the projects are a cocktail of underestimated costs, overestimated profits, underrated environmental implications, and overrated economic developmental effects. In sum these huge, complex projects come with extreme risks that are hidden from taxpayers and governments (Flyvbjerg et al. 2003).

In light of these empirical data, Hydro's project record, even without a systematic overview, seems indeed to be impressive. At the time of my entrance into this social landscape with the Azuqueca project in Spain, Hydro's previous project, one conducted in the US, was internally depicted as decidedly unsuccessful, though for reasons that were not easy to illuminate. As the saying goes, the suspects in an "unsuccess" vanish rapidly, as was the case in this instance. As Gard, a highly experienced, top-notch technical manager, once noted while we were exploring the subject: "The people in that project have all sublimated." Gard was somewhat ironically indicating that they seemed all to have diverted and transformed themselves into culturally higher or socially more acceptable activities. The story line that seemed to have stuck with most of the actors with whom I spoke of the matter, emphasized the reliance on *video* instructions as the main training tool, and thus unsatisfactory training, especially the lack of practical training, as the main reason for the failure. Pressed on the issue, themes like problems with US leadership styles, communication problems, and cultural differences surfaced. As Sigurd, the lifelong expert who travels the Hydro world to assist both new ventures in the making and old operations that suffer problems, once lamented: "You know, in their expressions these guys [in the US] are always world champions. They know everything and do not ask for help."

The video mistake stuck and became the main explanatory idiom. Intrigued by this puzzle, and by the combination of the obvious oversimplification in the video explanation and the high level of indeterminacy and intangibility in Hydro's own efforts to arrive at other explanations, the present chapter explores what I call "the social reality of construction." Situated in the world of investment project genesis, this phrasing alludes both to Berger and Luckmann's "The Social Construction of Reality" (1966) and Searle's "The Construction of Social Reality" (1995). Proceeding from the argumentation in the previous chapter, centered around technology and managing as processes of emergence in terms of "challenging forth," of "ordering revealing" and poietic complex causative "industrial arts," in the following I argue that the more subtle dimensions of this reality that makes possible the bringing forth of such projects, is a reality of process, flow, and "seamless" movement. It is a world struggling with the fixation of wholeness and compartmentalization, of concentrating conceptual flows, of "materializing abstracting," and of systematizing flows and flexibilities. It is a world of goals, objectives, and aims that guide projection and conceptualization.

The greatness of the industrial arts of bringing forth projects rests fundamentally upon these seamless movements and flows, but its grandeur in the pragmatic sense is arguably due to what Paglia (1990: 5) has called the "delusional certitude" and Einstein labeled the "optical delusion"[1] prevalent in the Western insistence of the discrete identity of objects— including the conception of the self as limited in space and time—and the mastering of these objects through naming and knowing them. These processes may adequately be labeled processes of "id-entification": the making of identity through conceptualization and externalization, in one sense through what anthropologist Tord Larsen labels processes and "acts of entification" whereby "something inchoate congeals into a thing (Latin: *ens*), a unit, a category with discernible boundaries" (2008: 203). I will argue that the "social reality of construction" is largely constituted through processes of "concentration and projection" of (inter)subjective imagination. These processes are not at all "purely" mental, ideational, and disembodied, but rather intimately connected to projections of passions and desire, and particularly related to male sexuality and communion (Røyrvik 2008a). As Camille Paglia attests: "Man's metaphors of concentration and projection are echoes of both body and mind" (1990: 21).

In the following I will describe and analyze a subset of practices and conceptions related to project genesis in Hydro. First, the chapter focuses on the processes of "structuring projects," which I will interpret as processes of "concentrating conceptual flows." Secondly I describe social conditions often referred to as "atmosphere," "ambience," or "ethos." These subtle conditions that are vital to project emergence are interpreted as contributing to the realization of projects in terms of its power to assemble, that is, to unconceal, or reveal "the real" (i.e., the truth), of imaginative anticipation and *intersubjective intentionality*. Finally, the analysis of core constitutive features of the genesis of investment projects is summarized by conceptions of *potentiality* and elevated under the heading "The Imagination Bank: The Art of Entangling."

Keepers of Gold and Processes of "Structuring"

It was in the very early phases of the Qatalum project. I was working out of my temporary fieldwork office space at the Hydro headquarters in Oslo. There had been some meetings, some interviews; I scanned and collected information from the internal web pages, and so on and so forth. Alexander had recently been appointed responsible for the "organizational" side of the slowly emerging Qatalum project. In his early forties, he was, relative to his age, very experienced in managing large industrial projects. He had successfully executed the role of project director of the largest project in Hydro in recent years. We had talked a lot about what makes for a good process in bringing forth a project, and his reflections were based on his own experiences. He was extremely skeptical of the vast and complicated "systems" and "tools" approach to managing projects, the standardized "Project Management Institute" (2004) kind of approach that, in his words, "administer[s] more complicated tools the more complicated the project seems to be." For him the key seemed to be the opposite: "the more complex project you are dealing with, the simpler, more straightforward approach you need. It all boils down to people and communication. You need to get a team together that works well, that understand each others positions, that talks plainly and directly."

Now, however, when discussing where to *start* in such a large and complex project as the Qatalum project—what to do first, as it were—he seemed to be saying something else. His position was nevertheless straightforward: "First now, we need to get some structures in place." Given my previous conversations with him, this statement seemed somewhat surprising. However, before long I realized what kind of "structures" he was referring to when he brought out his PDA (Personal Digital Assistant). "To be able to start enrolling the best people for the project you need to get the calendar out and start booking meetings." Getting structures "in place" was in the first instance to schedule meetings, which in turn was a lever to start enrolling "good people." Now his strategy became more coherent with my ideas of his approach to projects. He had to work within the institutionalized environment of the company, where among managers "meetings" were the primary organizing principle of daily work.

Fascinated by this use of the term "structures," I wanted to get a handle on what kind of "structures" managers in Hydro constructed and employed in their activities of project creation and realization. In the following I present some of the "structures" that I found most compelling. For brevity I have organized them in two main types of "structures": project *process* structures and project *organizational* structures, both strictly related to the emerging projects in question. Of process structures I have found two main types, first the *meeting structures* referred to above and second the CVP (Capital Value Process), the decision support model that all projects now need to follow in Hydro. In the following two sections I describe both of these two main types of "structure."

"Goldkeepers" and the CVP

The "decision support system," the CVP, at first seemed to me to be very complicated and bureaucratically "heavy." Thus I was in some bewilderment, because Alexander still had praised it as one of the reasons for the success of his last project. The CVP project itself—the project designed to establish the CVP throughout the organization—was launched late in 2001, instigated by the situation of their earlier decision support model having never "become firmly planted within the organization," as the manager of the CVP creation project put it. The group responsible looked at the systems other companies used and found that the model Amoco had could fit. When Amoco merged with British Petroleum in 1998, the latter adopted the Amoco model. The name itself and the basic design of it, with drawings and schematical layout, were also adopted from Amoco.

Then extensive work commenced throughout the organization's business units in clarifying purposes, defining contents, and enabling ownership of the CVP through participation of members. This was a long and complex process on which I will not dwell here. However, language was a problem because all business units wanted to get their "words" into it, whereas the CVP project team aimed at making the CVP universal within Hydro. The Hydro project's "native slide" in Figure 2 displays the agreed-upon concepts.

According to the CVP leaflet or folder that was printed and distributed internally, *Decision Gates* "[i]s a milestone at which a formal decision is made"; *Decision Gate Support Package* "[i]s a management summary of the key results of the work performed in each phase and including a clearly recommended statement"; *Decision Gate Reviews* is a "project external review to provide the degree of quality assurance required by the Gatekeeper"; and *Gatekeeper* "[i]s responsible and accountable for the decision made at the end of each phase. The appointed gatekeeper shall be proactive in defining Owner's objectives and requirements, and ensure that adequate control is exercised." The "Owner" is the business unit, seen as the actor that orders and owns the project, while the Projects organization, together with operations, is the organizational actor that mostly executes and "delivers" the project. The *Post Investment Review* is an "[e]valuation of [the] project after one year of operation to provide the basis to assess the success of a major business decision."

Each business unit also defined its own "best practices," which enables the CVP. The best practices are unique to the business unit, not universal in Hydro. For the Projects organizational unit, the best practices that are listed on the CVP folders are the following: "CVP General Description; Start-up Arena; Risk Management; Project Definition Rating Index

Figure 2. Slide from Hydro giving an overview of the basic principles of the Capital Value Process (CVP) decision support process for projects (Hydro Projects).

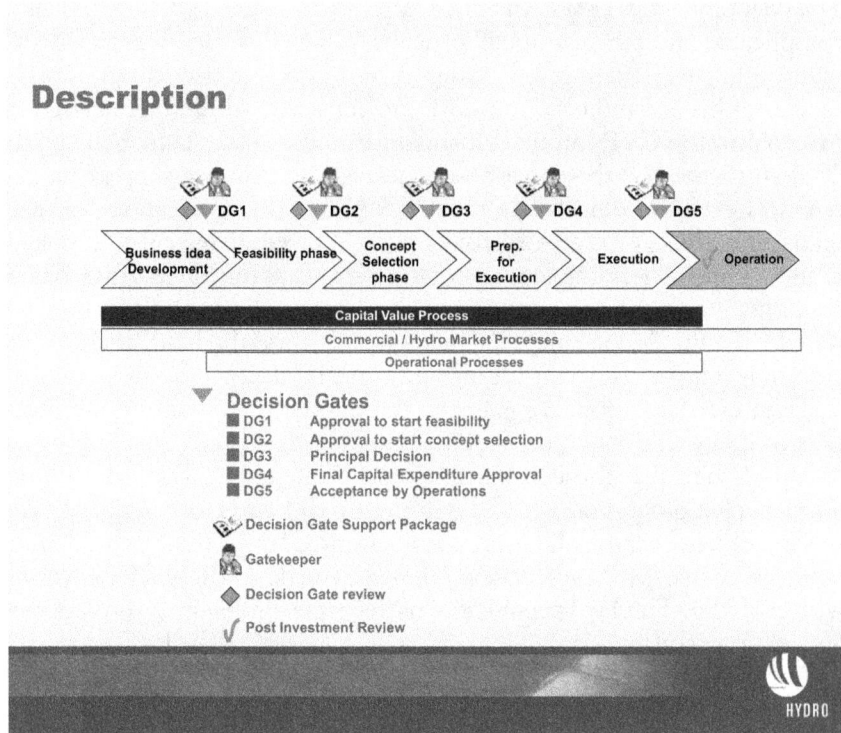

Source: Hydro.

(PDRI); Decision Gate Support Package; Decision Gate Review; Post Investment Review; Hydro Estimating System; Hydro Economic Analysis; Commisioning." By January 2002 it had been decided that oil and gas projects should use the CVP process, and the same was established for Aluminium as of 2004. By 2005 all projects in Hydro were supposed to be supported by the CVP. Projects not complying with the CVP risked not being supported by the corporate management board. Some of the labels, like "Gatekeeper," were new to experienced Hydro managers, and were sometimes the subject of a laugh. For example Hans, director of one Aluminium business unit, once said to a colleague and me as we walked together to a meeting: "The first time they said I was going to be a gatekeeper I did not have a clue what it entailed, and I thought it was 'goldkeeper,' so I was quite happy actually!"

Looking at the formal CVP process, the lists of best practices, and other adjoining systems, I figured it seemed complicated, possibly to the extent of "overkill" in many projects. Not until I spoke with the manager holding the overall organizational responsibility for the CVP could I fully comprehend Alexander's enthusiasm for the CVP. "It is completely flexible and adaptable," the CVP responsible manager said. "You can use it for the construction of a huge factory and also for buying only a fork lift. Obviously, you scale it differently for these two tasks." In his mind it was completely scalable. Meanwhile it turns out, upon talking to various project managers, directors, and participants, that projects were indeed carried out in much the same way as "earlier"—as before the CVP was implemented. The most common statement was a version of "The CVP formalized and explicated practices already existing earlier, but also added some new elements and concepts." As for Alexander, his main reason for praising the CVP was that it "was a structured way of facilitating necessary dialogues with all stakeholders in the project," and as such it enabled all parties to comprehend core dilemmas of project work. This in turn forged a shared meaning among participants that they "were together and in the same boat, and could see their place in the bigger picture," and that everybody had to, and wanted to, give and take to make the boat move forward and succeed in its adventure.

If we consider the power that is literally invested in naming in this case, the CVP is particularly interesting. The name "Capital Value Process" was simply adopted from Amoco and BP. With this adoption, however, the importance of the conception "capital value" was firmly rooted in the midst of the engineering process of industrial creation in the company. With the adoption of the CVP name and concepts, the former "engineering department," "where we sat in felt slippers and white coats with our rubbers and pairs of compasses," as Gard humorously once put it, had in a sense been transformed into the keepers and stewards of capital value. Figure 3 below illustrates how the scheduling of main project events in the Qatalum project was done at one point following the CVP process.

A brief gaze at another relevant case study, of the making of Fiat's Melfi factory, reveals some of the same dimensions of relevance that are touched upon above, and also anticipates some of the things that will be discussed below. Patriotta's (2003) main finding was that the factory, which in retrospect appears to be a ready-made product, a "black-box," is the visible outcome of a construction process also involving the future workforce. The processes of design and construction show six main phases underlying the construction of the factory and progressively leading to the sedimentation of a corpus of organizational knowledge: (1) the design concept, (2) recruitment, (3) formal training, (4) construction work, (5) learning to "disassemble" (technology), and (6) full production. Similar broad categories apply in the Hydro projects.

Figure 3. **Overall overview of the Qatalum project development plan, organized in terms of main activities and scheduled on a timeline.**
It was made in the early phases of the project and covered the entire project period, until "full production" of the finished plant was reached.

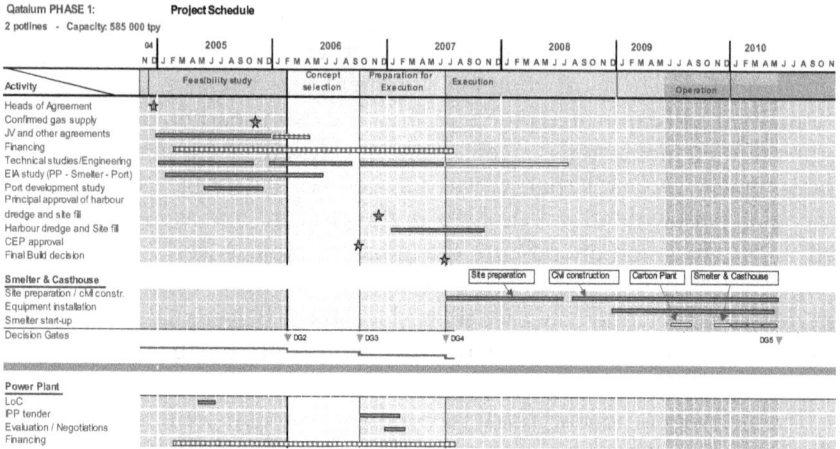

Support 6,
Qatalum - Project Development Plan

Qatalum Project

Source: Hydro.

Project Organizing "Structures"

All the projects investigated "grappled with" and seriously "played with," variously throughout different phases, the organizational "structures" that were brought fourth and then in turn guided their work efforts. All of the projects had different conceptualizations of their evolving "organizing structure." Here I will give a brief presentation, illustrated by their own figures, of some of these evolving and enabling organizing structures—these both structured and structuring "structures." To ease the interpretation of these figures it is useful to first consider an overall model of project-related interfaces. Figure 4 below outlines the main Hydro internal bodies involved in project creation.

External stakeholders like customers, suppliers, and governments are not included. The corporate owner is the body that finances and owns the project. The business unit operations side is the body responsible for running the plant when the project is finished. It is the business operations

Figure 4. Project-Related Organizational Interfaces

```
Corporate          ¦        ¦ Business Units/
Owner              ¦        ¦ Operations
- - - - - - - - - -¦ Project ¦- - - - - - - - - -
Business Units/    ¦        ¦ Corporate
Operations         ¦        ¦ Owner
```

side of the business owner. The project itself, including the main institutional managing body of the project, i.e., the Projects division, is created by these three actors. We see that in the earliest phases of a project it is the Owner role that is most pronounced, and thus placed on top of the dotted line interface. In the late phase of the project it is the Operations role that is of most significance and practical importance, as it is operations that are going to run the "end" result of the project, the materialized plant with all its technology and competent people.

Figure 5 below follows the organizational structure as it had evolved more or less halfway through the Azucueca project in Spain.

As the figure illustrates, the project was divided into three main subprojects: the "start-up project," the "building project," and the "IS/IT project." The project was perceived as being fueled by the experienced team of Hydro experts, as well as the local knowledge possessed by those already working for Hydro in Spain and those who were successively hired into the local workforce. In this project the concept of the "dream team"

Figure 5. The Overall Organizing Structure of the Azuqueca Project

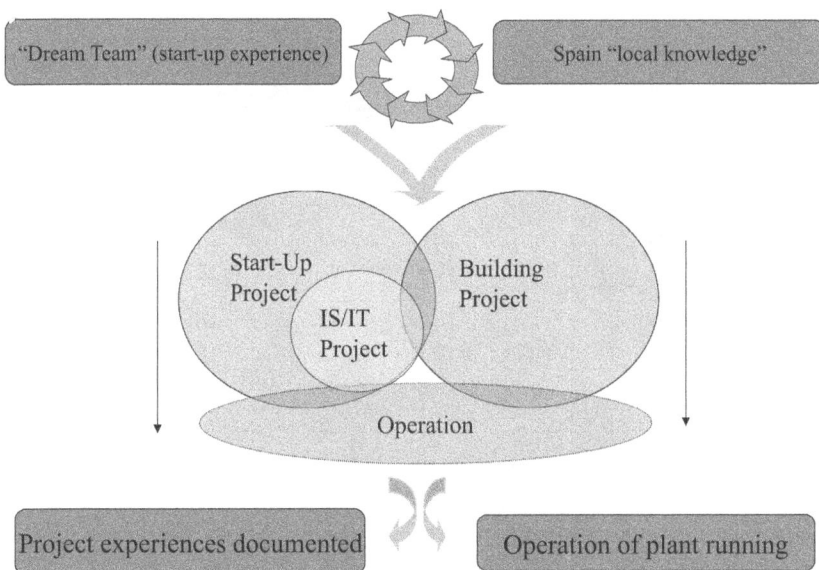

was born, intentionally somewhat humorously labeled. This team is made up of those experienced Hydro people throughout the system who contributed to the project's realization. Organization of the dream team in time and space is a whole separate issue. A key preliminary point is that the three sub-projects of the Azucueca project at first were seen as quite distinct, but during the emergence of the project the interface management became more and more pronounced and the three were increasingly seen in conjunction.

The "building project," seen as the "hard physical stuff of buildings and technology," was managed by Hydro Projects (HTP at the time), while the "start-up project," managed by a team of managers taken from various operational European Hydro businesses, was concerned with the "soft side" of the project and "everything else"—for instance, hiring employees, training, competence, establishing routines and procedures, legal formalities, customer relationships, etc. Figures 6 and 7 are formalized outlines of the project organizational structures in the Xi'an project in China, which was significantly differentiated in terms of its formal "organization" versus its practical "organizing."

Figure 6. The Formal *Organization* of the Xi'an Project
Notice the formally conventional hierarchical and "square-like" representation of the project organization given here.

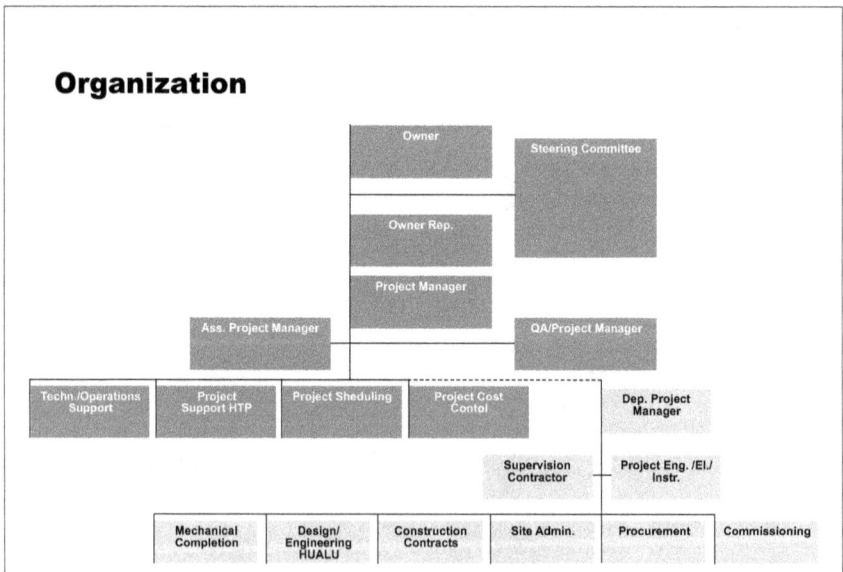

Organization

Source: Hydro.

Figure 7. Project *Organizing* in the Xi'an Project
Notice the much more fluid, dynamic, and circular representation of the organizing in the project. It reflects more the practitioners' view of entangled processes than the "formal structure" view above.

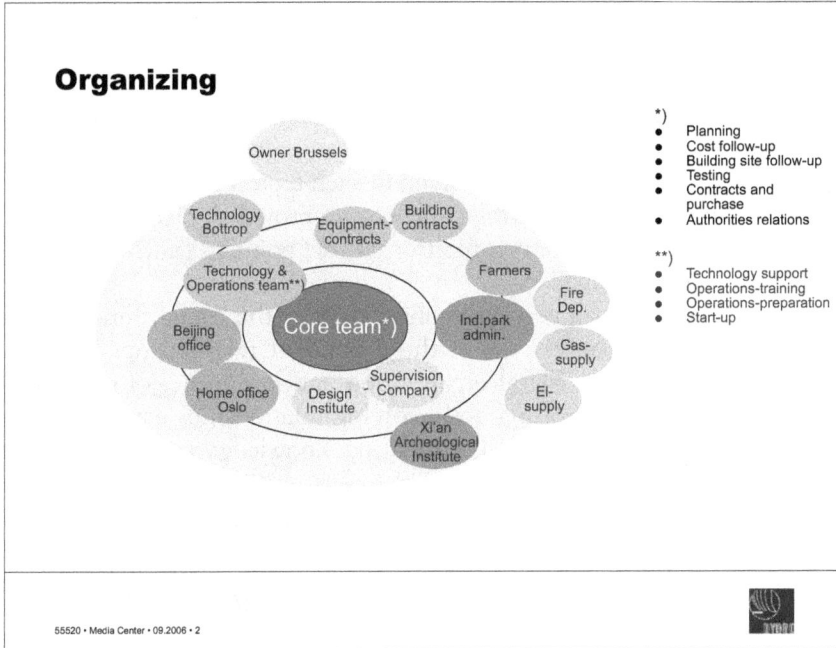

Source: Hydro.

Figure 6 illustrates the conventional, formal "organizational chart" way of presenting the many internal corporate bodies, roles, phases, and activities of the project. Figure 7 includes also, in a more complex and dynamic way, the project's organizing structures with Hydro external stakeholders included as well. The color coding is significant; it clusters actors according to main roles. Because it is in the magnesium business, the "Owner" is referred to as the magnesium headquarters in Brussels. Internal technology assistance is provided from Germany and Norway; corporate assistance is provided by the home office in Oslo and from the Beijing Rep. Office. The Design Institute, which supported the detailing of the plant concept design, and the "supervision company" were local in Xi'an; as were farmers, the "industrial park administration" where the plant was to be located, and the Xi'an Archeological Institute. The equipment and building contracts were drawn up in collaboration between the core team and the local assisting agencies.

This was a small project for Hydro, but the complexity of the effort is illustrated quite appropriately. Moving to the gigantic Qatalum project, the complexities become even more evident. As the project leader in the early phase of the Qatalum project laconically commented in a discussion about the dimensions of the project, "Just because it is big, it doesn't happen by itself." Gard once noted that small projects are more vulnerable to person dependencies because each person needs to take care of a broader area, whereas large projects have more redundancy as they accumulate more problems of complexity and coordination. To briefly illustrate some of the dimensions involved in such a project, two figures from the emerging project organizing concepts are provided. Figure 8 outlines what the Qatalum project organization at one point in time, during the early phases, had evolved into.

Figure 9 below was a very early-phase draft of the "same thing" as figure 8, trying to visualize some of the dependent relationships between the Hydro Aluminium Metal organization and key bodies of the Qatalum project. The functioning and evolving relationships across this interface are critical both to disseminating knowledge and experiences

Figure 8. An evolving "concentrated" instantiation of conceptual flows related to the organization and organizing of the Qatalum project

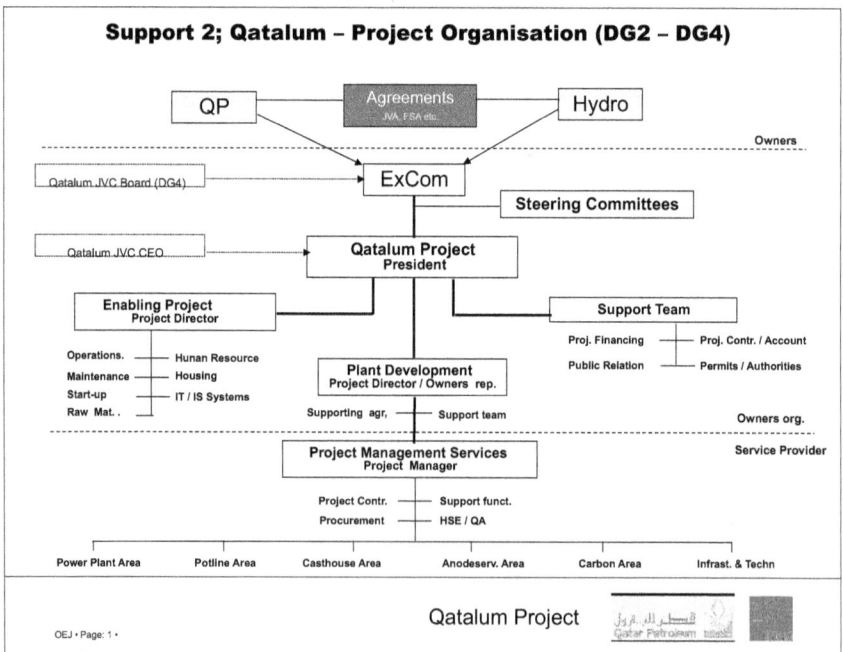

Source: Hydro.

Figure 9. An early draft trying to conceptualize and visualize some of the relationships between the Hydro Aluminium Metal "parent" organizational entities and the Qatalum project's key actors and organizational bodies

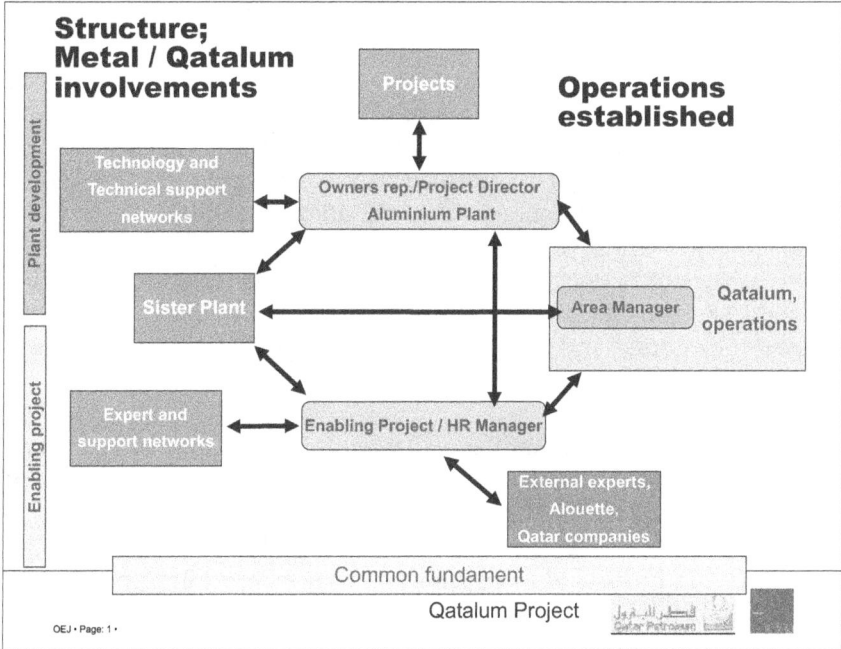

Source: Hydro.

from the Hydro organization to the project, and to using the project as an opportunity to strengthen the competence of the Hydro Metal "parent" organization.

In various presentations and discussions, the importance of clarity and responsibilities of roles was a major issue. This was even more pronounced in the Qatalum case because it was a 50/50 joint venture between Hydro and Qatar Petroleum. Thus, the organization of roles and responsibilities had also to be broken down into what belonged to Hydro, what belonged to Qatar Petroleum, and what were the "pure" activities and responsibilities of the Qatalum project and later the separate joint-venture Qatalum company. The bringing forth of these "organizing structures" and conceptual aids for action was the result of a complex series of communicative interactions over longer periods of time. These evolved and were re-created until a point in time when they were considered mature enough to be "frozen" and then used as more formal guiding principles in establishing the huge project organization and work organizing principles, with support functions and legal statuses, etc.

Concentrating Conceptual Flows

As demonstrated above, core managing practices in the early phases of projects are related to conceptualizing forms of organizing and "structuring" the work of the project. It is a simultaneous bringing forth of a holistic overview of the project—the core sub-elements in terms of actors, organizational bodies, and roles and responsibilities, as well as their interconnected relationships. The visualizations of these complex dynamics are evolving processes of intersubjective communicative interactions, where the models and figures are interconnected instruments and aids in a conceptualizing hermeneutic individual-collective sense-making spiral. In these processes the project is emerging out of both preexisting concepts and the creation of new concepts. In processes of "concentrating and projecting," and as such possible instantiations of creational arts (Paglia 1990), the project comes to life as a creation that is both abstracted and materialized.

On bringing forth a technological project into existence, Latour writes, "By definition, a technological project is a fiction, since at the outset it does not exist, and there is no way it can exist yet because it is in the project phase" (1996: 23). Latour seems to be saying that "a fiction" does not exist, and that it exists only insofar as it is materialized in physical technology. As such, technological projects are ripe with both epistemological and ontological concerns. How is something brought forward into existence? Why is there something, rather than nothing? He seems to suggest that such projects are constituted as a movement from nonexistence to existence in terms of physical realization. Latour continues, however, by saying that "[t]he observer of technologies has to be very careful not to differentiate too hastily between signs and things, between projects and objects, between fiction and reality, between a novel about feelings and what is inscribed in the nature of things…. Only a fiction that gains or loses reality can do justice to the engineers, those great despised figures of culture and history" (Latour 1996: 24).

Thus Latour seems to hint at a notion of different levels or modes of reality, similar to what I argue for. The passage above suggests that ideas, concepts, and expressed signs in a variety of media (drawings, slides, pictures, texts, etc.) certainly are "materially real." Indeed, it indicates that abstracting (often considered an upward movement from some kind of material base) is an interconnected process linked with "materialization" (considered conventionally as the downward movement from abstract to concrete). The "concentrating" of conceptions of organization and organizing structures above suggests a simultaneous movement of *abstracting materializations*, where signs *as objects* are brought forth from a background, first as still inchoate qualities and relations, then to ideas and concepts, which are again re-created, transformed, and concentrated in recursive cycles before "congealing" into a more rigid and permanent form. Credence then is given to what Picasso supposedly once said: "Everything you can imagine is real."

In the efforts of concentrating (abstracting/materializing) flows in projects, we catch a glimpse of a deeper nature of this reality. Reflecting on the bodily and psychological nature, or basis, of cultural production, Paglia notes: "Male concentration and projection are self-enhancing, leading to supreme achievements of Apollonian conceptualization" (1990: 22). Fueling the genesis of project conceptualizations are processes of concentration and projection, successively unfolded through time. To properly theorize these ontological relationships there seems, however, to be a lack of a coherent and *differential* ontology, to account for phenomena's relative positioning and reality status in the overall ontological field (Johansen 2004). In David Bohm's philosophy and terminology (1980, 2000), which has recently been gaining currency also in mainstream anthropological forums (Ingold 2007), we might say that whole-part project conceptions are abstracted and materialized in successive movements of unfolding, from the generative or "implicate order" to the "explicate order."

In this light we might quite literally propose that the "finished" result of projects, the physically operating plant, is a "fantastic reification of abstractions," though the expression signifies something quite other than what Radcliffe-Brown meant when using the phrase in his critique of the concept of culture (1940: 10). I pointed to elements of such an ontology in Chapter 2, and below I suggest that this ontology is also grounded in the new physics of quantum reality—the sciences of nature and the universe as fundamentally entangled, relational, "seamless and undivided" (Bohm and Hiley 1995; Nadeau and Kafatos 1999; Aczel 2002). First I turn to a set of empirical descriptions that might reveal some of these dimensions in managing practices in investment projects.

The Ambience of Enabling

As we have seen, the projects investigated here have invented different approaches to the organizing concepts and actions, and to bridging the "hard" and "soft" side of projects. In Azuqueca they started out with two separate projects, the "building project" and the "start-up project," as well as a smaller ICT project, and gradually made the interfaces and overlaps stronger. In Xi'an there was one project that was broken down into several activities. In Qatalum, the vast complexities and evolving models of organization are visualized above (see Figures 8 and 9). In this section I will describe how *both* the hard and soft sides of projects are seen by the participants as being underpinned and fundamentally enabled by "soft" processes of human, social communicative interaction. As noted by a president in Hydro Aluminium when we met during the inauguration of the Suzhou plant in China: "The hard aspects of projects we know how to handle. There we are really good. To a large extent it is extreme logistics, and in that area we have brilliant people. The main challenges are on the soft side of projects." Likewise, it was often noticed by managers and other experts involved one way or another in project work that the project methodologies or routines and procedures were mostly tuned to the "hard stuff," while the soft side was handled on a more ad hoc, person-dependent and improvised manner.

One of the major ways in which investment projects contribute to realizing a "long life" for a new production plant is by hiring and training all the new local managers and employees. Training is a key activity and interface for actualizing projects and allowing them to transform into an operational plant. In the Azuqueca project I participated in several training sessions taking place both in Spain and in Norway. During the first days of receiving and training the new staff for the plant, I was speaking with Bruno on-site in Azuqueca, in the almost-ready office section of the emerging plant. Bruno was the lively traveling engineering-manager type—cosmopolitan, unorthodox, with a surprising personality; there was no place he really considered home. He was commenting on the issues of safety, training, and pedagogical communication and illustrations. Bruno said, in his usual way of talking, at once entertaining and serious, "When the training is planned..." he paused for effect before continuing:

> it is important not to make it boring. You know you can take the people and put them in the front of a screen, or in front of the video-projector or in front of me. And I can explain them during thirty days about aluminium, about the market, about the customer, about the equipment, about everything. But in the end the people will be impressed by me, and will say: "Ah Bruno, very good!" And if I have said the truth or not that will be the same, OK? And then I can say, OK, you are ready to go and burn yourself to death there, because it is dangerous!—I'm being aggressive again...

He often joked about his own personality quirk of being too straightforward, direct, and "aggressive." "But we have to balance that, and I guess that the best way is to bring people to where you have the similar operation. And to pay for this training, and to pay what it costs to have people to stay for one week or two weeks or three weeks or four weeks or five weeks."

Here our discussion was joined by Sigurd, an impressive character: tall, energetic, and vigorous despite approaching retirement, with silvery gray hair brushed backward except for a stray lock that drummed his forehead as he gesticulated and nodded to underscore critical issues. Sigurd stated with confidence: "The money used for proper training is like a piss in the sea compared to the cost of sending expert support people for a long time after start-up, like we have done at the Henderson plant."

Susan, the project manager of the start-up subproject in Azuqueca and a much more diplomatic and systematic person than either Bruno or Sigurd, also emphasized the importance of practical, hands-on training:

> I don't think Henderson had a "dreamteam" in the way that we have had. They had training, lots of training actually. Too much maybe. And a lot of training was done in the classroom, but not so much in practice. And if there are people who have no clue about aluminium production, you can get an overload of information and cannot absorb it all. And it gets difficult to use it in practice. Then there has been a lot of people from the European system supporting afterwards as well in Henderson, but in a way it has been on an ad hoc basis, so when the problem occurred somebody was sent over and stayed one or two weeks to try to solve the problem.

Bruno beautifully explicated the pedagogical principles of practical exposure and experience:

> I will never say that if you are staying in a plant for two months you will know enough. But the main issue is the experience. If you can see small aluminium explosions.... You can ask Juan [the production manager in Azuqueca]. Juan has been at Clervaux [an established Hydro plant in Luxembourg], and we had one guy two years ago at the 27th of August. He burned his feet. And I said to the guy, and we know each other very well: "Could you show your feet today to Juan?" I don't know if you have this experience, but the feet are looking like a piece of meat at the butcher! It is not feet, it is something...

Not finding the right words, Bruno gesticulated dramatically, trying to give shape to some fuzzily bounded object in the air: "... you know, really a piece of nothing—meat.... And I can say that I am sure that Juan this evening was not sleeping well." He looked up, staring intensely through his glasses, his gaze entirely unwavering, anticipating a reaction. I just waited for more, and of course there was more:

> It is perhaps the best way? For me it is a good way to try to electroshock the people. Show something that is the reality! Don't explain that aluminium can be very dangerous. Aluminium is dangerous! And you can die from

liquid aluminium! So show that to the people, and I guess all people coming down to Clervaux, will have access at least to this picture. They have
a video at Clervaux, and I guess they are accessible in the company worldwide, showing a start-up of a big company with a big explosion, where
there were twenty wounded. If you show that to your people, and I have
experienced that at Clervaux, but three years after we started there people
are looking on it and say "it is so dangerous" and all. But when they are
familiar with the business they do perhaps not believe all that we show.
But for new people, if you can show that if you are not wearing the right
clothes, or protective equipment, if you are not respecting the regulations
to have dry tools to use with aluminium, if you have moisture somewhere
and you don't take care of it. You will have a big risk for your life!

The reference point for the managers of the Azuqueca project was the
Henderson project and the way it had used a lot of video material in the
training process. As Sigurd said: "You know, when the people entered
their built cast-house, and experienced for the first time on their own
body how hot the metal was, how hot the working conditions were, surprisingly since it looks like water—they were scared to death. Scared in a
serious way that inhibited their work."

In our many discussions about training, competence, projects, and
production Sigurd always stressed the communicative aspect of learning.
"What is often missing," he said during a workshop meeting in Sunndalsøra, Norway, "is the pedagogical skills to make learning happen! Models,
figures, procedures and everything is of no use if you cannot communicate, if you do not get across to the others." The whole Azucueqa team
visited Sunndalsøra to participate in different forms of production at a
fully operational and experienced plant. Bruno told about the first trip
the Spanish managers and employees made for training at the Sunndal
plant in Norway: "Some of the people were present when the cast started,
and some metal splashed two or three meters up in the air. Juan called
me and said he had seen something, and that all the people had been
'shocked.'" Bruno himself jumped in his office chair to underscore the
point. "700 degrees into the air! You know. Surprising, because before it
is so calm in there, beautiful when the metal is liquid, you can sit there
almost like at home in front of the fireplace … well not now during summer.… The wood burns, you are relaxed, it is so nice, grey and glowing,
silverlike, really beautiful, like at your cabin. But the danger is different,
yeah?" Sigurd explicated the purpose of the training trip to Sunndalsøra:
"We give the people classroom hours, a lot of practical training, a lot of
videos, plastics, how to behave, basics about aluminium, explosion, water, humidity, emergency procedures—you name it, we got it!" Both the
Spanish employees and the Norwegian "teachers" at the plant had a great
time during the practical training. Both parties praised the initiative.

"Everything Is Connected"

An additional corpus of ethnographic material I want to present is a collection of quotes taken from a host of interviews and discussions with various categories of managers who all have experience working with investment projects in Hydro. The quotes are clustered around a few key categories. First is a set of statements that focuses directly on the "soft side" of projects, emphasizing aspects of communicative practices:

> Underlying all of this is that you communicate well; that you communicate well between the different disciplinary groups in the project.

> So it's this thing about working in a team with other human beings, and the total dependency you have on each other to get the collaboration working well, that's what's fun in everyday work.

> It is when you have been struggling uphill for some time, perhaps having had problems communicating and creating alignment—really striving to get it right—and then people are beginning to see it and they put in that extra effort and they deliver.

> It is this thing about presence—actually taking the time to listen and talking to people, have a dialogue and discuss things.

> It is very important that you try to span out the entire solution space … and you have to be on guard for the sluggers that have strong opinions at an early stage.

> (One) should never forget that human beings are social creatures first and foremost, and the greatest need when we have had enough food and sleep and sex, that is participation. It's not money, really. It is participation, to be accepted, be involved.

> To listen and not just do the talking yourself.

> To be open for other angles, other sides of the issue, and to respect and make use of other people's competence. If there is someone else there who are in your discipline, then you should contact him.

A second set of quotes highlights issues related to seeing the "big picture" of projects, the "total concept" of the holistic view.

> [It is] important right from the start to think "totality" … a concept that is coherent.

> I feel that it should always be so that everybody feel they are part of building the cathedral and not lay brick by brick … that's really important.

It's great fun to be part of creating something and see that things are rising up out there in the field and that there are concrete results and not just on paper. Of course that gives you something of a kick.

To see yourself in the big picture, try to see totality: "What is my role in this and why is what I am doing important?"

This thing about working in a matrix is an external condition and it is hard for many. It is a big challenge, and I have no patented solution for it. I think it is important that you motivate people from a holistic thinking.

The project owner has an extremely important role—they need to see that everything is connected. It must be persons who care about getting things to work together, who do not dive into disciplinary details.

So, I am saying that if there is a group of ten, if more than two or three are creative, there will be chaos, right? And you need one or two who also think that total concept is fun. You need one or two in the group who are very conscious of and good at treating stakeholders, one who has a good network in Hydro, and of course you need good specialists in each of these disciplines.

Some of the most important things in the early phase is about seeing the totality, in particular that you manage to see the technical and the commercial picture in connection. The concept architects are those who have a very good holistic understanding, they know a bit about the underground, a bit about everything.

Finally, a small series of quotes is offered to illustrate the frequently emphasized aspects of projects as idea-driven, joyful creational efforts.

To execute projects is OK, but we don't live from that. We live from coming up with our own ideas that can be executed and from creating projects.

The most fun thing I do is projects—to be part of creating something.

[W]hat's exciting is that early, the project is lead by a type of people, a type of KPIs [Key Performance Indicators] … who don't have that feeling of (having to) deliver physical execution … they are very eager to find smart solutions. Creative smartness is really the driver.

Prior to DG2 [Decision Gate 2] the important thing is getting ideas to flourish, it is very important that you try to span out the entire solution space … so consider the entire solution space and explore that which to begin with does not feel right.

Celebrations are important. It has to do with team spirit and a sense that you are part of contributing with a product and that you make visible what you have done and the result of what you have done. It is very important that the one having done the job is credited.

Some of the material presented above might be interpreted in some strands of organization studies as representing the struggles and efforts of coordinating (independent parts), of establishing work routines and knowledge sharing (between autonomous individuals), or of getting all kinds of "systems" in place to make everything work. Such interpretations would in several ways be fair and reasonable. However, I argue that such explanations hold true only as far as that goes. Seen in synchrony, the empirical material presented above strongly signifies a set of recurring issues related to concepts, actions, and representations of project work as what we might call the materiality of imagination or anticipation. It instantiates the industrial arts as abstracting/materializing and co-evolving imaginative design work. It adds to the foregoing analysis of projects as "concentration and projection" while also lending further emphasis to the notion of *presence* in intersubjective communication and interaction, underscored for example by the importance of "listening." It highlights the centrality of coherence and seeing the big picture (the cathedral)—of holistic thinking, realizing that "everything is connected" and perceiving the "total concept," the totality of the project "field." It pushes to the forefront the sense that project work for members most fundamentally relates to participation, identification, and acceptance, and that project managing is "creation work," accentuating its deep sociality in terms of, for example, celebratory "rituals."

Projects as Situated Potentiality

The most intensely recurring themes in the genesis of projects have to do with concepts of wholeness, of totality, of intersubjective communication, of goals and objectives. The empirical analysis illustrates how participants "struggle with" and feel shortcomings in relating with, and communicating the wholeness and coherence of, their projects. It seems to be important not to get too lost in details but rather to see one's part in a bigger picture, constantly striving to avoid fragmentation as reality successively unfolds. The interpretation put forward here is that this is indicative of the participants' sense of an absence of an ontological space, and a corresponding epistemology, in which to fully acknowledge, accommodate, and finally, in their idiomatic vocabulary, "to manage" the wholeness of the projects. This more or less opaque realm of their projects, which in the ethnographic narratives is strongly emphasized as important, is like a shorthand for vast complexities, in "native speak" dubbed "the soft side of projects." The soft side, as it were, is the key, but a key that is mysterious and difficult to interpret, let alone "manage."

It has been described how projects and project work on the ontological level can be described most profoundly as involving *potentiality*, a potentiality that accounts for the deeper levels of the "social reality of construction," what might be designated a "situated potentiality." The realm of projects is a domain concerned with bringing forth, realizing, emerging, enabling a potentiality at all levels. Likewise, bringing forth a project and realizing it as a productive plant can fail at any juncture. Not until it has reached full production in the sense of its design capacity, can the project be assessed as a success or not. At this juncture in time the project can be evaluated as to whether this one particular path of potentiality *realization* brought forth the anticipated fruits. The temporality of the principle of potentiality, among other things, is illustrated in Figure 10 below.

In the project development phase the value is "created" and enfolded as the potentiality of the project. In the execution phase the potential value is controlled as materialized in a plant. In the next critical phase— from Decision Gate 5 (DG5), when the project is formally closed (and

Figure 10. Dynamics of potentiality and temporality in the CVP process, merged with the start-up phase in operations, and full production.
The different main phases in terms of conceptions of value are also indicated. Hydro native concepts of "value creation" and "value control" are supplemented by a construct I label "value release."

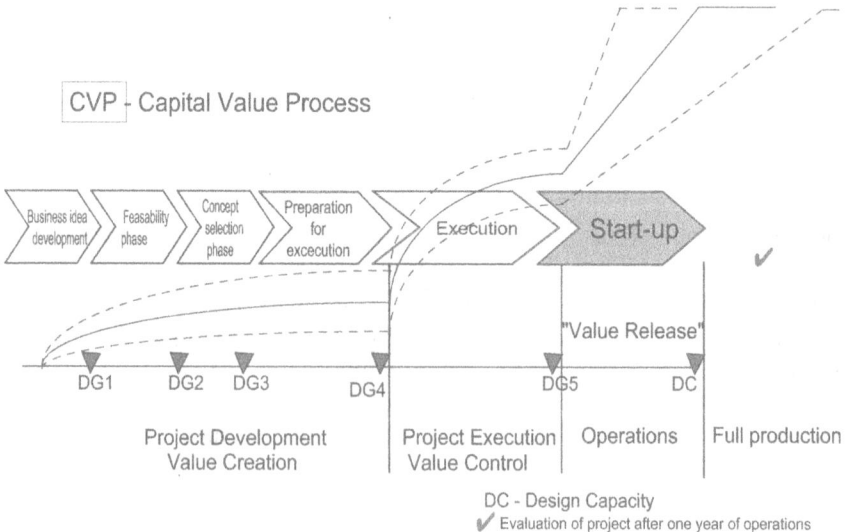

Operations has taken over) until the plant has reached its full production design capacity—the potentiality enfolded in the project must be "released" and realized in delivering quality production and products to the market. The project can break down and become a failure at almost any juncture, even after its transformation into a plant at DG5. If the customer side, the demand side, does not live up to expectations, or cannot be made to live up to expectations, the realization of the project, even if the plant is able to produce at design capacity, would be a "failure," in the capitalist sense of not making a profit. On the other hand, a "bad" project—one that makes the plant reach design capacity a year later than planned, for example—would also result in failure, possibly endowing the plant with the "curse" of not ever making a profit. This would be because the cost of the delay in terms of lost income, the expenses of expert consulting, and so on, lowers the internal rent to such a degree that the plant will struggle economically long into the future. The bringing forth of potentiality, as we have seen, involves a range of complex, polymorphous, embodied intercommunication and entangled "instrumentation" issues.

The domain of life and nature in which *potentiality* has been most rigorously described is the quantum reality as established by quantum physics. Since the early twentieth century quantum physics has provided a fundamentally new understanding of physical reality. In a word, it says that objects are not as separate as they seem, and that at the most fundamental levels interconnected relationships extend and transcend both space and time. These fundamental connections were called "spooky action at a distance" by Einstein and "passion at a distance" by Shimony, and Schrödinger labeled the phenomenon "entanglement" (Cohen et al. 1997). It is commonly known as "nonlocality,"[2] and the new physics has concluded that "nonlocality is a fundamental property of the entire universe" and that "mind, or human consciousness, must be viewed as an emergent phenomenon in a seamlessly interconnected whole called the cosmos" (Nadeau and Kafatos 1999: 4–5). Potentially vast consequences for the social and human sciences are implied by the new physics, far beyond what can be explored here,[3] but below I outline some key implications for the argument thus far.

A Set of Propositions

The issues that have been investigated in this chapter (and the former) point to the following preliminary propositions, summarized in a suggested conceptualization of an ontology of "situated potentiality" in the realm projects' "social reality of construction."

(a) The reality of the processes of bringing forth and realizing projects seems to be nothing like the reality of the product of the effort. The clockwork operations of a machine plant are preceded, or presenced, by a reality of processes in projects that are not at all clockwork-like. However, based on this investigation, we might also question the whole notion of the "clockworkings" of an industrial plant. It has been illustrated that the standard notion of "project management" as structural planning and prioritizing in an "atomic universe" of disaggregated elements and parts that need to be coordinated, is the outcome of the worldview or creation myth brought forth in inspiration and departure from classical physics. In the same way, we might question the clockwork perception of the operational reality of an industrial, mechanized plant. For example, the continuous "tuning" and complex problem-solving in the production process, to enable a stable quality of metal product, is embedded in various forms of tacit and implicit, contextual and procedural know-how, very far from being solely an explicit "knowing that," declarative "clockwork" process. This latter perception was made idiomatic in Charlie Chaplin's film *Modern Times*. However, the classical physics perspective, also as imported and as a source of thinking in social sciences, seems to be a surface point of view, a perspective of natural and social reality as a "flatland." The classical physics of Galileo, Descartes, Kepler, and Newton, to whom this worldview has been attributed, rests upon some basic assumptions about the status of reality: locality, object separation, simple causality, and mechanic determinism. Quantum mechanics and other related recent advances in physics have rendered all of these assumptions questionable and out-of-date as basic conceptions about fundamental reality. Out of these questions and findings emerges a new reality, and thus slowly a new worldview—indeed, a new ontology of modern man might be carved out.

(b) The field of knowledge constituting the genesis of productive projects is found to be a form of movement or a process of "bringing about" and "bringing forth." I support the proposal made by Bohm (1980), drawing upon the history of philosophy from Heraclitus to Whitehead, to consider reality and knowledge "itself" as process. What has been explored in this chapter are the particularities of the knowledge processes that constitute, at a deeper level, the bringing forth of productive industrial projects. The movements and flows of this co-creation are complex and multilayered, both differential and holistic, but wholeness is primary ("mono-plural"). In Bohm's jargon, it points toward the generative or implicate order. The "conventional way" of interpreting the imperative of seeing "the big picture"—of the cathedral, the totality, as expressed by the participants themselves—would possibly be that in order to construct unity and coherence out of the fragmented elements of an atomistic reality, a vast systematization machine of means of control, coordination and planning, and so on is necessary. Otherwise nothing would become, nothing would endure, and nothing will be. This is implied in the conventional view of "managing rationality." From the perspective advocated here, this narrative is wrong at its core, even if some of its peripheral manifestations, or "symptoms," might be similar and "correct." In the interpretation offered here, the fundamental aspects of creating projects entail efforts of "tuning in to," of "connecting with," of "getting in touch with" the wholeness that already is "present" at other levels or "orders" of reality. In project work these are the realms of ethos, of atmosphere and ambiences related to the subtleties of communicative action, of linking up to, of being part of and releasing the power of intersubjective intentionality—and of course, all the rest of the unfolding and objectifying trials and tribulations that follow. I argue, however, that without the former, projects are doomed to catastrophe, or at least to being unsuccessful. And as the track record, reviewed above, of a diversity of projects historically, cross-culturally, and across sectors shows: success is indeed difficult.

(c) Furthermore, this investigation invites a shift in how we understand the basics of "aggregation," or the underlying dynamics of the generativity of project genesis itself. Rather than focusing, as is commonly recommended in the literature on management and project management, on coordination and control, we suggest that the guiding conceptual heuristic of the ontology of "situated potentiality" should instead be that of (integral) coherence. The power of *intersubjective intentionality*, the *ambience of enabling*, the *materiality of anticipation*, all our major issues, suggest that the primary guiding conceptualization could be *coherence* rather than coordination. Instrumentally this implies an understanding of managing the processes of bringing forth projects as efforts of generating coherence of attention and energy toward goal finding and goal achievement.

(d) In relative opposition and complementation to the social constructivist position, I have argued that the "social reality of construction" is not constituted through a process of "bottom-up" construction of "building blocks" collectively weaving the social fabric. Rather, the "social reality of construction" is characterized by a whole-part and process-form dialectics that moves both vertically top-down and bottom-up, and horizontally outward and inward. Metaphorically it might be illustrated by the Klein-bottle (Johansen 2005). From the participants' imaginations about the whole—the end result, the purpose, the goal, the "cathedral" or "pyramid"—subsequent processes of id-entification are brought forth. This process is the achievement of the "delusional certitude" and "optical illusions" involved in conceptualization, objectification, and "thingmaking." This genesis of objectifying derives from a background of more or less inchoate "wit and will" modalities and emotional and sociotechnical flows and movement—and emerges as creations of "joy and pain." Temporary building blocks of some durability are thus constructed, and are again included in a process of reassembling and instantiating the whole in a new form. The key issue here is the notion that construction is considered the process of bringing forth, in a *combined materialized and abstracted sense*, objects of "id-entified" sub-wholes out of a background of flow—in Heidegger's terms, a process of revealing. The critical element is not the construction of wholes out of given building blocks, or the construction of building blocks from which to construct wholes. What is at stake in the social reality of construction, I argue, is the genesis of new forms of wholes, perceived as wholes of successively increasing "density," "rigidity," and durability (in the abstracting/materializing sense), out of a background of entangled flows or movement. Again, this argument is captured in the proposition of an ontology of "situated potentiality" for characterizing the social reality of construction.

In such a way we can understand Latour's phrase that "technology is society made durable" in another light. In fact, the term "presencing" as used by Heidegger comes from "*Wesen*" as "*Whären*," meaning to last or endure. In the expression "to come to presence" the meaning "endure" should be strongly heard (1977: 4–5). As for example Bergson and Piaget have informed us, our human logic is the logic of solid bodies, through our embodied experiences with discrete objects on the macro-level, fueled again by delusional certitude and optical illusions. However, the experiencing in Hydro projects also keeps people in touch with another reality, that of movement, flows, and transformations indicative of the implicate order or entangled "quantum reality" pulsating just below/above the surface. Figure 11 below outlines the basic steps of the present perspective on the social reality of construction.

Figure 11. An ontology of "situated potentiality," of whole-part relationships indicative of the experiencing in project work and also "midstream" production work.

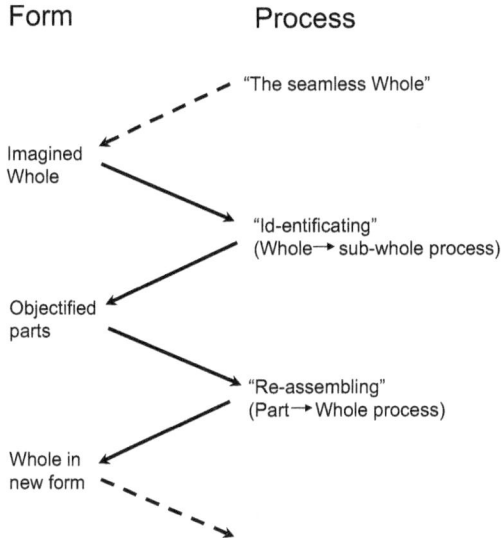

The Imagination Bank

In the empirical context of the social reality of construction investigated here, the processes of creating and re-creating, of making and unmaking, of the acute "processuality" and whole-part dynamism, push the fundamental interconnectedness that the new physics has revealed at the "micro-level" also to the forefront of human experiencing at the "macro-level." The vivid imaginative reality of an *unmade* plant, or "unconcealed" plant in Heidegger's terminology; the levels of recursivity in its realization in new co-evolving structures; the extreme bodily embedding and symbolism in the (re)assembling of technology and in the remelting and casting of metal production, and in the emphasis on totality and wholeness; and much more: all testify to a felt experience that the most solid of (all kinds of) objects are brought forth and informed by more fundamental processes of and in reality.

This more fundamental reality does not necessarily exist unnoticed. As Nadeau and Kafatos write, "even the human eye is capable of registering the impact of a single photon, and the structure of everyday objects is emergent from quantum mechanical events" (1999: 97). The sensing and experiencing reality of "construction work" engenders constant awareness of the fact that even the most solid of objects can melt, mold, change, and be re-created in numerous ways. In the remelt casthouse for example, the operators and others are (sub)consciously and bodily, indeed emotionally, informed that the stability of bulk metal matter, and the rigidity, uniformity and coherence of the matter and its mechanical, thermal, chemical and optical properties, are all fundamentally subject to the rules of quantum mechanics. In the genesis of greenfield projects this experiencing reality is arguably even more pronounced. These characteristics of the project as a form of holistic imaginative anticipation, and of production as flows and fundamental transformations, are furthermore mirrored in the entire integrated value chain logic of aluminum production in Hydro, i.e., in its conceptualizations of "upstream," "midstream," and "downstream" production and business. The conventional way of thinking is that upstream is closer to the raw materials and thus more "primitive." The more downstream, the more processed the goods are, the more advanced and "knowledge-intensive" it is. This conception might be fundamentally questioned.

What is flowing upstream—flowing "up the river," as it were—are different types of requirements of use: this alloy must meet these and those requirements, dependent upon which type of use context it is to be applied in, be it housing, packaging, transportation, ICT, or whatever. Downstream, downward "in the stream," flow, of course, metal products—which are not, from the perspective pursued here, the most significant content of the flow, however. More important here are all the ideational and knowledge elements that are enfolded in the metal manifestations flowing downstream. All kinds of knowledge related to the constitution of the metal and the variety of potential uses for it, the limits and the horizon of use, so to speak, are enfolded. Metallurgical knowledge is heavily research-intensive. This interpretation is supported by the fact that Hydro and its research partners acknowledge that their downstream innovation efforts have been targeted more toward development than research. It is their upstream business that has been most engaged in basic types of research efforts—a contention also supported by independent assessments (Wulff 1992; Øye and Ryum 1997; Sand et al. 2005; Karlsen 2008). Although it is somewhat controversial, upstream and not least midstream may indeed be perceived to be *more* research- and knowledge-intensive than downstream. This also explains why process innovations have been continuous over so many years, re-creating the capacity for new and better processes and products.

The reason for the conceptualization of downstream as the most knowledge-intensive section of the value chain might lie in the conflated worldviews and models that researchers use in understanding these mechanisms. While no doubt upstream is "closer" to raw materials, upstream is also, at least in the perspective discussed here, where the *situated potentiality* for diverse unfoldments resides. And vast faculties of anticipation, creation, innovation, ideas, spirituality, and technology are involved in the manufacture of material potential.

How can this be reconciled with the notion that upstream/midstream along the value chain is the farthest away from the customer, and in this sense perceived as less knowledge-intensive? Above I stress the importance of anticipation. There is reason to say that all the things that emerge out of customer interaction and market-based innovation flow all the way up to the engineers of material potential. Far up in the river, all these constraints and possibilities need to be anticipated, and the ideas need to be manifested in the material metal, for all of the downstream potentials to be utilized, or better, in the terminology of a possible "quantum ontology," to be "actualized." The flows are, however, obviously never optimal or perfect, and they depend upon the subtle factors discussed here. We might then argue that a key issue in creating industrial activities of high value-creating potential is to build capacity for "transformability." In one sense this can be explained as engaging in economic activities that are brimful of *learning potential*. Again the significance of potentiality. Industrial aluminum business has been conducted for over a hundred years since the birth of hydrometallurgy in the late 1880s, with the invention of the electrolytic aluminum process in 1886, the cyanidation process in 1887, and the Bayer process in 1888 (Habashi 2005). These basic technological inventions provided the foundation upon which the aluminum industry was built, a history that until the present day has been fueled by continuous technological changes and innovations. High learning potential is related to the phenomenon of increasing returns in the economics of knowledge-based production (Arthur 1994), heavily stressed in the "other canon" of economic theory and history (Reinert 2007).

Even though upstream is closer to the raw materials, the upstream I have been talking about is the *processing* of raw materials, not the assembling or reaping of them. Norway never had the raw materials for aluminum production. What Norway had was power. Its huge waterfalls were tamed at the turn of the century by Hydro and others and turned into energy. At Hydro, first for the production of fertilizers and now for the aluminum industry, energy is potential. As described earlier, Hydro sometimes refers to aluminum products as "energy banks," and the lack of the raw materials may even have been a factor that contributed to Hydro's success. This proposition is made by aluminum historian Jan Thomas Kobberød (2008). More generally, as noted by Reinert, "Paradoxically, being poor in natural resources could be a key to becoming wealthy" (2007: 7). This has been systematically understood at least since Antonio Serra produced the first theory of uneven economic development in 1613. Serra wanted to explain why Naples remained so poor in spite of its vast natural resources, while Venice, with its lack of such resources, was "at the very centre of the world's economy" (ibid.). The key, according to Serra, was the manufacturing sector in Venice, displaying many different economic activities all subject to the falling costs of increasing returns, while Naples relied on cultivating its land and thus was dependent upon economic activities subject to diminishing returns.

In the terminology of Bohm, then, upstream (but not *the* raw natural resources) and midstream production is a form of enfolded knowledge and technology potential. In terms of economy, it is enfolded wealth potential. It is also not only an energy bank, but more importantly an abstracted/ materialized idea and *imagination bank*. The diverse downstream and customer physical products are "all" anticipated in the idea bank. The downstream is an unfolding realization and actualization, a successive series of explications of the enfolded potential. In Part II of the present work the lens is turned toward the dynamics of the *wealth creating* potential of the imagination bank. Attention is drawn to issues of economy and finance, not least the technologies of economics and finance, and how they are instantiated through managing actions in the realm of investment projects, in both the Hydro corporation and in the context of global capitalism. As will be shown, the value- and wealth-creating potential of the "imagination bank" can be interpreted and actualized in substantially different forms and with quite radically different outcomes. The coming chapters will explore how the "creative powers of production" enfolded in the imagination bank have substantially been turned to constructing and commodifying abstract notions of value as new, capital "goods," and have also, along the way, refunctioned social relations of technology and political economy in the name of finance—thus commodifying and "financializing" cultural relations on an unprecedented scale.

Notes

1. The quote from Einstein is the following: "A human being is part of the whole, called by us 'Universe,' a part limited in time and space. He experiences himself, his thoughts and feelings and something separate from the rest—a kind of optical delusion of his consciousness." The quote is apparently from a letter Einstein wrote, dated 15 February 1950 (quoted in Calaprice 2005: 206).
2. Several groundbreaking physical experiments have established that physical reality is indeed nonlocal (Aspect et al. 1981, 1982a; Aspect et al. 1982b; Tittel et al. 1998; Marcikic et al. 2004).
3. For a more in-depth discussion see Røyrvik (2008a).

Part II

High Finance and Contemporary Crisis Capitalism

Chapter 4

THE TURN TO ENCHANTMENT
Investing in Projects

Accumulate, accumulate! That is Moses and the prophets!
—Karl Marx, *Capital: Volume I*

Globalization must not become financial imperialism.
—Muhammed Yunus, 2006 Nobel Peace Prize Inauguration Speech

The practices of investing in new projects in Hydro provide fertile soil for a fascinating study of some of the ambivalences enfolded in the economic logic of financing new industrial "ad-ventures." As outlined in Chapters 2 and 3, Hydro employs structuring and structured models for both process and organizing issues. Of particular importance for the decision-making process in projects is the Capital Value Process (CVP). The CVP process model is perceived as a support, in all of the aspects of the project, for investment decisions. The model is thus quite appropriately designated by the name "Capital Value Process" (see Figure 2). As noted in the former chapter, however, what's in a name is far from trivial. And concerning the financial aspects of the project life cycle, the major institutional event and "turning point" is "Decision Gate four" (DG4) of the CVP. In this chapter I am concerned with the financial and more broadly economic aspects of projects, and subsequently the wider ramifications of the "financial turn" that instilled the principles of "value based management" throughout the Hydro organization since 1999, following its strategy process called "Focus for the Future" (Lie 2005).

As mentioned, following the CVP the DG4 is the main event in the project life cycle in terms of life and death for the emerging project. It is at this juncture that the Final Capital Expenditure Approval (CEP) is made—or not made. The corporate management board meets and, in the name of Hydro as a legal person, definitely declares the "to be or not to be" of the burgeoning project, giving the proverbial Caesarean thumbs-up or thumbs-down. Thus, the first part of this chapter is a description, based on participant observation, of the DG4 meeting of the Qatalum project—the largest aluminum plant project the world has ever seen. A joint-venture with Qatar Petroleum, it represented an investment of $4.8 billion and was planned to be in full production with a gas power plant, a smelter, and a casthouse by late 2010. Having just reached full production capacity, due to a power plant failure in August 2010 the production plant was shut down. "The doomsday scenario" occurred, as one Qatalum manager put it. The production cells had to be cleaned out, and expectations for reaching full production capacity were now adjusted to the end of the first quarter of 2011.

The subsequent sections are first a description of the introduction and partial "takeover" of financial means of managing and control, followed by some of the engineers responses to this shift. Afterward, discussions of the wider context of Hydro "value-based management" and the "shareholder value" paradigm as it has been embedded in Hydro practices are offered. Subsequently I discuss this turn in light of Hydro's tradition and strong emphasis on "knowledgeable expert management" and industrial democracy. Backed by figures, statistics, and historical data, I conclude the chapter by discussing how projects can be depicted as cultural idioms for the whole of the Hydro corporation, and note that there has been a significant shift in some of the central legitimizing idioms of managing in Hydro project and corporate work. This transformation, I argue in the chapters below, is moreover illustrative of the financialized "turn to enchantment" in the globalized economy—of the allure of capitalism.

Decision Gate Four

Once again I was approaching "the house of glass." The brand-new glass and metal corporate headquarters building at Vækerø in Oslo was the site of the "ritualized" meeting of the day: the Qatalum project was to pass through "Decision Gate 4" (DG4). The Aluminium management board was to decide upon the final approval, or—a somewhat less likely possibility—the disapproval, of the project by way of deciding upon "the final capital expenditure approval." As I approached the location by way of all the major modern means of transportation—taxi, airplane, train—I was far more excited than I could remember being on any of my numerous earlier visits to the headquarters. One reason for the anticipation was the secretive buildup to the meeting. Almost exactly two years earlier I had unsuccessfully attempted to gain access to a meeting of the Aluminium management board while participating in the opening ceremony in Suzhou, China. I had therefore expended no little strategic thought about different approaches to securing participation in this meeting. After I interviewed members of the corporate management board the request was accepted, and I was positively surprised. Meanwhile, the way in which the "green light" was communicated heightened the anticipation: in the confirmation e-mail from my "gatekeeper" (not the DG4 gatekeeper), or rather, my gate opener, who made my participation possible, I read the following:

> … can in the meantime happily inform you that we take a positive view of your attendance when the corporate management board discusses the project in preparation for a final recommendation to Hydro's Board of Directors (it will also be treated in the Corporate Assembly). Conditions are, however, that we are allowed to read through your description of the meeting/discussion before you finalize your thesis, and that the discussion/decision in the meeting is treated confidentially until we publicize the final building decision (probably during summer). The meeting is of course only the last step in many discussions about the project over the last years, but if you think it can be of use to be a "fly on the wall," you are hereby welcome. I will ask our corporate secretary [*direksjonssekretæren*] … to notify you of the date (probably during May) when it is decided, and ask you to keep the time in question to yourself as we never publicize [*kringkaster*] date and time for administrative discussions and decisions, nor the agenda of the Board. The decision will be made public when it is treated by the Board, with a recommendation to the Corporate Assembly. (My trans.)

Practices of secrecy produce many different social effects, not least an aura of exclusiveness and importance, and have a certain appeal to many different people's psychology. Examples as diverse as the successful conscious strategy of secrecy as a means to disseminate the "Shell scenarios" within the organization, and thus spread the word of corporate strategy (Davies-Floyd 1998) on the one hand, and the dramatic employment of secrecy in ritual initiations for the purpose of disseminating cultural knowledge, for example among the Baktaman of New Guinea (Barth 1975), on the other, testify to the power of secrecy in the unfolding of social reality. Thus Hydro members' talk about discussions, opinions, and decisions made by "KL" (Konsernledelsen), the corporate management board, or the top Hydro management, instigated considerable interest, spreading informal information and rumors. These board meetings therefore had a symbolic significance that transcended the "actual" content agenda of the meetings. The meeting's symbolic power, partly invested by the ritualistic construction of secretive boundaries, certainly had an effect on me as well. After asking, I was given friendly advice by another corporate assistant about the dress code. "People always ask about that," she laughed, "but persons attending these meeting usually wear a suit and a tie, so that could be an idea."

Thus I entered the "glass house" prepared for any question I might get about the projects I had been working on in collaboration with Hydro or about my dissertation work. I waited in the lobby somewhat anxiously, given the experiences of the last two interviews I had conducted at the same place. One of them was with a member of the corporate management board, and the other with President and CEO Eivind Reiten. On both occasions the lobby somehow managed to forget to inform the executives' secretaries about my arrival, so they came down to fetch me 10–15 minutes later than the time agreed upon. Time schedules are not something that is dealt with as one pleases at the headquarters. This time around I made absolutely certain that my arrival had been communicated to the right person. After being guided through the locked entrance gates, the friendly "dress code" assistant guided me to the elevator and into the office spaces where the top management meetings are held.

I met other attendees in an open space with stylish furniture, surrounded by glass offices and, most notably, an informal conference room behind glass walls and doors, with a large artificial open fireplace and two adjacently positioned designer couches. Taken altogether, that particular room, into which we had a clear view from the open space, gave an initial aesthetic impression of being an intimate seating arrangement at some exclusive mountain holiday resort. Fascinatingly, its glass enclosure and its position on a stylish office floor gave the room the appearance of being on display in an art gallery. I greeted the five other people present, most of whom seemed to know each other already. The corporate secretary announced that the meeting taking place was a bit behind schedule and that we would have to wait some minutes to enter the conference room. Everybody present small-talked about business related issues. I asked a man who turned out to be the economic "controller" about his assessments of risk in the project. I jokingly announced, "I guess there are no risks in such a well-managed project?" which prompted laughter from the controller and the assistant to the head of the Aluminium division. "Well," the controller replied, "there are of course quite large values at stake in the project."

We were standing beside the main seating arrangement in the open space, in which sat the president of the Qatalum project and the head of the Aluminium division (the Executive Vice-President). They were discussing different aspects of the project, progress, and challenges, particularly a month's delay that had recently surfaced with reference to the official project schedule. One month in the course of a five-year project did not seem like a big problem, but as the discussion unfolded it emerged as something possibly serious. The head of Aluminium explained that due to the way sales contracts are made for a whole year, this one-month delay could in the worst case lead to problems securing contracts for the first year of operation of the Qatalum plant. This scenario could unfold if the plant was completed too late to reach the qualification process of the product qualities. In this case, securing sales contracts for 2010 could be problematic. Thus the one-month delay could possibly have consequences for the whole year. During the discussion of the delay in the meeting that took place some minutes later, the concern about the sales contracts for the whole year was not aired explicitly, but different strategies, such as starting up some of the production cells earlier than others to secure "customer qualification" even if the plant was not entirely ready, were indeed discussed.

In the open space sofa group, still outside the conference room, the two executives also discussed the political positioning of the project in Qatar. "Will the project get fast enough and high enough on the table of the Emir?" one of them asked. They were discussing whether, in the competitive environment for industrial projects in Qatar, their project had sufficient support from high-level politicians. Three others joined the open space, among them the project manager. He voiced concern over the delay as well, anticipating the discussion later in the meeting. In a brief intermezzo, prompted by the Aluminium head's combined question and statement "You are aware that what is discussed here is meant for this room only"—directed at me—I had to explain my role and confirm that agreements concerning confidentiality had been secured. Two financial managers, seemingly appearing out of thin air, entered the "holiday resort room," closed the glass doors, and had a private conversation. It was a fascinating scene. Even here, where access was strictly regulated and predictable, there seemed to be a need for secluded space. The need could easily be explained in situations of business negotiations. The actual use of the space, however, had a paradoxical effect. The combination of the absolute visual transparency and the complete auditory impediment imparted to the social significance of its use the effect of broadcasting to the group outside the conceptual categories of secrecy, importance, and exclusivity themselves.

The corporate secretary announced that we could now enter the big meeting room (different from the "holiday resort room"). A large conference table in what looked like mahogany dominated the room, framed on one of the long sides by a window wall with a view of trees and the sea, and an adjacent wall dominated by intense works of colorful abstract art. The ten or so people already present (it was difficult to account for everybody all the time, as some people came and went discreetly) rose and welcomed us. Unsure about the custom, I found a place along the table close to the door. The attendees I had not met earlier came over to me and we shook hands. Eivind Reiten, the CEO, came over as well, remembering me from the interview I had recently conducted with him in his office. The meeting resumed quickly. I noticed to my astonishment that the brown leather tray for plates and cups at each place around the table had a small engraving of a Roman-style helmeted soldier's head. My private and speculative metaphorical conception of Hydro managers as incarnating modern "aluminum-armored Apollonians" (Røyrvik 2008a) suddenly had a very concrete symbolic representation.

Reiten, seated in the second-to-last chair with his back to the windows, announced that today's meeting was essentially the plucking of fruits that had been cultivated and groomed over a long process of development. The meeting was conducted in the Norwegian language, reflecting the composition of top management and the persons present. He invited the Hydro "owner's representative" in the Qatalum joint-venture company to present an overview and status report of the project development. The self-evident Powerpoint slideshow, always present in managing meetings, was projected on a canvas. Several issues were raised: cost numbers, market price forecasts, margins, LME, Alumina, Amperage. A brief discussion emerged with respect to the efficiency of the power plant, to which the hot outdoor temperature in Qatar posed a challenge. The project president announced that "we should have built it in Norway … here it is optimal in this respect." Quiet laughter spread around the table. "Yes," replied Reiten, "we are entitled a few advantages up here in the cold. To bad we are lacking the gas." More soft and appreciative chuckling. The presenter lined up the assumptions made at the previous Decision Gate, DG3, and changes and adjustments made in the project since then.

The major issue in the discussion was the new month-long delay, which was related to a problem with the supply of sand to the site. A new road was to be built to enable transportation. The representative said, "It really takes a long time to get the necessary approvals for an alterative road, we have to go to the police, and they refuse to meet more often than once a week." The head of Aluminium added: "With this last month delay we lose 0.2 percent on the internal rent. The two months we have lost earlier in the project had combined only a 0.1 percent negative effect on the internal rent." In the Powerpoint presentation all major adjustments and changes with reference to assumptions made at DG3 had their effects measured in positive and negative changes to the project's projected internal rent, i.e., to the future profitability of the project. The development of the LME [London Metal Exchange] real prices had a positive effect, as did expansion of the power plant capacity and changes in the tax situation.

When the one-month delay had been discussed at some length, Reiten announced: "The challenge in the project is not *that* month, but the general observation that things take time in Qatar. We will have to face more such crossroads. And we have to hold fast to the edge of the table [bite oss fast i bordkanten], to keep the schedule. It is mostly psychology ... not that we here around the table do not know what is really at stake." The project manager wanted to clarify something: "I just want to stress that the problem with sand and the road may seem insignificant, something that should be easily handled, but to cater for the 1,000 trucks coming in and out of the site every 24 hours we need to set up a roundabout in the middle of a four field motorway where cars fly by at speeds reaching 150 km/h." Around the table the point was taken. Reiten replied: "We need to take into account that next time it is something else. In relation to our partners, the key is that if we start moving the schedule it quickly becomes a slippery slope, time will be eaten again and again."

Later in the meeting, the project manager came back to this issue, asking: "The time pressure, is it on us or on our partners? Because I cannot see how we can drive ourselves out of this problem." Reiten clarified: "It is on them, for sure, but it is a tactical issue from our side [to communicate that the schedule was fixed]." And he added, in an expressive tone of voice, looking at different people down the table, "There might be other roundabouts emerging down the road..." The project manager agreed: "In relation to our partners I believe this attitude is the correct one." Reiten closed this round of discussion: "As always, you just have to be rational and do the right thing."

A mixed formal and informal atmosphere characterized the discussions. Participants seemed to have their say when they had something relevant to contribute. When a discussion went on for too long Reiten smoothly, deploying both humor and mild authority, closed the subject and directed the meeting forward. Tax issues were thoroughly discussed: tax holidays, tax rates, tax in profits brought to Norway, owner issues in terms of country registrations, tax agreements with governments, and so on and so forth. The theme of "major risks" was introduced by the presenter with what he calls "an oddity." On his slide he had covered drawings of the plant site with soccer fields. "The Ormen Lange site at Aukra covered 100 soccer fields," he said in cool anticipation of his key point. Everybody in the room knew that the Ormen Lange was the largest industrial project ever commenced in Norway, and that Hydro had the project management.[1] "Now, have a look at our site in Mesaieed … it covers 250–260 soccer fields," he smiled. The others chuckled, and Reiten said, "Yes, this tiny little Ormen Lange project…"

Reiten subsequently turned his attention down the table. The presentation phase seemed to be over, and he gave the word explicitly to the controller for an assessment of the risk picture: "Does the controller have anything to add or ask?" The controller took the floor: "Yes, the project seems to be well balanced. The concern is related to schedule, this is a distinct concern. And also progress in terms of access to gas." Reiten summarized: "In respect to changes that have happened since DG3, they are mainly on the positive side, [that is] from an arithmetic accounting type of perspective [regnestykkeperspektiv]. Concern is foremost related to schedule, the time it takes to 'drive things through' the bureaucracy." Then he turned his attention to the project people and asked, "Do you have the right people?" The project president replied: "We have a challenge in getting more. The average age is also high, 58 plus." "After project completion they are 62 plus," laughed Reiten. The chief financial officer in Hydro then announced that "there is a considerable riskiness related to currencies," and the head of corporate finance downplayed the risk involved: "That is fair enough, but in Qatar we know the currencies toward which we are exposed."

The meeting drew to a close with a discussion about the formal procedures and timing of the announcement of the final approval decision. There were a few tactical issues to consider to "receive applause," as Reiten put it, in the other forums that subsequently would need to consent to the final decision. There were issues of obligation in terms of information dissemination, and what should be the proper chain of information events. After reaching some sort of consensus on these issues, Reiten declared, "With this then, I take it that the management board approves the project and will send a recommendation to the Board of Directors." Silent agreement. Some final words from Reiten closed the meeting:

DG3 was the steep hill [tunge kneika] for us, to adjust ourselves toward a new cost picture. It is not every day we commit ourselves to a 2.5 billion dollar investment. And also in days and periods with other aluminium prices we need the mental readiness [beredskap]. However, it will only be for a short time that this plant will be the most expensive one built in the world. This is the start of a new strategic chapter, with phase two of the project the plant will produce more aluminium than the whole of Norway combined. The general development since DG3 has been positive, something good, something bad, but in sum a positive development. But that our main challenge in Qatar turned out to be the lack of sand! I'm sure we will learn even more.

Shortly thereafter I was whisked out of the conference room by the corporate secretary. Though I managed to secure some agreements to interviews in the stairway down, in the rush of things I forgot my coat in the conference room wardrobe. I was fortunately rescued by the helpful "dress code" assistant, who then guided me through the locked gates to exit the glass house as I wrote furiously in my notebook. Outside, waiting for the taxi, I struck up a brief conversation with the main presenter from the meeting. "You see," he explained, "we need sand to build, but they protect their sand mounds more or less like we protect our fjords."

I concluded afterward that I had participated in an organizational ritual of establishing an institutional fact of huge consequence and significance—an interpretation somewhat different in tone from the CEO's remark that the meeting was more the plucking of fruits that had already been planted and cultivated. In the trajectory of an emerging project, the performativity of the utterances of approving the Capital Expenditure Proposal (CEP) is, according to speech act theory (Searle 1969), the moment when the project is turned into an objective institutional fact. As Searle notes: "Performative utterances are members of the class of speech acts I call 'declarations.'… These utterances create the very state of affairs that they represent; and in each case, the state of affairs is an institutional fact" (1995: 34). The declaration of the CEP instills the project with financial muscle and breathes institutionally objective life into it. From being very much alive and well in the social realms of organizational practice it is transformed, by the utterance of a few words, into an institutional reality with a future. This calls to mind the issue of the perception of projects and their ontological reality status, in the process of origin until CEP approval (see Chapters 2 and 3 for in-depth ontological reflections).

The CEP approval declaration is metaphorically the finger of God, as it were, which in one brief statement transforms a potential future reality into an effective (future) reality. After the CEP declaration, there is, de facto, an existing project in the institutional sense. Even though the project had already been developed to a quite mature state by means of formal and informal organizational practices before the CEP approval, the ontological status of the project before and after the CEP approval is very different. The CEP signifies an institutional belief in creating the future.

A number of interesting aspects related to project management practices are illustrated in the empirical exposition above. Throughout the rest of the chapter I will refer back to various issues from the DG4 event. First let us explore one of the most significant features of the meeting. The exchange consisted of a combination of personal and "organizational" anecdotes, conveyance of institutional "facts," and not least the communication of numbers as a regulatory and controlling mechanism. The major numerical device for assessing the project development as a whole was the internal rent, the measure of the future profitability of the project. Every major change in the project was assessed by an equivalent amendment of the internal rent estimate, which is thus a financial control mechanism for the emerging project as a whole. This mechanism, with its numerical representation, is a crystalline expression of the profitability concerns embedded in the practices and the name itself of the project decision support process—the Capital Value Process. Therefore we might say that the CVP, with its internal rent orientation, shows that the life of projects at Hydro is marked by the corporate rise of finance control.

CROGIism: Inventing Finance Control

The developments and changes in the complex activities and interdependent relationships in the Qatalum project over time were, in a series of analytical steps, translated into internal rent effects prior to, and conveyed in, the DG4 event. This analytical approach as a strategy for project control is based upon "sensitivity analysis," whereby the variation in the output of a model can be apportioned to different sources of variation. The aim of the analysis is to enable managers to understand the underlying variables. Sensitivity analysis is used in several domains, including financial applications and risk analysis (Rees 2008). However, a number of problems are associated with such analysis in the context we are exploring. For example, it does not properly take into account that variables are often highly interdependent, that change in one variable changes others. Also, it is contingent upon subjective interpretation in terms of assigning value ("pessimistic and optimistic") in various parts of the analysis.

For example, judging from the DG4 event, time delay was one variable producing an effect on the internal rent, but underlying the time variable is a complex composition of myriad entangled and interacting activities. In short, the rhetoric of the sensitivity analysis masks complexity and subjectivity in its translation of project practices into "internal rent" effects. Although Hydro members are conscious of this, the "analytical concealment" in the representational rhetoric nevertheless displays a logic of "computational determinism." Such analysis and mechanisms are viewed by the Hydro members I spoke to about it as tools for management, and not as direct representations of reality. However, although this has not been studied directly, keeping such mechanisms in a concurrent double standard, of both "just tools" for interpretation and control as well as rhetorically powerful "direct" representations of reality, must entail considerable acts of advanced cognitive "juggling" on members' behalf. The tension between viewing the objects of description as real things versus seeing them as the result of analytical conventions embedded in the actual work is well known, but as Alain Desrosiéres argues in *The Politics of Large Numbers*, "it is difficult to think *simultaneously* that the objects being measured really do exist, and that this is only a convention" (1998: 1, italics in original). As one senior engineer once noted in relation to the modeling tools in oil exploration: "Sometimes we are caught by the vividness of our own constructed models. We can blow too much life into them. Then reality can hit us back hard."

An example of how the "internal rent" focus affects project life is the way a project is assessed in advance in light of its potential to return profits, based on the level of the "internal rent." As one project manager once noted, half jokingly: "With the internal rent requirements these days, it is an open question whether we can do many more projects in the future." Some consider the requirements so high that most projects can never reach the target, and thus are not ventured upon or realized. The internal rent is in this way a decisive guiding tool in determining which goals to find, choose, and realize. Indeed, during my years of fieldwork Hydro undertook a major strategic shift of focus from downstream projects to upstream and midstream, the latter two exemplified by the Qatalum project. Corporate management explicitly stated in 2005 that new investments would mostly be directed toward upstream/midstream activities. The main reason was the difference in profitability in their downstream versus mid/upstream activities, the latter having had a much higher profitability in recent years.

Nevertheless, the majority of workplaces are found downstream. At Hydro's Capital Markets Day in 2006, CEO Eivind Reiten was asked by one of Hydro's American investment banking shareholders why they did not simply sell the downstream businesses, due to its low profitability. Ultimately, during the substantial downturn the company suffered as the finance crisis unfolded, it did sell a portion of the downstream business in 2009. Reiten explained in a research interview, however, that he found the finance community also to be concerned with the long-term view, as long as rational reasons were given for it. In a Hydro internal company-wide intranet "Netcafé," the head of Hydro Aluminium at the time was asked about the recent strategic shift toward up/midstream activities, and answered:

Hydro Aluminium and the other large integrated aluminium companies are all struggling in achieving sufficient returns. Therefore, in our strategic process this year we had to evaluate different portfolio alternatives like should we still be an integrated company, should we be a more upstream focused company, should we have more downstream focus, our future cash flow and the financial requirements for the different strategic directions. As you have already seen, our choice was to remain an integrated company but with more resources allocated to the upstream area in order to win the comprehensive restructuring that will take place in the industry. We will continue to capitalize on the unique position midstream and work to improve profitability and cash flow downstream. In order to justify this kind of portfolio, we need to create more value across the sectors than each and everyone would be able to do on their own. (Netcafé, 22 September 2005)

When talking to project managers, plant managers, corporate managers, and line managers at Hydro, I found myself often discussing different types of financial instruments of control. These are concepts with tantalizing abbreviations like CROGI, EBITDA, and RoaCE. "We struggled the first years, but last year we met the CROGI by quite a margin," said Peter, one of the GMs in Xi'an. We were sitting in a hotel lobby one evening, and the head of Magnesium was also there for a short visit. He stepped in: "We call it 'CROGI-ism', everybody is talking about it these days. Even in Bécancour, a plant that is repaid and makes millions every year." Peter followed his lead, saying:

Here we are making just small money compared to Bécancour, but because our CROGI is good we get positive feedback from "the management" while Bécancour gets the heat because they struggle with their CROGI. As you know, the Bécancour project exceeded the budget with more than one billion NOK, and was troubled by a host of unforeseen issues. Because of that, their CROGI will never be satisfactory. The plant operation, however, is excellent now, so the whole thing is very much unfair in my view.

CROGI is an especially interesting abbreviation in relation to Hydro and investment projects because it is an in-house invention. Meaning "cash return on gross investments," it was developed prior to the Focus for the Future strategy process Hydro ran in 1999 and introduced to the organization along with EBITDA[2] in the year 2000 (Lie 2005: 429). At the same time that these two measures of return on capital were introduced, Hydro terminated the ordinary operations budgeting, in which expected revenues, costs, and results were presented. A problem with these older budgets was that they were not well suited to follow up the results in the various business units and thus did not give a picture of the performance of the different operations. The most important performance measure thus became the CROGI, an indicator of the relationship between cash flow and investments.[3]

In discussions it often seemed on the surface that these terms were completely natural parts of corporate life—that there was an eternal flavor to them, a self-evident status and legitimation. And not only that, they seemed to be very, very important. That is not to say that managers in Hydro were not constantly asking why they were so stringently monitored and measured on the basis of these oftentimes incomprehensible terms. Often the more engineering-minded managers, meaning those whose educational background and experience were mostly in engineering, voiced considerable skepticism toward these instruments as major tools for steering projects and the operations of a company. As these instruments were developed by the accounting discipline, this skepticism should not come as a surprise. However, while interpretations and judgments of these instruments are highly heterogeneous throughout the different manager groups, and vary individually across employee functions and educational backgrounds, there seems overall to be a shared understanding of the need for some form of financial control throughout the company, as far as I have been able to observe.

CROGI was discontinued in 2004 and RoaCE (return on average capital employed) continued as the major performance measure. Officially this change was made due to the demerger of Hydro's fertilizer operations. Agri was established as a separate company listed on the stock exchange in 2004, and subsequently more of Hydro's total revenues came from oil and energy. RoaCE is the most commonly used measure in the oil business. After Hydro continued as a dedicated aluminum company, having merged its oil and energy operations with Statoil in 2007, Hydro kept to reporting on RoaCE and simplified EBITDA to instead report on EBIT (earnings before financial items and tax).

The recent introduction of finance control measures at Hydro is part of a global trend of the last thirty years or so, generated especially by the Anglo-American corporate tradition, which has increasingly introduced "batteries of sophisticated financial indicators and controls" (Armstrong 1987: 416). In a self-reinforcing cycle, accountants have more frequently been occupying managerial positions, which has in turn enabled a shift from "production" to "financial" controls. This has "increased the salience of financial as against other forms of control and extended financial controls deeper into the organization in the direction of the labor process itself" (ibid.). This is a significant reading of an aspect of the wider context of the idioms of the name and of the practices of the CVP process in Hydro. As we saw in the DG4 ritual, the finance "controller" and other economic and financial managers played key roles, while the critical measure for the development of the whole project was the numerical representation of the projected "internal rent." The CVP thus embeds "capital value" concerns and controls directly into the mostly technically oriented engineering process of creating projects for future production.

As a corollary to the more thorough discussions of the practices and premises of managerial authority earlier, it might here be argued that when authority appears fragile or fails, managers frequently employ a second dimension of power. Zuboff call this dimension "technique," the material aspect of power (1988: 313). While authority to a large extent is linked with, and based upon, a spiritual, sacred, or "transcendent" reference of faith beyond the authorities themselves, "technique" concerns the concrete practices that can shape and control behavior. "Techniques of control, are used for monitoring, surveillance, detection, or record keeping" (ibid.). They can be a comfort to those in power, but simultaneously they reveal a crisis of confidence in the system of belief that, under circumstances of legitimate authority, ought to constrain behavior. Numbers have a special appeal to bureaucratic officials who are lacking in legitimate authority, as Porter notes: "Objectivity [from numbers] lends authority to officials who have very little of their own" (1995: 8). This perspective on the rise of mechanisms of finance control should be kept in mind. Legitimate authority and techniques of control could possibly be seen as co-originating the spaces and conceptions of power under "reflexive modernity" (Beck et al. 1994).

Indeed, this recent turn to financial control at Hydro was part of a comprehensive and concerted effort to bring about a wider financial (re)orientation throughout the whole of the company since 1999. By way of anticipation, before turning to the wider efforts and consequences of this quite radical turn to finance, let us examine an empirical snapshot of how a group of project managing engineers described from their point of view the situation of the increasing power of what they called "the economists."

Blåruss-blues

I am heading for dinner together with three engineers from Hydro Projects. It is almost Christmas on a cold evening in Suzhou. As always, the discussion revolves about where and what to eat. No one in the company speaks any Chinese. In their forties and fifties, Roger, Jonas, and Gard are all very experienced project engineers, specialists, and managers. Due to health problems, Roger is very conservative and cautious about what he eats, and every time someone suggests one of the plentiful restaurants along the road he insists that we move on. After a while, as frustration builds up, we realize he is heading toward a known restaurant, "the one with the yellow chairs." It was number 262.

Gard, the top-notch technical specialist who sometimes travels 250 days a year and over 100 times across the Atlantic—a his-own-excavator-in-the-garden kind of guy—exclaims calmly, always calmly, and with a stead-fast, humorous keen eye fixed upon you, indicating some double meaning or another: "We have been here three days in a row now." He looks around, smiling at everybody. "Yes," replies Roger, "that's exactly why we're head-ing there. We know what we eat, they even have a guy speaking some English. Remember last time we improvised?" He shakes his head, the other two chuckle, and some prudent hints surface about the implica-tions for his podagra. "Yes, yes," says Jonas, "but today I have a note with Chinese signs explaining what we want to eat. Lin made it for me." Jonas, the incarnation of the stereotypical Norwegian man "from the woods and mountains," always wearing his skiing cap and walking at high speed, is very pleased with the note. Roger, however, does not give in: "The note is based upon *this* very restaurant! What makes you think you can get the same food at another place?" It is not a question. You do not negotiate with podagra. We enter the restaurant with the yellow chairs. During the ordering of the meal, Lin must nevertheless be called by cell phone.

Back on the sidewalk, before we went in, discussions of project life had already been alternating with the dining decisions dialogue. "There is too little recognition for project work in Hydro," said Jonas. "The decision makers are 'blåruss' who know nothing about value creation. There is really some arrogance upward in the system. There are soon only econo-mists left among top management." *Blåruss* is a Norwegian native con-cept literally meaning a last-year student or graduate from high school, with a specialization in business and commerce. In Norwegian it has a range of connotations, partly depending upon context. In the present situation Jonas is implying a derogatory meaning of "yuppies" without ex-perience, expertise, or knowledge of the "real issues" related to industrial value creation.

Gard stepped in: "All the contemporary focus on separate business units kills new ideas and long-term vision. You see, the engineering peo-ple used to be part of staff, the 'engineering department.' We sat in white lab coats, felt slippers, with erasers and compasses and enjoyed ourselves. So you see, today we are missionaries." Jonas laughed and remarked dryly: "The white coats I remember, but not the felt slippers." Gard continued: "Today it is the impression that project people 'are so expensive.' Our jobs are almost on 'tender,' that is the situation today. Internal hourly invoicing is brewing in the background regarding every activity you are carrying out." Gard was hitting hard now, but as always huge doses of humor were embedded in his speech: "The path we are now taking is the economists' death march toward becoming a trading company. As Jonas said, they don't know value creation, view technology as something you are burdened with, think that everything can be bought, that a factory can be set up in a day. These guys don't build anything. Right? You can buy a factory at the grocery store. Yes?"

Later, in a chance meeting in the garage at the corporate headquarters, Gard vividly illustrated this point. With a seriousness that almost made his statement comically absurd, he said insistently: "You have to take into account that these people [alluding to both to "top management" and "the economists"] do not build anything themselves. They don't fix anything themselves. I mean, these guys do not even build their own outdoor lavatory at their mountain cabin!" Presumably responding to my big smile and internal voice noting my own lack of lavatory construction capabilities, he chuckled briefly. Then seriously again: "It is their everyday experience to buy everything. Remember that."

At the restaurant with the yellow chairs in Suzhou, speaking of the liberalization of the power market and the struggles with "competitive" power prices for industry in relation to the consumer market, Gard further contends:

> Comparing power prices for industry and consumers is just nonsense, because the latter does not account for the cost of the net. You gain on the swings and lose on the roundabouts. The "blåruss," when disguised as regulators, live with the belief that you get the same societal value from power when used for your bathroom heating cables as when used in aluminium production! Reiten, I am sure, he wants to create something, but there is no will to create value in Norway—only distribution. There is no political will.

Jonas steps in: "There is little new recruitment in Hydro, we are moving toward a trading company, and toward no onshore industry in Norway. It doesn't matter at all what the engineers are saying, they can talk as much as they want." Gard humorously adds: "We have to learn from the French truck drivers, to just block the road." The discussion picks up again once we are seated, and the joke cracking and brief anxiety occasioned by ordering the food have settled. "You know," says Gard,

> The competencies are diluted upwards in our system. We have to teach them over and over again, ten generations. The "blåruss" are not aware that it takes at least ten years to build project competencies. I have to teach new

people casting economy all the time. They have to learn it from top to bottom and up again, otherwise it just becomes nonsense. But at the next moment these people move quickly out the door. There is no status for the "blåruss" in doing this.

Jonas joins in again. "The recruitment of decision makers is done through a process of inbreeding, but then again, project people would not enjoy themselves in a staff function." Roger doesn't say much; he is busy evaluating the food. Chopsticks are not the most practical of tools, according to him. A small army of young female waitresses dressed up in orange uniforms is continuously at our service. Having finished the meal, we settle the check—indifferent to both local customs and local prices—by each person putting exactly the cost of what he himself has eaten on the table to aggregate the total sum. "Otherwise," as Gard explains, "it just creates an economic mess when getting reimbursed back home."

The CVP process, owned by Hydro Projects, is—however they felt about "the economists"—defended by the engineers. As Gard points out at one juncture: "The CVP is in fact very educational [oppdragende] for the economists. It builds shared understandings of the project between the owner and the project. It secures involvement, or highlights lack of it, from the owner side. For example, when the corporate management board terminated the project for a new casthouse in China as late as at DG4, I think it was due to lack of involvement from the owner side earlier in the process." Gard's assessment of the casthouse project termination was later confirmed to me by Reiten. He noted that the corporate management (ledelsen) got acquainted with the project too late and upon finally reviewing it found it unsustainable.

Gard sees the process surrounding the casthouse project, and its late termination, as a consequence of the project being "market-driven" and thus bound by customer contracts. "In such a case, it may happen that many links in the chain are superseded because things have to move fast. Involvement [from the top] is then often lacking…. Also," adds Gard, seemingly wishing to balance the picture somewhat: "The economists and the lawyers think that postponing a decision does not entail implications. They don't easily see the consequences of decisions at all. Thus they become a bottleneck in the system. And remember," he said, emphasizing the phrasing, "*not* making a decision is *also* a decision. And it might very well be the wrong one." Jonas later called me up. He had checked the facts. In all fairness, there were still engineers in top management. He had been wrong in stating otherwise.

The theme underlying this discussion among the project engineers is the underpinnings defining different "worldviews" among engineers and economists, as they see it. "The economists" don't recognize that technology is created, that production is complex, that industrial efforts take training, skill, competence, and time. That is why the CVP, despite its very strong financial connotations, functions in the eyes of the engineers as "educational for the economists," as Gard puts it. More importantly, they have a strong conviction that various economic activities are *qualitatively* different. You don't get the same value from energy power when used for bathroom heating cables as when used for aluminum production. Some economic activities are seen as more valuable to society than others, because of their potential for wealth *creation*. This is the same argument made by the "other canon" economists (Reinert 2007), who argue that this insight is lost in contemporary mainstream economic theory and policies guided by it.

The engineers are also alluding, wittingly or not, to the perennially significant relationship, sometimes symbiotic, sometimes parasitic, between production and financial capital. In the context of Hydro, engineers sometimes refer to "finance" pejoratively as "*økonomene*," "the economists." This because they epitomize the idea of taking production capabilities for granted, "buying them at the grocery store." The "economists'" concern, in their view, is to maximize return on already given production capabilities at any given point in time. This logic is also illustrated by the "internal rent" that was projected up and down, varying with various incidents and forecasts, at the Qatalum DG4.

The engineering managers are worried that Hydro is turning into "a trading company," into a financial corporation. As noted by, for instance, economist Michael Hudson,[4] the industrial worldview, in contrast to the financial, emphasizes economic potential and how best to finance a higher economic horizon. This was exemplified by nineteenth-century German, French, Japanese, Scottish, and Russian industrial banking as it evolved along a different line from Anglo-Dutch mercantile banking, producing very different financial philosophies. Hydro itself, which was then in its inception and development phases, financed by Swedish, French, and German industrial banking, was very much born out of that particular "production capitalist" financial tradition (Andersen 2005). As Hudson remarks, the classical way of extending the economic horizon was by providing returns to entrepreneurs for investing savings in building new factories, hiring more labor, and undertaking more research and development. Hydro's history could not be a more fitting example of all these three elements. However, the issues of a "turn to finance" in projects, raised above, is part of a larger reorientation within Hydro since 1999, in the name of "value-based management," or "shareholder value." This shift was in several ways a turn away from Hydro's own financial tradition, spurred largely by the global rise to domination of a reinvented version of the "mercantile" finance tradition.

The Surge of "Shareholder Value"

Following the "Focus for the Future" strategy process in 1999, guided by the American consultancy Boston Consulting Group (BCG), a wide array of efforts, actions, and principles were put in place at Hydro (Lie 2005: 424–433). One major result was the initiation of "value-based management." Value was here understood as shareholder value, that is, return on shareholders' invested capital. BCG's analysis of Hydro's 10–15 previous years concluded that shareholder returns had been good until the middle of the 1990s, whereas in the following 5–6 years they had fallen. Hydro concluded that the return on capital had been too low and subsequently defined higher shareholder returns as Hydro's overarching goal. A set of measures was launched to reach the goal, based on the principles of so-called value-based management: detailed performance indicators, development of a composite portfolio, and control and incentive systems. On the Hydro website, under the heading "Value based management," which accompanies a figure illustrating that value-based management comprises all processes, from portfolio strategy and business strategy to business planning and performance management, the text reads:

> Value creation is the basis of all our processes. Key elements of this philosophy are:
>
> - Prioritization of investment funds:
>   – to ensure better correspondences between allocation of resources and strategy
>
> - Tightening of capital expenditure discipline:
>   – to focus on supporting strategic potential within business units
>
> - Introduction of value-based management tools:
>   – to measure results in terms of profitability and capital input throughout the organization, and increase understanding of how value is created
>
> - Introduction of performance related pay systems at all levels of the company in the near future will further encourage creation of value.[5]

A key question about what this entailed was whether other interests, such as growth, creating work places, contributing to society—in short other "stakeholders'" interests—were sidestepped by the new focus. The board of directors concluded that they were not. The BCG consultants' level of understanding of the issues at stake was, however, vividly illustrated when they explained that this was not a problem because the shareholders got their compensation last, after employees, suppliers, banks, and the state. As Lie notes: "The question of how production results are to be distributed among labor and capital, presented as a Gordian knot in economic theory at least since Adam Smith and David Ricardo, was apparently solved just by saying 'value-based management' and pointing to the trivial fact that the dividend is disbursed after wages and taxes" (2005: 426, my trans.).

Lie further contends that the consequences of the new shareholder value orientation should not be overemphasized. Nevertheless, at the same time as the turn toward financial forms of control, most of the top management changed. To some extent this was owed to older bosses retiring, but it was also because Eivind Reiten, the new CEO as of 2001, intended for larger changes to be effected to introduce a more performance-oriented culture at Hydro. For example, a new position and director for "management and culture" was hired. She reoriented Hydro's "culture-building" project from primarily creating shared understandings between employees and management, to creating shared conceptions between top management and shareholders demanding return on capital—the latter as represented by a dispersed investor and analyst community (ibid.).

A performance-oriented personnel policy was also implemented via the introduction of "key performance indicators," result-based compensation was implemented for both management and employees, and an options programs for the higher echelons of management was installed from 1999 and expanded in several later waves (more in Chapter 5). Illustrative of the cultural premises pertaining to indicators and performance-oriented ratings is an entry from the diary of the Hydro expatriate manager Kurt in China. On 26 February 2005, he wrote about the evaluations the members of the plant management team gave to each other:

> [L]ast week we had some discussion about the appraisal ratings. I found that we in Europe normally take a much softer approach if we have to evaluate people's attitude, behavior etc. I personally give a rating [of others] between 1 (worst) and 5 (outstanding) as the lowest rating "3." When I saw later the ratings of my managers of their direct reports there was a significant difference. 2, 3 and 4 was a widespread rating. I brought this up because I thought that if you give too low scores people are rather unmotivated than encouraged. No. The Chinese found that this shows people a nice gap where they can improve.

In continuation of the new "finance control"–oriented policies, employees were also given the opportunity to buy company stock at a discount.

The whole system was designed to support the principles of "value-based management" and weave top management and shareholders' values and goals tighter. Out of a wish to appear shareholder-oriented, as early as 1995 Hydro had begun to hold special "Capital Markets Days." Not wanting to give the impression of being (half) "state-owned," Hydro became attentive to signals from the investor communities. A brand-new design and structure of the www.hydro.com website was launched in 2002/2003. An interesting aspect of this was that the new main menu, which was labeled "Investor relations," provided all the major information and details about the business of Hydro, including its annual reports.

The newfound strong attention toward the shareholder community was in line with the dominant US-driven shareholder value movement that took hold in global economic relations starting in the 1980s (Ho 2009). The ideology of the whole shareholder value paradigm was drawn from mainstream neoclassical economics and its recognition *only* of the owner-entrepreneur as a legitimate actor. The advocates of shareholder value thus sought to substitute only "shareholders" for all of the corporation's various socially interrelated "stakeholders" and "worked to replace the social organization of the corporation—the multiplicity of claimants and constituents engaged in labor and production—with the singular 'owned' concern of the individual in his quest for profit" (ibid.: 174). The shareholders now supposedly instantiated and "embodied" the whole of the corporation. This collapse rationalized, in the neoclassically driven shareholder value movement, that the profit-making self-interest of the shareholders was identical with the corporate interest. This shareholder-focused pressure and the underpinning neoclassical values and premises were strongly at odds with some of Hydro's core social values. Thus the overall turn to finance in Hydro, however strong at one level, turned out in the end, as we shall see, to be only partial and highly ambivalent.

An early indication of the new CEO Reiten's ambitions in the direction of a financial reorientation was signaled in his new program slogan for Hydro: "People, Performance, Portfolio." As we have seen, both of the first two P's had major, but indirect and complex, "turn to finance" implications. The latter symbolized the turn directly. The concept of "portfolio management" indicated a shift away from top management being experts in key aspects of the business, to managers as "generalists" viewing the company and its sub-units as "liquid assets" that could be managed as a financial investment portfolio. As Crotty (2005) notes, this development was part of the "conglomerate" surge of the 1960s that picked up speed in the "takeover" movement of the 1980s, though not until the 1990s was the financial or portfolio view promoted or forced upon the managers of nonfinancial corporations. With regard to the P for "People," in the next chapter I discuss the introduction of new financial incentives and compensation schemes like the stock options program.

"Scientific Management," Collaboration, and Democratization

The Hydro case illustrates the ambivalences of this broader development. While several other large companies in Norway, like Statoil, definitively adopted the "manager as generalist" notion, Hydro continues to the present day with a strong focus upon top managers as experts in the business and operations of the company. The "native" term for this kind of management in Hydro is *faglig ledelse*, roughly translated as expert, knowledgeable leadership. Discussing the role of experts and specialists in relation to top management in Hydro, Geir, a highly experienced project director, noted:

> I would say so. In reality, yes. The top management is very concerned to be informed about what the experts say. And not only because they think it is "nice," that is. When we approached concept selection in the Ormen Lange project, three days prior to deciding upon the partnership, Hydro also arranged the, what is it called… capital markets day. Reiten wanted to tell them something about the project, so he called me the prior day. He asked me, "Geir, do you have the flow assurance under control"? He asked that, [pausing], so he knew it was the last thing left [in the project before the selection of the concept could be made]. I told him "yes," he said "great," and chose the concept. I think it says something about him as well; engagement, participation, understanding, and the form of communication we had throughout. Excellent accordance between the expectations and ideas about what we were supposed to be doing.

Reiten himself elaborated upon this theme from his perspective in an interview with me in his office.

> I am immensely conscious about it [*faglig ledelse*, to be professionally and scientifically informed and on top of business activities]. Therefore I work an incredible number of hours a day, and I work those hours to continually be professionally up to date with what we are doing. I believe that my authority, and not only mine, but the whole of top management, but also my authority as a leader here is dependent upon the organization realizing that "he knows this"; that they recognize that when they join a meeting in the corporate management board they will be challenged by someone who knows what he is talking about, someone who has read and worked himself through it [the material]. If I was seen in a way as "surfing" on my title, only walking in and out of black cars, surrounded by security guards, and all of this fuss that is a part of it [*alt dette styret som følger med*], that day you

are definitely finished here. You have to go in, embed yourself in the matters [være i materien]. This adds a lot of working hours to my day, because you need to command a huge area. It is enormous value creating potential in that of challenging the organization, so that when they exit the meeting they think; "he was knowledgeable, not what we had expected on this level, we thought maybe…" At the same time you need to focus on the big picture. It [faglig ledelse] doesn't work perfectly everywhere, but as our main philosophy, yes. Our organization is allergic to such things [as the Kenning philosophy of the generalist manger who without specific domain knowledge can "manage" everything]. There is absolutely no room for such things in Hydro. They are allergic to "strange notions" [påfunn], as I call it; trends, fancy ideas, all kinds of mess and buzz [surr og ball]. You can positively be resilient, but you have to be sober, serious, keep your feet on the ground, know what you are talking about. In Hydro words weigh no more than the quality of them. They carry no more weight because the sender has some title. It is not possible, I'll tell you, to throw around various "leadership slogans" in this organization. It will not be well received [det bare faller igjennom]. The organization is deeply sober and serious [grunn-nøktern].

In Hydro's focus on faglig ledelse, as "expert management" or "knowledgeable management," and even a bit of "scientific management," we also notice its legacy to the original emergence of the subsequently globally "triumphant" managerial rationality, as it developed out of the American engineering tradition in the period 1880–1932. As noted by Shenhav: "The American scientific justification of management practices and ideas sets it apart from European countries where more importance was attached to religious, nationalistic, and culture-specific ideas determining human relations at the workplace" (1999: 5). Thus, while the logic of the "managerial vision" was disseminated worldwide, it had very different local justifications. As has been shown earlier, particularities of both the "Norwegian model" and of the German engineering tradition have also shaped managerialism in Hydro.

In a certain respect the Norwegian model also resembled the British. Here debates about management were dressed more in moral and ideological terms than the "merely" scientific, and thus neutral and non-ideological, productivity discourse in the US. In Britain, as in Norway, the main arguments for introducing human relations programs echoed the ideology of enhancing democracy at the workplace. The major collaborative effort to introduce these programs, on the researcher side, was a joint British-Norwegian team (Emery and Thorsrud 1976). A key concern of the project in Norway was to link human relations more directly to production and the "core of the issues," which the researchers felt had not been done in Britain (Johannessen et al. 2005: 308).

We might also note that the major program, the Norwegian Industrial Democracy Program from 1962, seems to have been much more successfully implemented in Norway than in Britain (Thorsrud and Emery 1970; Emery and Thorsrud 1976). A national strategy for the "humanization of work" came out of these initiatives. It led to the idiosyncratic "Norwegian model" of work life relations, manifested both at the macro-level as major agreements on collaboration between the key work life organization parties, and at the micro-level as particular collaborative, democratized ways of working in each organization (Byrkjeflot et al. 2001; Hernes 2007). The program had three main phases: first, creating improved representative systems of joint consultation, involving establishing "worker managers"; second, the program moved to workplace democracy with employees gaining both resources and power to change their own work organization when and where they deemed it was necessary and appropriate; the third phase was four major experiments in Norwegian industry on work reorganization (Mumford 2006).

The national strategy emerging out of the program included a part of the Norwegian law on working conditions, which gave workers the right to demand jobs conforming to certain sociotechnical and psychological principles and requirements of work practice, such as variety of work, having one's own decision-making power, learning opportunities and organizational support, a desirable future, and social recognition. Subsequently a program emerged for increasing trade union competence in technology and thereby, implicitly, trade union power (ibid.). In addition to the many issues above, concepts that emerged out of the Norwegian Industrial Democracy Program, later to be disseminated worldwide and quite successfully implemented in Japan, were for example the ideas of "autonomous work groups," or "semi-autonomous work groups" [*selvstyrte grupper*], forerunners of concepts like "self managing" and "self directed work teams". And from the late 1960s Hydro was a pioneer in this area (Mumford 1997: 310). Importantly, when these notions were exported out of Norway, for example to Sweden and other places, the core democratization and humanization values were to some extent lost. In the discourse of management, Emery and Thorsrud also interestingly discuss the possibility of a shift in the function of management, from internal coordination and control to regulation of the company's "boundary conditions."

Of noticeable relevance here is, of course, that Hydro was arguably the most important Norwegian company participating in the program. In light of both the Norwegian case and my own empirical material from China, it is problematic when Shenhav, in presenting supposedly one of the most "differentiated" and "non-reified" histories of the "managerial revolution," proposes that managerial techniques may now be similar or identical globally, and that it was only in their inception that they were substantially different and culture-bound (1999: 6). Although it is arguably difficult to deny a globalizing homogenization of managerialism, like possible others the Norwegian case stands out. Furthermore, and not least, the Chinese local managers in my cases had quite uniform perceptions about the radical difference in managerial styles between the international companies localizing in China. Typically they differentiated between American, German, Japanese, Korean, Taiwanese, and Scandinavian companies. And their interaction with companies from these various countries was marked by different anticipations of what they could expect from the companies. As covered in Chapter 2, one of the main reasons the Chinese managers—and to the extent I have direct and indirect knowledge, other employees as well—wanted to work for Hydro was its "soft," participative managerial style, favoring low hierarchies with much delegation of responsibility. To sustain an idea of a globally uniform managerialism is thus difficult.

Boltanski and Chiapello's analysis of the "new spirit of capitalism" underscores, however, that what they label the modalities of control in *neomanagement* entails the significant transition from control to self-control, and that ensuring self-control is achieved by subsuming the inner life— the emotions, values, and personal relations of workers—under productivity and profit motives (2007: 78–86). They identify the practice of organizing the workers in "autonomous teams" as a significant mechanism inducing people to control themselves. This analysis certainly has merit, and it is in line with some of the discussion in Chapter 1, relating among other things to Sørhaug's concept of "managementality" as a form of self-management (2004). However, in the Hydro case, as is true for broader aspects of the Norwegian model, democratization as illustrated in the Xi'an case is still a strong *"eigenvalue,"* alongside productivity and profit considerations. As shown in the Xi'an case, this applies to a large extent also when Hydro exports the Norwegian model abroad. This is contrary to the general notion noted above, that the core democratization value was lost when key aspects of the Norwegian model were adopted in many other countries, and it is a case that runs counter to findings that suggest that Norwegian-based companies expanding abroad also discard core values of the model (Løken et al. 2008). Furthermore, in the unique cross-cultural encounters that occur in investment projects, new cultural forms, also related to managing, are created. In Xi'an we saw how a hybrid type of plant, a Hydro/Norwegian/local/American/"international" style of "democratized" workplace, emerged in just a few years.

Projects as Cultural Idiom

Nevertheless, and despite these significant historical trajectories, the shareholder value focus in Hydro was reaffirmed by a very thorough "brand process" conducted with the aid of the Siegelgale consultancy firm in 2003.[6]
Based upon extensive Hydro executive interviews, focus group interviews
throughout the global organization, and surveys of Hydro internal audiences, in addition to viewpoints gathered from customers, partners, and
suppliers, the report concluded: "Three external forces have conspired to
put Hydro at a crossroads, where the company must take a fresh look at
how it will create value in the future." One of the external forces was seen
as: "A *more demanding shareholder* places pressure on Hydro to emphasize
profits first, which calls into question traditional values" (emphasis in original). Following are some utterances by different Hydro members, taken
from the report, that exemplify this "external force."

> Last year, it was performance and sustainability, today it is people, perfor-
> mance and portfolio. But financial performance remains consistent.

> Hydro's shareholders put pressure on everyone these days, and so we're told
> we have to live up to that.

> The shareholder was never mentioned ten years ago. But now it's "share-
> holder this" and "shareholder that." It's taken a front seat.

> Our company is being driven by economists. Shareholder value is a text-
> book phrase.

In his "history of Hydro" from 1977 to 2005, Lie concludes, however, that
the core of the new orientation was rather a much stronger focus upon
the *daily operations*, a more thorough follow-up on the economic results of
the various business units in Hydro (2005). He maintains that from the
1970s throughout most of the 1990s, Hydro was not characterized by such
an operations orientation. It is interesting, from the present investigative
approach to Hydro investment projects, that the company's newer history
documents that its capacity to handle large, complex investment projects
has been one of its foremost qualities. That means project competence in
a wide meaning of the word. As Lie notes: "The company's resources in
engineering, research, finance, contract design, human resource management have been mobilized on a broad basis [in such projects], along with
Hydro's well developed talents for handling authorities and their other
surroundings" (ibid.: 434–435, my trans.). Following Lie, Hydro's systematic development and maintenance of this competence has been a critical
factor in Hydro's generation of wealth and profitability. Hydro's history

the last thirty years or so thus documents that it has not been an especially "operations-oriented" company, but rather a *project-oriented* culture
in the widest sense of the word.

A concrete example of this continuing legacy was when Head of Projects Tom Røtjer in 2007 was promoted to executive vice-president and
awarded a place on the corporate management board. As of 2007, Projects
became one of four divisions in Hydro, on par with Energy, Aluminium
Metal, and Aluminium Products. Projects are also frequently cited within
Hydro management as key to Hydro's continuing success. As Reiten said,
their inclusion on the corporate management board attests to that. Historical records thus deem that a study of Hydro's investment projects may
have generalizable value to the company as a whole.

I argue here and in the following two chapters, however, that the financial turn as of 1999 has had quite dramatic and unforeseeable consequences, besides a mere reorientation toward daily operations, as Lie
seems to conclude. As I will show, its consequences point also in the opposite direction, not only "downward" toward the production and daily
operations, but also "upward" to the "imaginary" and "virtual" realm of
abstract "financial wizardry" in the name of what I call "value origination
and appreciation." I will continue to show how this wider context of "financialization of the global economy" imposed significant constraints on
Hydro investment projects and the corporation in general

As we have seen, the "worship" of shareholder value entered Hydro
with full force from 1999 onward. Whether the financial turn took place
at the expense of other concerns remains an open question. The Norwegian and Hydro work life model of "democratic capitalism" (Sejersted
1993) may have buffered and slowed down, and transformed the particularities of, the entrance and the impact of the turn to finance. What the
changes in Hydro since 1999 illustrate, as is implied in their own hints
about the "driving forces," I will interpret first as an indication that the
legitimizing idioms of managing authority have been transformed considerably, from being based in engineering and a technocratic rationality to
increasingly being justified in terms of economy and finance.

The invention of "finance control" along a variety of dimensions illustrates this. As will be further elaborated in the next chapter, this shift
can be seen as a "turn to enchantment," a sign of a captivated capitalism.
It illustrates a quite radical development in the globalized economy in the
direction of "financialization": a finance economy increasingly decoupled
and classificatorily "autonomized" from the economic life of people and
societies everywhere, and also from the productive activities of key industrial institutions like Hydro. For now, we must recognize that financial
mechanisms of control and follow-up have been actively socialized into

the core practices of production in projects and internalized in other aspects of corporate "everyday life" in Hydro.

To be able to account for the financial turn in Hydro projects and in the Hydro company at large, however, we also need to look beyond Hydro itself. We need to describe some of the wider historical and structural contexts, both nationally and "globally," that provided the impetus for the changes and co-produced the financialized "driving forces" that Hydro to some extent has obeyed, and in some senses thrived under. Although continuing to be situated in the "local" case of Hydro and its investment projects, the next two chapters extend the field outward to situate the case within its broader contextual constraints.

Notes

1. The oil and gas division of Hydro merged with Statoil in 2007, forming the new StatoilHydro corporation. In 2009 the name was changed to "Statoil". For some facts about Ormen Lange see: http://www.statoil.com/en/NewsAndMedia/FeatureStories/ OrmenLange/Pages/default.aspx (accessed 23 May 2011).
2. EBITDA is "earnings before interest, tax, depreciation, and amortization."
3. See the Hydro annual reports for their definitions and usages of the various finance control terms, available at hydro.com.
4. "Capital, Capital Everywhere: How to Invest It Wisely?" Report to the Norwegian Shipowners' Association, 2000. See http://www.michael-hudson.com/speeches/0008 norway_1.html (accessed 15 August 2007).
5. See http://www.hydro.com/en/Investor-relations/Analytical-information/Value-based-management/ (accessed 10 December 2009).
6. "Clarifying the Potential of the Norsk Hydro Brand," *siegelgale report*, 2003.

Chapter 5

WAGGING THE DOG
The Financialization of Sociality

We've seen why commitment is in increasingly scarce supply in the
new capitalism, in terms of institutional loyalty ... how can you
commit to an institution which is not committed to you?
—Richard Sennett, *The Culture of the New Capitalism*

They wanted something for nothing.
I gave them nothing for something.
—J. R. "Yellow Kid" Weil, *"Yellow Kid" Weil:*
The Autobiography of America's Master Swindler

On 29 January 2005, Kurt, the Hydro expatriate manager in China, wrote
the following entry in his diary:

I went to Europe with my wife in the beginning of January to attend two
meetings. The first one was the so-called "Hydro Summit" in Oslo. During
this meeting we were generally aligned for the upcoming challenges. Our
CEO wanted to make his point and share the good results and his concerns
with the key managers. Hydro has changed recently very much and the
former freedom we had in the Sector was substituted by a strong top down
approach. This opinion is shared across the sector and across people. There
were one reflection on that item but Mr. Reiten says he does not believe
that Hydro has become more bureaucratic and mentioned a lot of projects
that were carried out quickly and with no bureaucracy. It was the most dis-

cussed point in the corridors. Another fact is that at the moment it is the finance people ruling the company and the shareholders and the financial community are setting the tone of the music. Customers don't count and very little is said about their satisfaction with Hydro. "Deliver" is the key word, and if you don't deliver, for sure you will get some troubles.

As the former chapter concludes, since the late 1990s Hydro projects and the entire corporation have undergone a shift toward "shareholder value," a shift that I will document illustrates a dramatic, worldwide financial expansion in the global capitalist system over the last thirty years or so. I indicated that this development might appropriately be labeled a financialized "turn to enchantment," a captivated capitalism, and examined this turn by empirically discussing changes in Hydro's orientation toward "shareholder value," "value-based management," and other "financial" idioms of its managing practices. Broader driving forces of this shift, as will be explored in the present and the next chapter, affected and re-formed actors in the Anglo-American tradition first, the continental tradition later, and arguably the Nordic and Norwegian economies and organizations even later.

As we saw, the fundamental shift at Hydro can be dated relatively accurately to the year 1999, forged and explicated by their Boston Consulting Group–led strategy process Focus for the Future, which instigated a massive strategic turn in the company toward "shareholder value." Some of the various corporate implications were outlined above. Judged in terms of its ambitions of a real change toward a financial reorientation, Hydro has been fantastically successful. The market value of the company increased sixfold during the period from 1999 to 2007, putting Hydro at the top of its league in comparison to relevant companies.

In the present chapter I will try to put this extraordinary financial success into wider perspective. I will unfold some of the major contextual circumstances that enveloped the case of financing projects and the financial turn the company took since 1999 along some key dimensions. The turn, in terms of projects or corporate culture or knowledge traditions, was by no means developed in a vacuum. Rather it was part and parcel of fundamental transformational processes of the capitalist economy on a planetary scale. I will argue that Hydro's "turn to finance" is symptomatic of several dramatic new trends since the 1970s in the operations of capitalism on both the domestic or national, and the global scale. In this chapter and the next I will show that the turn taking place within Hydro was part of: (a) a political reorientation among the international and national (Norwegian) administrative elite toward market mechanisms and neoliberal ideologies, (b) a historically recurring phase shift and new triumph of "high finance" in the capitalist *fourth* systemic cycle of accumulation (Arrighi 1994), and finally (c), a shift in the globalized interstate capitalist system of global money creation and management.

This is far from implying that the particular financial path taken at the fin de siècle by Hydro, which was crowned with formidable success on its own terms, was in any way determined or inevitable. Rather, I will show how Hydro's idiosyncratic trajectory comprises a skilled, "advanced" act of balancing several of the global trends and transformations of vast depth, reach, and consequence that has been played out over the last thirty years or so. President and CEO Eivind Reiten himself signified this balancing act when he said, regarding the large portfolio restructuring and the subsequent dramatic rise in Hydro "value creation and appreciation," that "the driving forces are powerful. We had to cultivate each of these huge areas of Hydro."[1] At the same time he indicated that to date Hydro has exploited these major trends and shifts in the global economy to its advantage. I will argue that in terms of the recent years' fabulous economic results, until the finance crisis hit, Hydro might serve as an illustrative example of what Arrighi (1994) has termed a "wonderful moment" in the midst of a deep global crisis in the capitalist system of accumulation.

The analysis will convey that the "wonderful moment" of the millennium, exemplified by the Hydro case, is a reminder of an underlying reality that was ripped open when the finance crisis, once unleashed, indicated to most people the possibility of a postcapitalist world. Prior to embarking upon the more general analysis, I will ground the discussion first with a brief documentation of Hydro's financial results and transformation since 1999, using the company's own financial reporting. Subsequently I describe and discuss the Hydro stock options compensation scheme and the public debacle it instigated in Norway. From that illustration I go on to discuss the Norwegian context of "democratic capitalism," within which Hydro is heavily constituted and contributive, and discuss the pressures upon and possible demise of this form of capitalism. The options case is furthermore extended toward a discussion of Hydro's uses of other new financial instruments, especially in "risk management," and broader implications of this are analyzed.

Hydro's Financial Transformation

In the decade or so before Hydro's "shareholder turn" in 1999, Hydro's share price performance was on par with, and for the years 1996–2000 even considerably below, the average performance of the Oslo stock exchange. In 1999 payouts to shareholders jumped, and actual shareholder returns reached a total of NOK 37 billion in the period 2000–2006, with an average payout ratio of 50 percent for 2004–2006.[2] In the same period the level of investments was fairly stable. Most significantly, from 1999 to 2007 the market value and stock price of Hydro increased by approximately 600 percent.[3] This put Hydro at the top of its league, compared to competitors in the aluminum and oil and energy sectors. The share price reached its peak of NOK 85.50 on 15 May 2008 before it plunged to NOK 21.20 by 21 November 2008. Measured by share values, when the finance crisis hit Hydro lost 75.2 percent of its value in half a year. The market capitalization—"total net value"—of Hydro reached its peak in July 2007 with NOK 99 billion. It then dropped to 88 billion in February 2008 and 75 billion by July 2008, then plummeting to NOK 33 billion by February 2009.

From the above figures we might conclude that Hydro conforms to the overall trends in the global economy described as *financialization*. As empirically described by Crotty (2005), comparing the 1960s–1970s to the 1980s–1990s, US nonfinancial corporations more than doubled their payouts as a share of their cash flow. I argue that the kind of developments evident in the Hydro shares and value appreciation since 1999 represent an overall development from a focus on production to a focus on "value creation" and finally to a focus on "value origination and appreciation," which is characteristic of the contemporary financialized global economic system.

The strategies for the buildup of financial values during the "wonderful moment" are illustrated by then President Reiten in the first "Letter to shareholders," a communicative genre launched for the first time in 2001: "In my first shareholders' letter, it is natural to underscore my commitment to promoting the company's further growth—by getting the best out of our employees, developing our portfolio and, not least, by improving our own, and our shareholders', results.... Active development of our portfolio is a key factor in our effort to create shareholder value. Our three core areas all have a good basis for competitive value creation."[4]

The concept of value creation, as it is embedded in the CVP and management rhetoric in Hydro, is positioned in between productive creation on the one side and financial "value origination and appreciation" on the other side. Practices and talk about value creation thus tap into and feed on both the broadly defined traditions of "productive capitalism" (including "productive finance") on the one hand, and "financial capitalism" on the other hand. Viewing the two as poles on an interdependent continuum, we can appreciate how, depending upon context, situation, and circumstance, the concept of value creation may "slide" toward one pole or the other. A debate from the newspapers could illustrate the point further.

According to the Norwegian business newspaper *Dagens Næringsliv*, Reiten received criticism from one of Norway's most ardent industrial conglomerate leaders, Jens P. Heyerdahl, during a presentation the latter held. He supposedly commented that with Reiten at the top, the only focus of Hydro was the share price, and that there was a difference between building industrial strength and shareholder value. Reiten replied in the same edition of the paper: "Each and all of the major changes in Hydro the last years have been industrially justified, both the separation of Yara, the fusion with Statoil and the commitment forward as a focused industrial company. If the fact that Hydro's industrial development over time also creates major shareholder values is an embarrassment to Jens P. Heyerdahl, I can live quite well with it" (my trans.).[5] He also described the restructuring of the Hydro conglomerate as an "industrial revolution." When I asked Reiten what he would hope to see as the legacy from his years as president and CEO of Hydro, he emphasized the importance of restructuring of the portfolio, of the way three strong companies had been created out of the former Hydro conglomerate. Questions that emerge are: is the process Reiten has led most adequately described as an industrial or a financial revolution, or both or none of them?

In the newspaper interview, Reiten continued: "There is no doubt that completing such major changes in the diverse Hydro organization entails melancholy and a couple of seconds afterthought about whether it is correct. Whoever does not say that is not being honest." He continued: "But the driving forces are powerful. We had to cultivate each of these huge areas of Hydro." He stressed that today's investors want focused companies to be able to assemble their own portfolio and risk profile independently. Also, he emphasized that the market focus at Hydro had contributed to its continuing success: "There is a tendency to talk about share prices as if they mean nothing. But Hydro has lasted 102 years because the management always has been concerned with this."[6]

Hydro has been extraordinarily successful in elevating the value of its stock and creating shareholder value since its turn to finance in the late 1990s, particularly since 1999 and especially since 2003. It has been both praised and criticized for this, but Reiten regards the changes made in recent years as an "industrial revolution." As discussed earlier, considerable critique has been focused on the shareholder value approach in general by organizational and management scholars as well. That corporations exist to maximize shareholders' value is a doctrine with too much power, according to commentators like Mintzberg, Simons, and Basu (2002), who argue that analysts, institutional stock traders, and the media reward and assess companies and their CEOs based on this single standard of performance. Through an analysis of statements from a group of chief executives representing America's 200 largest corporations, these authors identify a shift in their priorities between 1981, when a balanced view of the corporation's and management's justification and responsibilities toward a broad set of stakeholders and societal interests was advocated, and 1997. A report from the round table announced, in the words of Mintzberg, Simons, and Basu: "The paramount duty of managers and of boards of directors is to the corporation's stockholders. Period. The customer may be 'king,' and the employee may the corporation's greatest asset (at least in rhetoric), but the shareholder is the bottom line" (2002: 69). One significant feature of Hydro's adoption of the shareholder value management goal was the implementation of performance-related compensation schemes. For top managers this included a stock option program.

The "Stock Options Carnival"

The events described and analyzed below played out in an intense public debate in a short time span during the summer of 2007. The background was that in 2000, Hydro implemented a stock option–based incentive system for top managers. The justification for the scheme, as described in the Annual Report, was that

> [o]ne of the board's most important areas of responsibility is to ensure that the company's top management meets international standards. Greater demand with respect to competitive compensation and career developments means that the board will have to take greater responsibility for ensuring that the company as a whole continues to develop as an attractive and challenging employer. The implementation of incentive schemes will provide a stimulus for the achievement of the company's goals, as well as contribute to a better understanding of the shareholder's requirement for a satisfactory rate of return. (2000: 32)

Eleven pages later, the same report discloses exactly what kind of incentive schemes the board has in mind: "In line with the strategy concerning increased emphasis on performance and value creation…. The scheme consists of share options and an annual bonus linked to the attainment of the business plan" (ibid.: 43). The option programs of the large Norwegian companies received irregular attention and occasioned various degrees of public outcry and denunciation in the years after the millennium, and the events described in more detail below were preceded by a shorter and not quite as intense and consequential debate in 2006.

In November that year a heated debate over options in the big, partly state-owned companies of Norway was all over the media in newspapers, on radio, and on the televised debate programs.[7] The main reason for the intense debate in November 2006 was that the CEO of the recently privatized telecom company Telenor had redeemed his options. Hydro was also highly involved in the debate. It reached the highest levels of the government: Prime Minister Jens Stoltenberg was "grilled" in the question hour in Stortinget (the Parliament), and the Minister of Finance and the new Minister for Trade and Industry appeared on television discussing the issue. The major Norwegian labor union, LO, was also involved, as well as the NHO, the Confederation of Norwegian Enterprise (the main representative body for Norwegian employers). What was the buzz about? As the LO representative presented it on television,[8] nothing less than the Norwegian social model ("den norske samfunnsmodellen") was at stake. To better understand the background and vast implications adhering to the option incentive schemes in the Norwegian public debate, it is appropriate to describe the even more intense debate about the same issue that reemerged a bit more than half a year later. This time around, Hydro management was fixed in the spotlight.

The options program at Hydro was terminated in 2007 after the implementation of Norwegian laws restricting (partly) state-owned companies from applying such compensation schemes. In conjunction with the program's closure, the board of directors decided to disburse NOK 210 million to thirty-five top leaders at Hydro. Reiten alone got NOK 27.8 million. The decision sparked heated debate over its legality in the news media,[9] and the first part of the debate culminated in a statement made by the Ministry of Trade and Industry that an inquiry would be initiated into the legality of the disbursement of the options. Several of the other big Norwegian owners of Hydro, like Folketrygdfondet, Storebrand, and KLP, also announced that they would investigate whether the board was within its judicial rights to end the options program the way it did. Hydro's own lawyers concluded quickly that the board did not exceed its authority; they seemed rather to have advised the board not to "shave" the options disbursements due to possible lawsuits from the affected directors.[10] This advice was also interpreted as somewhat suspect in the media based on the fact that the leader of Hydro's judicial department was himself included in the options program.

The strong reaction from the Ministry, however, seemed somewhat peremptory in view of information coming out that the government had already been informed about the options disbursements the previous month[11] but reacted strongly only after the case broke in the media. Reiten had personally informed the prime minister of this four weeks prior to the media headlines.[12] Some maintain that the information provided was too general and misleading to claim that the agreements to be terminated were changed in favor of the top management.[13] Undersecretary Rikke Lind of the Ministry of Trade and Industry was quoted as saying: "This is horrible. Reiten has of course not deserved all this money."[14] She continued to say that the huge payout in effect was the exact opposite of what the state had intended with its guidelines for (partly) state-owned companies, which had led to the termination of the options program. She maintained that these schemes threatened the "Nordic model" characteristic of societies with low levels of social inequality.

The leader of the Oslo Labor Party and the leaders of SV, both parties in the government coalition, among others, demanded that the director of the board had to be removed,[15] and speculations surfaced about the end of Reiten as CEO of Hydro, and also about stopping him from becoming the first director of the board of the merged StatoilHydro energy company.[16] This was one episode in a series of media events that were highly critical of Reiten.[17] The director of the board of Yara, the former Hydro fertilizer division, stated that he would have taken the issue to the general assembly before any such disbursements would have taken place. Meanwhile, Yara continued its already existing options contracts.[18] The hedge fund managers, on the other hand, feared that Hydro would suffer from "brain drain," losing its "best people" because of the closure of the options program.[19]

Reiten and the corporate board of managers also received some support from Senterpartiet, a party in the coalition government. The party's finance-political spokesperson understood the frustrations of the Hydro management and put the blame for the option story on the Minister of Trade and Industry.[20] The vice-chairman of the party said he knew Reiten *not* to be a man of greed.[21] Reiten himself is a former politician and Minister of Oil and Energy from Senterpartiet. The media storm was further aggravated by speculations that the board had disbursed NOK 46 million more than the options contracts demanded.[22] Intellectuals interpreted the options case as both a symptom of moral and cultural degeneration and a threat to the Norwegian "societal model" (*samfunnsmodell*). They labeled the options disbursements as "moral striptease"[23] and "the money that disintegrates Norway."[24] Fuel to the fire was provided by newspapers reporting that Reiten at one point allegedly had referred to the public debate surrounding manager compensations as "the annual carnival."[25]

Relevant to the debate was speculation that five of the Norwegian board members, among them the three employee representatives, were the most critical toward the options disbursements, whereas the three foreigners on the board seemed to have been the most positive. The latter three also later chose to discontinue their engagement as members of the board, allegedly because of the way the state intervened in the options case. The director of the board dismissed speculations about dissent on the board and said the final decision was made unanimously.[26] After what Director of the Board Jan Reinås felt as "pressure" from the government, however, he resigned his post. He described the process in strong and vivid rhetoric, at least in light of being a member of the national corporate elite: "To get a boot behind, for doing a good job, I find quite surprising" ("å få en fot i ræva for å gjøre en god job synes jeg er overraskende"),[27] and he also described it as being "stabbed in the back by the government" ("jeg ble dolket i ryggen av regjeringen").[28] The minister contended they had not fired him but had expressed mistrust on behalf of the state as one of the owners of Hydro. Reiten said he regretted but accepted Reinås's decision. The opposition parties, especially Høyre, Venstre, and Fremskrittspartiet, used the occasion to criticize the government, and the latter stated that it was the minister who should be leaving.

The debate raged on. Subsequently the rest of the board and CEO Reiten's role and position became more pronounced in the debate. At least among some of the coalition partners in the government, the position seemed to be that if Reiten and the corporate management themselves were responsible for creating the proposal of the NOK 210 million disbursements, Reiten and possibly the board of directors ought to be removed.[29] Before Reinås's resignation the board had submitted its decision-making process to be scrutinized and assessed by the Corporate Assembly, to reach a conclusion about trust or mistrust of the board. Before its decision was made, Hydro announced that Reiten and others in the options program had renounced in total about NOK 20 million of their options compensation. Reiten himself waived NOK 7.8 million.[30] The Minister of Trade and Industry replied somewhat ambivalently that this seemed to be "enough" and that doing it now contributed to establishing order ["ro"] in relation to the Hydro options case. Others in the government commented that it was not enough, and that Reiten's position was still threatened.[31] Some commentators ironically noted that in the reduction from 210 to 190 million it was now made clear where the border between the acceptable and the outrageous was to be found.[32]

The Corporate Assembly reached a unanimous conclusion of trust in the way the board had handled the termination of the options program. However, reports still indicated that elements within the government wanted to remove Reiten.[33] Simultaneously several reports described the substantial stock value increase Hydro had created under Reiten's management. The paper Dagens Næringsliv calculated that, compared to their most significant competitors in the aluminum and energy businesses, Hydro under Reiten had outcompeted its rivals by a sum in excess of NOK 100 billion.[34]

Reiten himself finally broke his silence and responded to the allegations against himself and Hydro, stating that he understood some of the reactions in the public but firmly disagreed with the strong allegations, "both untrue and malicious" ("usanne og ondskapsfulle"), that had been put forth in the process.[35] He reacted especially strongly to charges of disorganization and impropriety ("ordentlighet og ryddighet"), asserting that "when it comes to form of procedure [saksbehandling], quality in the ways things are done, and role clarity, I have always put my honor in that being well organized [ordentlig]." The only thing he regretted was that the general meeting of shareholders had not been informed about the decision to terminate the options program in a one-time disbursement. One Hydro historian labeled the Hydro options drama as the company's largest leadership crisis since 1917, when Sam Eyde, the famous co-founder of Hydro, was forced out of the company by the Wallenberg financial interest, whose Marcus Wallenberg held the position of the director of the board.[36]

After sixteen days of intense media storm the debate faded out, and in the "closing phase" the minister of oil and energy stated that Reiten's future second position, as director of the board of StatoilHydro, was secure.[37] The minister of finance, representing also SV, probably the most critical government party in relation to options and Reiten's position, also dismissed the "possibility" of removing Reiten.[38] The case did not go silent, however; for example, the Oslo Labor Party's board voted unanimously against Reiten becoming the first director of the board in the new StatoilHydro company about a week later.[39]

The government announced that its handling of the options case was the proof of the new red-green government's policies of "active ownership," which had been frequently ridiculed since the launch of the slogan. The option theme promises to remain an issue until 2013, when the options contracts in the major partly state-owned Norwegian companies are finally phased out. Both Aftenposten and Dagens Næringsliv published huge feature stories summarizing the Hydro options case.[40] Interestingly, Dagens Næringsliv, the daily paper whose editorials and staff commentators had been most positive toward Hydro and most negative toward the government's handling of the case, turned out to be highly critical of Hydro in its summarizing feature story, conveying how the value of the stock options had fluctuated widely in just a short time span.

On 13 June, when the board of directors had decided to terminate the options program, the value of the options was NOK 157 million. By 23 July, when the official decision of closure was taken by the board of directors, the market value had risen to NOK 210 million. But by 6 August, the day of the "crisis meeting" of the Corporate Assembly, the value had fallen to NOK 147 million. At this meeting Reiten "gave back" 20 of the NOK 210 million, and the head of the Corporate Assembly confirmed that this act had been critical to ensure the continuing trust in CEO Reiten and the board of directors. He further answered "no comment" to the question about whether the Corporate Assembly during the meeting knew that the total value of the option compensation package had fallen to NOK 147 million the very day of the meeting. Ten days later the value of the program was down to NOK 127 million.[41] From a purely pecuniary perspective, the Hydro managers benefited maximally. In a dramatic postscript to the options commotion, at least according to the popular media dramaturgy, Reiten announced rather surprisingly that he was resigning from his post as the chairman of the board of StatoilHydro only two weeks after his "inauguration." The reason was a self-judgment of role conflicts in terms of his double position also as CEO of Hydro, at a time when some older Hydro contracts, from before his time as CEO, had come under investigation in relation to possible corruption.

"Options" in a Moral Economy

What then, can account for the huge amount of attention, debate, consternation, and dismay pouring out toward Hydro's top management during the options media storm? Contextualizing the debate might enable a better grasp of the underlying themes. One commentator points to the obvious paradox that in Norway there are several company owners, most notably Kjell Inge Røkke, that earn many times the money Reiten did, but nevertheless are perceived positively in the public debate (Bjerke 2007). He asks: "'People' hate Reiten, but love Røkke. Why?" Some rudiments of an explanation are suggested in the same commentary. First, people seem to have had the impression that Røkke, like some others, earned his money from scratch himself. The image of the self-made man seems to be alive and well in Norway.

However, other historical cases of similar flavor indicate that this parameter is just one among many, one that might very well be overlooked in the public's eyes. Secondly, the commentator suggests, people may distinctively divide the elite into "owners" and "wage earners," whereupon directors like Reiten, in a certain sense, may surprisingly fall within the latter category. Expanding upon this commentary, we might say that the rage against extortionate compensation is perceived as morally legitimate and necessary within the common social categorical sphere of "wage earners." "Owners," on the other hand, seem to be perceived as outside this particular sphere of moral judgment. At a further remove, we may easily appreciate that the owner vs. wage-earner categories and relations reflect the historical relationship between capital and labor as framed in the Norwegian context. The notable conservative historian Francis Sejersted has labeled this particular context "democratic capitalism," in which a strong state combines with strong communalism and connects with the broadly based petit bourgeois and its ideals of equality and democracy (1993).

Democracy has been a fundamental characterizing value of Norwegian work life relations, as testified and described for example in the Norwegian Industrial Democracy Program (Emery and Thorsrud 1976). A core question has been how the economic domain can enable democratically participatory citizens and democratic societal development. In this view democracy is the overarching system value of capitalism (Slagstad 2001: 527). Historically "democratic capitalism" has characterized the Norwegian system since the late nineteenth century, though it has come increasingly under pressure during the last decades (Byrkjeflot et al. 2001). Variants of this form of capitalism might throughout the world more broadly be applied to the capitalist period of "managed" or "embedded" capitalism, also described as "embedded liberalism" (Harvey 2005), which will be further expanded upon below.

In the public debate on options, capitalist owners are seen as playing another game. It gets really interesting, then, in the Hydro options case, that it was the Norwegian capitalist state—a highly speculative one, in its millennial financial outlook[42]—as the largest, although minority, owner, that found it necessary, after multiple pressures, to act morally against the perceived "wage earner" directors. The moral lesson of this symbolic exchange seems to be that wage earners, in the eyes of the public, as incarnated in this respect by the state and the media and various expert commentators, must display moral decency, defy greed, and "show moderation." The latter is a favorite slogan of the NHO (the main representative body for Norwegian employers) to discipline labor in the yearly wage settlements. Without moderation, an accelerating wage spiral that is believed to undermine the welfare state is projected as a threat. The Norwegian welfare model rests upon the premise that labor is "modest" in terms of wage demands.

From the options debate we might further infer that the directors of the largest companies of Norway are perceived as belonging to the same social community as labor, as "the common people." As the prime minister noted during the debate: "To be a top leader in these types of companies is not all about own income and gains. It is about managing trust on behalf of the whole Norwegian population. Thus being a top leader is a position of trust. This means that such top leaders are constrained by special requirements. That is an issue of prudence and respect."[43] He also used the term "representative" (*tillitsmann*) and in doing so evoked a normative and historical metaphor-machinery. The word is the title of arguably the most famous book of the whole Norwegian labor movement, written in 1931 by the future Prime Minister Einar Gerhardsen; both remain strong symbols of the emergence of the whole post–World War II social democratic welfare state.

A highly paradoxical situation thus emerged. The board of Hydro introduced a financial incentive instrument for top managers, the stock options program, to shrink the historical gap and role differentiation between managers and owners of a corporation. This role division had been a key capitalist institution since the invention and widespread establishment of the "limited liability joint-stock company," incorporated as a "legal person" in the latter half of the nineteenth century (Bakan 2004; Micklethwait and Wooldridge 2003). The option measure was introduced by the Hydro board to align the interests of the managers, by turning them in part into owners themselves, with those of the corporation as an incarnation of the owners at large. This aim was in line with the theoretical legitimation of stock options measures. Nevertheless it was the largest owner, the state, that put an end to the options schemes.

Option incentives were initially introduced into the world of corporations to *stop* the abuse of power among managers. At the time of the inception of the idea of separating ownership and management, it was by many believed to be a recipe for corruption and scandal. Adam Smith, for example, warned in his 1776 classic *The Wealth of Nations* that managers could not be entrusted to "steward other people's money." "'Negligence and profusion' would inevitably result when businesses organized as corporations" (quoted in Bakan 2004: 6). The idea that came to be developed, in effect, was the following: upon becoming afraid that top leaders have too much power compared to the shareholders, those in power should be rewarded even more in the belief that they, behaving under the assumption of "economic man" notions as self-interested "rational egoists," will work more honestly in favor of the company rather than for themselves. Using options programs is a way to try to resolve the challenge of aligning the benefits for the managers with what is best for the company (seen as shareholders).

The problem of separating owners and managers is particularly accentuated from the point of view of the neoclassical premises of the self-interested economic man, alongside its assumption that the only two entities allowed to be present are individual owners and private property seen as an exclusive unit (Ho 2009). Herein arises an almost insurmountable

problem. In neoclassical thinking, the tradition from Adam Smith is continued with a form of economic organization Smith believed was destined
to fail. The tight unity of ownership and control, which Smith and classical as well as neoclassical followers perceived as the atom of property and
economic activity, was dissolved with the invention of management. The
premises upon which classical self-interest and neoclassical theory extensions are built are wholly inadequate to the modern corporate social organization. To simply equate the shareholders of the modern corporation
with the "ideal" of private and individually owned enterprises, the "family
model," is severely problematic, because "the stock price becomes a reification of the corporation as a whole, rather than merely one attribute of a
social entity with many attributes" (ibid.: 190). No proper reconciliation,
nor even a conflict, can emerge or exist between shareholder value and
any other interests within or related to the corporation, because the collapse into shareholder value is so fundamental that "by measuring shareholder value, one could measure everything" (ibid.: 212). Thus the nearly
totalizing victory of shareholder value has contributed greatly to the demise of the corporation, and the sinking of global capitalism itself, both of
which have been partly dismantled on the altar of finance capital.

The huge monetary incentives for directors and top managers are, as we
have seen, based in shareholder value thinking, but they are influenced by
some related ideas coming from "principal agent theory." The latter idea
is linked to the notion of information asymmetry. CEOs and top managers
are perceived as possessing the upper hand in terms of information surplus.
Because this advantage enables them to form other people's understanding of challenges and the overall situation for the corporation, they may
subsequently manipulate the board and the owners. According to Trangy,
herein lies a short circuit in thinking: the stock option measures try to
solve a problem of power by giving incentives to the more powerful (2006:
128). Judging by the market value increase in Hydro, the effect realized
may seem to be the contrary—that the options incentives indeed contributed to top management's working, and succeeding, at increasing the
shareholder value. However, what portion of this market value increase, if
any, might be attributed to the options program is impossible to assess. In
the media debate Reiten, at least, stated that the options program was an
incentive mechanism that worked. This contention raises yet other questions about the state of affairs in management motivation in the first place,
and so on and so forth. The media focus on "greed" as a major motivational force could, however, also be perceived as overly speculative, meanwhile simultaneously reflecting the hegemony of mainstream neoclassical
premises and neoliberal ideology as it relates to human nature in terms of
the egoistic and individually acquisitive economic man.

On the other hand, as discussed since the inception of "the corpo-ration," there is no doubt that shareholders have tried to manipulate managers into favoring shareholders in relation to other stakeholders in companies. True, this tendency has not emerged without reason. Several scholarly works have testified to how managers seized control over large corporations and manipulated shareholders for their own purposes (Gal-braith 1967). This situation led to counter-pressure from the investor and owner communities. The neoclassical defense of shareholder value, and critique of managerialism, turned into a forceful narrative of the "abused shareholder," a drama with the "shareholder as a victim, denied his right-ful role in the modern corporation by manager-usurpers" (Ho 2009: 190). According to one analysis, "the problem was fixed, all right, but the pen-dulum swung the other way—with a vengeance" (Mintzberg et al. 2002: 70). Following these authors the shift was achieved by co-opting the chief executives by "rewarding them disproportionately for the performance of the entire enterprise. Through options and bonuses they have bought off the chiefs" (ibid.).

The authors refer to one study showing that during the 1990s CEO pay in corporate America rose by 570 percent, while profits rose by 114 per-cent and the average worker pay by 37 percent—the latter barely ahead of inflation, which was 32 percent over the same period. The legitimation for this stark asymmetry in compensations is related to the "fabricated" notion of "heroic leaders," the leader who singlehandedly steers the busi-ness to success, who alone is responsible for its performance—at least, as long as the performance is good. Maintaining this illusion enables the shareholders to overcompensate top management with the aim of ma-nipulating them to act more or less uniformly in the name of shareholder value. One might speculate that what is also behind slogans among corpo-rate managers like "internationally competitive compensation," is related to prestige and reputation. In a knowledge economy, and not least in its contemporary neoliberal financialized version, characterized by value ap-preciations and thus an economy of signs, salaries and compensations are symbols of knowledge, power, and prestige. Money is the mechanism that makes managers comparable in status. That is to say, in the ecology of management discourse, a low salary is translated into an image of a less capable manager. This applies obviously even more strongly in an overall "money manager capitalism" (see Chapter 6 of this volume).

In the public debate, however, as we have seen, the Hydro board's ac-tions and the top managers' role were judged as belonging more to the moral community of labor relations, while the state, acting as a supreme judge both judicially and morally, did so as a capitalist owner-state acting apparently in the interests of the working class and against "greed" and the elite capitalist class. Indeed, a complex spectacle of moral symbolism. To better unfold these complexities, we also need a more thorough understanding of the changes recent decades have wrought in the national political climate and its perception of control, administration, and regulation of the economic sphere. This is pursued in the next section below.

The Gospel of Egoism?

However one assesses the options debacle, the Hydro board and top management miscalculated, and lacked the necessary musicality to anticipate, the media attention and intense public debate that emerged around these financial instruments. The complex and changing idioms of the domestic capitalist relationships may at least partly account for some of it. The fact that the Norwegian state, through its gigantic NOK 3 trillion (USD 525 billion) pension fund,[44] invests most of the money in capital markets, pure money management, and financial speculation does not seem to bother the public to a considerable degree. The state is thus both an incarnation of the common people's moral community of modesty and "class compromise," for the sake of the preservation of the welfare state, while simultaneously an incarnation of the "purest" capitalist credo of using money directly to make more money (without passing it through productive investments). These latter practices are surely embedded in quite different moral connotations. Balancing this paradoxical role of the state requires considerable political skill, as the options case has illustrated.

To reconcile the paradox, one might speculate that "people" are outraged when top leaders, perceived to be wage earners, are overcompensated. "Real capitalists," on the other hand, might be seen as more or less tacitly outside of the moral community, and are silently accepted when the benefits of their speculation seem beneficial to Norwegian society, as in the case of the pension fund. In one respect, then, the "problem" of the Hydro management is that they are not seen in the public as representing "true capitalists" that make money both for themselves and for society as a whole. At least it seems that the level of public acceptance of Hydro managers also working "for themselves" is relatively much lower than for "true capitalists." This is significant in relation to a company like Hydro, arguably the most important "industrial locomotive" throughout Norway's history. The top managers seem to be caught in the middle, as it were, not properly defined on either side of the capitalist-labor relations compromise. And this middle ground might just as well signify something significant about the Nordic and Norway's model of welfare or democratic capitalism.

As described above, the intense and heated public debate in 2007 about the Hydro stock options compensation program was preceded by a smaller one in 2006. The former one involved several of the same significant themes related to the functioning of contemporary capitalism. Like its successor, the former debate was ambivalent as to where the contextual limits for the debate were to be drawn. Some participants used the global outlook, while some referred to Norway as the relevant context. Hydro was an exemplary case in this matter, a partly state-owned company, while at the same time the vast majority of its business operations and employees were located outside of Norway. Secondly, the earlier debate in 2006 also turned into a discourse on moral values, as noted for example by Minister of Finance Kristin Halvorsen, who stated on national TV: "This is a debate about moral values" ("Dette er en verdidebatt").[45]

In the newspapers, the debate was also framed in terms of moral questions. It evolved around notions of "greedy leaders," leaders driven by avarice, allegations of envy, about cultural conceptions of decency and putting price tags on people's heads. It was about personal gain versus long-term interests, and about company profits and stock prices versus their societal obligations. As the headline of one academic's op-ed in a daily newspaper stated: "The Gospel of Egoism."[46] From a relatively marginal debate about a financial instrument most people had never heard about until recently, it evolved into an extraordinarily energetic debate about the contents and the basis of the Norwegian social contract at large; about the national identity and democracy in a global world; about deep questions of value, both moral values and economic values of types of work and people; about ownership rights and roles, and the role the large, "flagship" companies of Norway were to play both in Norwegian society and in the global context. In short, it pinpointed how the so-called "global" companies and the globalized capitalist economic system make up a deeply ambivalent moral economy still firmly rooted in the nation-state and national cultural discourse. It led to the conclusion that on one level we must talk of capitalisms, in the plural, rather than capitalism in the singular, in the global economy as well.

This insight propels us into a more thorough investigation of the Norwegian system of capitalist relations, as a significant context for Hydro project and corporate managing and economic activities. Related to the above interpretations of the paradoxes of the options case, an adjacent perspective is that politicians and the public have "given up" controlling, and thus judging, especially *finance* capitalism. In this perspective finance capitalism and contemporary corporations have grown so strong, riding the waves of perceived deterministic forces of economic globalization, that they are seen as outside of state regulative control, indeed outside of the entire interstate system of regulation. This perception, if indeed prevalent, is obviously wrong. The current "global financial casino" (described below), like all previous historical forms of capitalism, is sanctioned and partly constituted by the political interstate system. For example, deregulation of capital flows has been extensive under neoliberalization (Arrighi 1994; Bhagwati 2004: 202), and today it is also (de)regulated by various international semi-state organizational bodies like the IMF, WTO, and World Bank.

A Neoliberal Dismantling of
Norwegian Democratic Capitalism?

Privatization, deregulation of the economic sphere, free flow of capital in particular, and market mechanisms in the public sector—in short, the "neoliberalization of society" (Harvey 2005; Duménil and Lévy 2004)— have since the 1970s constituted the main transformatory processes also of Norwegian society, as has been the case throughout most of the world. Neoliberalism is by now the most common term used to describe the transformations capitalism and capitalist societies nationally and globally underwent at the turning points of the 1970s and 1980s. Following Harvey, as noted in Chapter 1, by neoliberalism I mean

> in the first instance a theory of political economic practices that proposes that human well-being can best be advanced by liberating individual entrepreneurial freedoms and skills within an institutional framework characterized by strong private property rights, free markets, and free trade. The role of the state is to create and preserve an institutional framework appropriate to such practices. (2005: 2)

There is a crucial distinction between classical liberalism and neoliberalism in the assigned role of the state. In the words of Mark Olssen:

> Whereas classical liberalism represents a negative conception of state power in that the individual was to be taken as an object to be freed from the interventions of the state ... neoliberalism has come to represent a positive conception of the state's role, seeing the state as the active agent which creates the appropriate market by providing the conditions, laws and institutions necessary for its operation.... In neoliberalism ... the state seeks to create an individual that is an enterprising and competitive entrepreneur. (2003: 199)

Also, there is a significant twist in the neoliberal conception of human nature. The postulates of liberalism, including the idea of universal egoism, the self-interested individual, the invisible hand that provides also the best outcome for society as a whole, and the political maxim of laissez-faire, are all continued in neoliberalist ideology. However, a further element is added, one that "involves a change in subject position from 'homo economicus', who naturally behaves out of self-interest and is relatively detached from the state, to 'manipulatable man', who is created by the state and who is continually encouraged to be perpetually responsive" (Olssen 2003: 199.). Under neoliberalism the state itself is increasingly a subject of commercialization. One symptom of this is the much-discussed increase of "audit cultures" and the "audit society" (Power 1997; Strathern 2000; Leys 2001). As we have seen with the Norwegian state, the most significant state in Hydro's network of relations, this ideological bent has paved the way for the mega-scale "finance investment fund state." A financial investment state has developed in just a few years, and it is unprecedented in Norwegian history.

Individual freedom was a wise choice for the "core value" of neoliberalism, as something that easily appeals to most people. However, freedom is a complex philosophical concept that may mean a number of different things in various contexts. There is also, meanwhile, a marked gap between neoliberal theory and practices of neoliberalization (Harvey 2005). In Glyn's review, it was the "unleashing" of capitalism from the challenging 1970s that ushered in the current area, characterized by a new policy framework of austere macroeconomic policies, privatization of nationalized industries, and the deregulation of markets (2006). However, according to Glyn, and a growing literature on globalized neoliberalization, the overall record of neoliberalism has been slower economic growth and greater instability, widening inequalities, and diminishing levels of social welfare.

Looking at Norway in particular, it seems that a partial dismantling, or at least a major transformation of the social democratic state and the Norwegian model of democratic capitalism (Sejersted 1993), has in effect been a partial result of the active political processes of neoliberalization in Norway. The concept of "democratic capitalism" is conceived of as complementary to Chandler's categorization of US "competitive capitalism," British "personal capitalism," and German "cooperative capitalism." One of the main processes by which this transformation is achieved, on a global scale and of high relevance to our empirical context in Hydro, is the way neoliberal globalization, or financialization, "is also destroying conditions of both product and financial markets that are necessary for the successful long-term performance of large nonfinancial firms" (Crotty 2005: 107). This process in turn has serious consequences for societal reproduction, if one accepts the general view of Schumpeter and Chandler that large nonfinancial corporations operating in oligopolistic markets, like Hydro, have been the main sources of capital investment, technological change, and productivity growth in capitalist countries for the major part of the twentieth century.

The recent shift in Norwegian political economic social relations is extensively documented and described, for example by historian Berge Furre (1992), who in his *Norwegian History 1905–1990* labels the period from 1981 to 1990 as "the years of the market" (*Marknadens år*). In this review, it was during this period that belief in the market became ideology, and he states that this "market fetishism" in effect contributed in such a way that the "social democratic order lost its moral sustainability as a meaningful vision" (ibid.: 489, my trans.). As described by historian of political ideas Rune Slagstad, the shift in the mode of governance of the public sector was led by the coming to power of a new "market-technocratic steering elite" (*markedsteknokratisk styringselite*) (2001: 503–524). An analysis of the extensive "marketization" of Norwegian society and institutions can be found in Tranøy (2006), who concludes that a deterioration of liberal ideals has occurred in the "market society." As recent assessments indicate, the exact nature of the changes is, quite logically, in some dispute. An anthology by the political science establishment in Norway concludes that the reforms that commenced in the Norwegian public sector in recent decades have been a "loosening up" and deregulation of public tasks, putting a greater emphasis upon economic efficiency and "profitability" in the public sector, while other neoliberal measures and aims such as privatization and reduction of the public sector have not been so widespread (Mydske et al. 2007).

Another recent contribution (Veggeland 2007) argues that the most radical changes to the Norwegian welfare model occurred not in the 1980s, but rather in the 1990s and 2000s. The main issue has been a market-oriented competitive organizing of the public sector under neoliberal influences. He argues that in terms of "outsourcing" public services, Norway has been in the forefront also globally, lagging only behind the UK and the US. The neoliberal penetration of the public sector happened, for example, through the breaking down of public service monopolies, the exposure of the public sector to market competition, and the liberalization of the labor market. Nevertheless, in Veggeland's view it is still adequate to speak of a particular Nordic welfare model, although it has been considerably changed in the direction of "market-friendly solutions."

The broader picture thus seems relatively clear. A host of neoliberal changes have taken place. Privatization has commenced, but arguably not as extensively as in many other countries, while considerable use of market mechanisms, "market organizing," and deregulation have indeed been heavily introduced in spheres ranging from infrastructures such as tele-communications, transportation, and power supply, to health, education, and broadcasting. Versions of "New Public Management," described by Veggeland as a global pandemic, were widely implemented in the Norwe-gian public sector (Hernes 2007). Many new "markets" have been created domestically, some of them also linked to the global market. For example, the Norwegian government, especially in the person of Jens Stoltenberg even before he became prime minister, has been a strong advocate and one of the ideational originators of the global CO_2 exchange market.

A particularly interesting example for our present study, and an area in which Norway was a liberalization pioneer, is in the creation of the power market. The main architect behind the liberalization of the power market was Tormod Hermansen, who from his position as secretary general of the Ministry of Finance was one of the prime leaders of the new market-technocratic steering elite. Slagstad notes that

> Hermansen has realized his market-technocratic program of reform in two key areas. The first was el-power. During a few years around 1990 Norway became a "leading example" [foregangsland] of power liberalism. Using the market-economic expertise of the Norwegian School of Economics and Business Administration (NHH), Hermansen strategically outmaneuvered other initiatives and political players. The report produced by NHH was important when the new law was established. Interestingly it was the later president and CEO of Hydro, Eivind Reiten, in his capacity as minister of oil and energy at the time who, based upon the report, proposed the new energy law. (2001: 515, my trans.)

Prior to his post as minister of oil and energy, Reiten served as the direc-tor of Energy at Hydro. Simplifying a vastly more complex process, we might say that it was Hermansen who designed and informally prepared the ground for "the world's most advanced power market," as he himself later labeled it (2007), while it was Reiten in his role as minister who enabled the necessary formal and institutional procedures. Hermansen's other liberalization success was the privatization of the telecommunica-tions arena.

Thus, it is of paradoxical significance that the same Hermansen, fif-teen years later, wrote a highly critical essay about the Hydro options case (2007). The government's handling of the case also received critical com-ments. Interpreting the essay in strategic terms, it is an effort by Herman-sen to position himself in line with the potential coming of new political trends—in line with the public consternation and the government's interventionist handling of the options case, a break with the so-called "Hydro-model" of passive state ownership—and to interpret history in light of these new trends. Hermansen's ambivalent positioning with re-spect to these issues is highlighted by comparing two passages of his essay. Concerning the role of the state and the Ministry of Trade and Industry as the major owner in Hydro, he writes: "As performer [utfører, a New Public Management term], of the ownership ... the Minister must partici-pate in the shareholder community and contribute to maximize the value creation for the company, from a shareholder perspective" (ibid.: 124, my trans.).

On the next page he describes how Hydro in recent years has become "unrecognizable." Once the star example of Norway's emergence as an in-dustrial nation, with a unique capacity for technical and industrial devel-opment and with socially acceptable ways of creating new opportunities and managing extensive reorganization processes, Hydro is described has having been exemplary in terms of cooperation between private and state capital, and also between labor unions and management. Hermansen writes: "Hydro had ... the characteristics of being an industrial locomo-tive where value creation based on industrial development had priority ahead of stock price and development of owner values" (2007: 125, my trans.). Now, by contrast, he states that Hydro is increasingly anchored in, and even controlled by, the globalized financially oriented capital market. He is obviously right in describing a turn toward finance, but he overemphasizes the turn, fails to recognize its multiple sources, and most tellingly fails to acknowledge the fundamental neoliberalized changes in the Norwegian context of capitalist social relations behind which he, as a prominent member of the new market-technocratic steering elite, was himself one of the major architects. The paradox entailed in the juxtapo-sition of the two quotes above highlights these issues.

It seems as though both Hermansen, with respect to his earlier key role in the neoliberalization of Norwegian society, and Reiten—who, in his capacity as president and CEO of Hydro and in need of cheap energy for aluminum production, sought a secluded (from the free consumer mar-ket), industrially regulated power regime—both face some of the possibly unintended consequences of their own prior roles and actions.

"Financial Weapons of Mass Destruction"

One question that begs an answer is why the turn to shareholder value appeared as late as it did, in 1999, in the most "global" of the large Nor-wegian corporations, positioned with one leg in the increasingly neoliber-alized national political regime of Norway and the other firmly embedded in the increasingly financialized global capitalist system. The brief historical answer is that Hydro has possibly been, and arguably continues to be until the present day, one of the most profound culture-bearing institutions of democratic capitalism. In this simplified sense, Hydro preserved some of the core values embedded in democratic capitalism somewhat longer than the Norwegian state. But then again, as discussed above, the major neoliberal changes in the Norwegian public sector arguably did not occur until the 1990s and 2000s. And as the Norwegian state might still be said to embody a particular form of the Nordic welfare model, Hydro continues to instantiate values of democratic capitalism. For example, the closures of the key plants in Høyanger, Årdal, and Herøya in Norway, the Bécancour plant in Canada, and the fascinatingly documented closure process of the Hydro Aluminium Motorcast foundry in West Yorkshire, England (Heads Together Productions 2004), were all done "in socially acceptable ways," to use Hermansen's own phrasing. And all of these closures happened after the millennium and Hydro's "turn to finance."

As touched upon above, however, internally in Hydro there must have been a lack of anticipation of how dramatic an effect the options program would have on the public debate. This rings true in an assessment of neoliberal attitudes among Norwegian constituents (Hellevik and Knutsen 2007). Although the overall differences were not profound in terms of "social indicators," for example, neoliberal attitudes found their strongest support among private-sector managers, especially in banking, insurance, finance, and business services; the lowest following was found among workers and subordinates, especially in the public sector and in agriculture. Another reason for this possible lack of preparedness is the fact that these instruments are relatively new financial inventions. Some of their unintended consequences have possibly not been clear even to major players. For example, derivatives, the master instruments of the financialized economy, are usually not included in state financial accounting. Even more troublesome is that derivatives are "completely outside the conceptual realm of traditional accounting, which can think of debt and equity, liabilities and assets, but not more insubstantial instruments like options, futures, and inverse floaters" (Henwood 2005: 192). The very opacity and immeasurability of an economy of abstract derivatives precisely emphasizes the case of financialization: "layers of claims have been piled upon layers of claims, most of them furiously traded, with some resisting definition and measurement" (ibid.). Derivatives, which have become the major instrument in the globally circulating financialized economy, are of course at the core of the current crisis, and Hydro is engaged in derivatives trading as a form of "risk management."

While generally acknowledged as being complex and virtual, and as circulating primarily in the closed circuits of investment banks, hedge funds, financial trading firms, and transnational corporations, and as having an imperative role in global speculation, the understanding of the functions and impacts of derivatives is still largely lacking. As LiPuma and Lee report (2004), derivatives seem at the surface level to be extensions of historically well-known financial vehicles, but they turn out on a deeper level to be considerably more complex than generally perceived in conventional economic accounts. At the simple level a derivative is a number of types of transactable contracts deriving their value from underlying assets of all sorts. With derivatives contracts there is no movement of capital before their settlement: change in the price of the underlying asset dictates the value of the derivative, and the contract has a decided expiration date in the future that determines the time horizon the contract can be realized within.

The speed of innovation in financial instruments, it seems, has taken aback not only the general public, but also leaders and control systems in major industrial corporations and governance institutions—like the case seems to be with Hydro. Drawing upon studies from the inside of the economic establishment of Wall Street banks, the IMF, and the WTO itself (e.g. Alexander et al. 2005; Schinasi 2005), this argument is eloquently outlined by historian Gabriel Kolko in his essay "Weapons of Mass Financial Destruction" (2006). The title alludes to a description made by the Forbes-listed second richest person in the world, Warren Buffet, concerning credit derivatives, one of the relatively new financial instruments of great significance today. Warren Buffet wrote in 2002 that "derivatives are financial weapons of mass destruction," describing them as a "megacatastrophe risk" and as "time bombs, both for the parties that deal in them and the economic system."[47] The Norwegian translation of Kolko's essay, as it appeared in *Le Monde Diplomatique*, was telling: "Finansielle trolldomskunster" ("The wizardry of finance").[48]

That the derivatives "market," barely known in 1980, had grown to ten times the size of global GDP in 2008, is illustrative of this economic wizardry. As LiPuma and Lee note, the economistic view not only hides the creative effects of speculative derivatives, but possibly more significantly also substitutes surface appearance for underlying reality: "Derivatives create their surface appearance by creatively presupposing social contexts of use, which economistic analysis then (mis)takes as an objective, external, and imposed reality. This move guarantees that the field of financial practice will never include the principles of its own genesis, construction, or encompassment of other peoples and places" (2004: 64–65). This cultural space of derivative relations, argue LiPuma and Lee, "posits itself as a space lying beyond the power of representation" (ibid.). A story about China's approach to derivatives, reported by the *Financial Times* and widely circulated, metaphorically defines derivatives at this deeper and more complex level.

At a secret meeting of top Communist officials at the start of this decade, Zhu Rongji, then China's premier, summoned senior academics and finance officials to teach a crash course on complex financial instruments. Financial derivatives, in the best explanation provided that day, were described as like putting a mirror in front of another mirror, allowing a physical object to be reflected into infinity. China's leaders, most of whom are engineers by training, decided to take a cautious approach toward these exotic products and still have yet to allow most kinds of derivatives.[49]

As the derivatives market by 2008 had indeed been reflected into something approximating "infinity," the Chinese metaphor proved to be precise.

On the innovations in the finance sector, noted economist Paul Krugman wrote in late 2007, in relation to what was still framed as the so-called subprime mortgage crisis: "The bottom line is that policy makers left the financial industry free to innovate—and what it did was to innovate itself, and the rest of us, into a big, nasty mess."[50] Krugman quotes one of the players in the game, a bond manager who indicates that not even the chairman of the world's most important central bank understands the workings of the contemporary economy: "What we are witnessing, is essentially the breakdown of our modern-day banking system, a complex of leveraged lending so hard to understand that Federal Reserve Chairman Ben Bernanke required a face-to-face refresher course from hedge fund managers in mid-August" (ibid.). Anthropologist Gillian Tett has exposed some of the key actors, agents, and events of the abstract financial instruments innovation game, especially the invention of securitized credit derivatives, in particular so-called collateralized debt obligations (CDOs), which eventually played a significant part in the latest stage of transforming the basis of banks' dealings with credit (2009). At Hydro it seems that neither the board of directors nor corporate management anticipated the full perspective of the possible consequences, neither monetary or morally, of the options packages.

As mentioned above, the neoliberalized changes have put the Norwegian model of democratic capitalism under heavy pressure. The Hydro turn to finance and the more or less concomitant neoliberalized turn of Norwegian institutional relations, led by the new market-technocratic steering elite, must both be analyzed in the wider globalized capitalist context, however. This might be interpreted as a local version of the global turn to finance," the implementation of "remarketized capitalism" (Fulcher 2004), described by several authors as a "financialization of the world economy" (Arrighi 1994; Epstein 2005). According to the historical scheme of Arrighi, drawing on Braudel's analysis, the 1970s marked the beginning of the *fourth wave* of financialization of the capitalist world economy. All these waves were similar in the respect that the financial expansion signaled a fundamental crisis in the system of accumulation. However, each wave had its unique features. The fourth wave is unique because it is not based in any country's regulated banking system but in the stateless and unregulated "banking system" of the "Eurodollar market" (Arrighi 1994; Dickens 2005; Appendix).

To provide another ethnographic vignette in the exploration of the financialized global economic context in which both the Norwegian and the Hydro shifts must be interpreted, further addressed in chapter six of this volume, a brief description of so-called financial risk management in relation to Hydro and its projects is given below, because it is here that Hydro became most significantly engaged with these new financial instruments.

Managing "Financial Risk" in Projects

To manage the multiple varieties of "risks" that are associated with Hydro investment projects, a vast battery of practices is mobilized, related to, in the words of Hydro: "all aspects of value creation, including strategy, finance, commercial matters, organization, HSE, reputation, corporate responsibility, regulatory and legal matters."[51] Here I want to focus solely on those practices associated with handling the risks related to financing projects and operations. Elements of this were also briefly described in the section "Decision Gate Four" (see Chapter 4).

To handle financial risk, Hydro is immersed in various types of financial markets in numerous ways. Risk management related to investment projects (and daily operations) is conducted through a variety of practices at various levels. These markets trade in various "paper assets" like stocks, derivatives like futures, swaps, options, foreign exchange, notes, mortgages, treasuries, bonds, and other paper property titles. More appropriately these assets would arguably be labeled "virtual," "digit," or "sign assets." As reported in its annual reports, Hydro is engaged in the majority of the financial instruments listed above. From the annual report I quote some of the major activities:

> The overall objective of financial and commercial risk management is to safeguard Hydro's ability to continuously meet its cash commitments and maintain a strong financial position. This includes identifying and monitoring the Company's main risk exposures, quantifying the potential impact on key financial ratios and proposing corrective actions when deemed

appropriate. Shortfalls in operational cash flow due to unfavorable developments in prices of main products, raw materials and/or exchange rates could substantially impact Hydro's financial position. Cash commitments are risk evaluated against cash flow from operations. Probabilities of not meeting set financial targets, such as maintaining the adjusted net debt/equity ratio target of 0.5, are monitored. Simulations of cash flow scenarios, using a 5-year rolling horizon, are carried out for this purpose. The outcome of this analysis is reported to management on a quarterly basis. Mitigating financial and commercial risk exposures through the use of derivative instruments is done only to some extent. For this purpose, Hydro utilizes financial derivatives as well as commodity derivatives. The most common use of financial and exchange traded commodity derivatives relates to currency hedging and LME-hedging as part of the Company's day-to-day aluminium operations.

It is appropriate to utilize derivatives to mitigate financial risk, because "a derivative is a transaction that is designed to create price exposure and thereby transfer risk by having its value determined—or derived—from the value of the underlying commodity, security, index, rate or event" (Dodd 2005: 170). From the longtime head of Federal Reserve Board, Alan Greenspan, through to the rest of the financial system, derivatives have been actively promoted as the major tool to offset financial and economic risk. In "Note 23. Market risk management and derivative instruments," of the Hydro Annual report (2006), it is written:

> Hydro is exposed to market risks from prices on commodities bought and sold, prices of other raw materials, currency exchange rates and interest rates. Depending on the degree of price volatility, such fluctuations in market prices may create fluctuations in Hydro's results. To manage this exposure, Hydro's main strategy is to maintain a strong financial position to be able to meet fluctuations in results. Market risk exposures are evaluated based on a portfolio view in order to take advantage of offsetting positions and to manage risk on a net exposure basis. Natural hedging positions are established where possible and if economically viable. Hydro uses financial derivatives to some extent to manage financial and commercial risk exposures.[52]

Hedging is the strategic process by which financial risk is taken out, or reduced, in relation to some investment. It can involve currencies or derivatives and many other measures. Regarding Hydro's activities in the electricity market, Hydro "utilizes both physical contracts and financial derivative instruments such as futures, forwards and options. These are traded either bilaterally or over electricity exchanges such as the Nordic power exchange (Nord Pool). *Hydro participates in limited speculative trading*" (ibid., my emphasis).

In the aluminum business a host of financial instruments are mobilized in the service of financial risk management. For a detailed exposition of the multitude of instruments employed by Hydro, I refer the reader to their annual reports. In an earlier publication I (2008a) documented significant aspects of this at some length, because at the time, long before the finance crisis unleashed, it was imperative to chronicle such unfashionable financial constructs. Since the finance crisis started unfolding, the media and the populace have become substantially more informed about these issues, including the critical "financial risks" Hydro seeks to manage and the financial instruments they employ to do it, like derivative trading, foreign currency and interest rate risk, and cash flow and other economic hedging.

This empirical vignette illustrates a portion of the innovations that have taken place in the realm of the financial economy, highlighting some of the vast arsenal of financial instruments now available. For Hydro the use of these instruments is first and foremost in terms of "risk management," not utilization for speculative gains. The use of financial derivatives and speculation is, as noted several times in their Annual Report, allowed to only a "limited" or "some" extent. The reason for this, as noted also by "traders" at Hydro, is in their opinion straightforward: Hydro is and should continue to be an industrially based nonfinancial corporation, not a trading company or a financial organization.

In discussion of these issues with the traders themselves, this perception seems to be very clear, although some of them emphasize that they could have made a lot of money from pure trading activities. But it is also corporate policy, as one trader said: "Guidelines for the 'limits to trading' are set by the corporate management, and they also relate to various aspects of law. In certain domains the law is different for non-financial and financial companies." Hydro's trading activities—the extensive use of various financial instruments and activities in the financial markets—are thus adaptations to a changing environment, where increasing and complex use of these instruments is a requirement to securely "manage the risk" of their industrial projects and operations. For example, Hydro has developed in-house a sophisticated software system to manage its London Metal Exchange (LME) derivative hedging operations. However, in addition to a pure adaptation, the financial instrument use itself expands the very field of risks and risk management. As financialized globalization unfolds, it in fact creates, through financial instrument innovations, the effect of a larger and larger realm of "risk exposure," a globalization of risk (LiPuma and Lee 2004), and concomitantly a more and more sophisticated set of financial instruments for managing the risks. The full-blown finance crisis has exposed this kind of risk management as both a chimera and a catastrophic Trojan horse for large portions of the economy.

In the context of the engineer-economist disputes in Hydro projects (see Chapter Four), the engineering experts' fear that Hydro is on a "death march" toward becoming a trading company can now be analyzed more in its proper context. The frustration coming from the engineering community, that "economists" and financial measures are more and more steering Hydro, had difficult finding a proper outlet. Hydro's top management was often singled out as the source of this change for the worse. The engineers were often ambivalent, however, even in their critique of top management, as exemplified by one of the core project specialists. In one sentence he accuses the top management of being *blåruss*, finance economists, and in the next sentence he says: "I'm sure Reiten wants to create something, but there is no will to create value in Norway."

To some extent the "blaming" of top management for the recent changes has strong merit. The turn to shareholder value since 1999, with all its accompanying practices, certainly resulted from a strategic effort by top management. As the present chapter has conveyed, however, there exist several layers of contextually significant "forces" above that of top management, which have to be take into account. As the quote above indicates, the Norwegian system was also considered. Judging by the contentions of the traders themselves, however, Hydro is far from the path to becoming a trading company. What has been receiving too little focus in the "native perspectives" among practitioners in Hydro, however, is the extreme financialization of the entire world economy. In the case of Hydro a paradoxical effect thus emerges. It spends a massive amount of energy, competence, and capital in the financial markets to ensure that the company may continue to thrive as a technology-based industrial "locomotive." However, all of its financial market activities concurrently contribute to the expansion of the volume of transactions in the "casino capitalism" (Strange 1986) that they employ these measures to "defend themselves" from. To continue to thrive in the financialized economy too, large nonfinancial production capitalist actors like Hydro contribute to the expansion of the casino. The notion of the "casino" was noted by Keynes in 1936, when he stated:

> Speculators may do no harm as bubbles on a steady stream of enterprise. But the position is serious when enterprise becomes the bubble on a whirlpool of speculation. When the capital development of a country becomes the by-product of the activities of a casino, the job is likely to be ill-done. The measure of success attained by Wall Street, regarded as an institution of which the proper social purpose is to direct new investment into the most profitable channels in terms of future yield cannot be claimed as one of the outstanding triumphs of laissez-faire capitalism. ([1936] 2008: 159)

Here Keynes alludes to the transformation in the reproduction of relations of capitalism from production to financially dominated, as reflected in the title of the present chapter; "Wagging the Dog." However, the casino metaphor is applicable only as far as it goes, as for example former Treasury Secretary Lawrence Summers in a 1989 paper quoted the following statement with approval: "The freeing of financial markets to pursue their casino instincts heightens the odds of crisis.... Because unlike the casino, the financial markets are inextricably linked with the world outside, the real economy pays the price" (Summers and Summers 1989: 262). As Paul M. Sweezy noted in the essay "The Triumph of Financial Capital" of 1994, incidentally the same year that Arrighi published his major work on the financialization-driven recurring systemic crisis in accumulation cycles:

> The locus of economic and political power has shifted along with the ascendancy of financial capital. It has long been taken for granted, especially among radicals, that the seat of power in capitalist society was in the boardrooms of a few hundred giant multinational corporations. While there is no doubt about the role of these entities in the allocation of resources and other significant matters as well, I think there is an added consideration that needs to be stressed. The occupants of these boardrooms are themselves to an increasing extent constrained and controlled by financial capital as it operates through the global network of financial markets. In other words, real power is not so much in corporate boardrooms as in the financial markets. Here a footnote: the giant corporations are also major players in these markets and help to give them their importance.

Although a substantial decoupling of the financial economy from the "world outside" has occurred, a relationship still remains, though the quality of that relationship might better be understood in relative terms than absolute. Chapter 6 will explore in greater depth the characteristics of the contemporary "real-life financial casino," and Hydro's investment projects and corporation as constrained and occasioned by large-scale financialization. It will show the emergence of a "money manager capitalism" that cannot be fully understood outside of its redistributive effects and context.

Notes

1. *Dagens Næringsliv*, 22 June 2007.
2. "Hydro Investor Presentation, February 2007." www.hydro.com.
3. The development of the share price from 1 January 1999 to 20 July 2007 was a remarkable 574 percent on the NYSE ("Hydro Investor presentation, July 2007." www

.hydro.com). Likewise, the market value assessment of Hydro rose by 638 percent if comparing the market value of Hydro as a conglomerate comprising three main divisions (Oil and Energy, Aluminium, and Agri) in 1999, with the combined market value of these three divisions as divested into three separate companies in 2007 ("Hydro Investor Presentation, July 2007").

4. Hydro Annual Report 2001.
5. "Samtlige store endringer i Hydro de siste årene har hatt en industriell begrunnelse, enten det gjelder utskillelsen av Yara, fusjonen med Statoil eller satsingen videre som et fokusert industriselskap. At det sjenerer Jens P. Heyerdahl at Hydros industrielle utvikling over tid også skaper store aksjonærverdier, lever jeg godt med." *Dagens Næringsliv*, 22 June 2007.
6. "Det er ikke tvil om at det å gjøre så store endringer i mangfoldige Hydro, innebærer vemod og et par sekunders ettertanke om det er riktig. Den som ikke sier det, er ikke ærlig... Men drivkreftene er sterke. Vi var nødt til å rendyrke disse store delene av Hydro... Det er en tendens til å snakke som om børskurs ikke skulle bety noe. Men Hydro er blitt 102 år fordi ledelsen alltid har vært opptatt av dette." *Dagens Næringsliv*, 22 June 2007.
7. Interestingly, the word "options" is *opsjoner* in Norwegian, and the word in both English and Norwegian also denotes "choices" or *valg* in Norwegian. As will be substantiated below, the public debate indeed developed into a discourse not only about financial options, but also about different options for society, and of moral choices.
8. NRK, "Redaksjon EN," 16 November 2006.
9. See for example *E24*, 27-30 August 2007 (http://e24.no/naeringsliv/article1907535 .ece#AF; http://e24.no/naeringsliv/article1911028.ece#AF; http://e24.no/boers-og-finans/article1911510.ece#AF, accessed 23 May 2011), and NRK, 27–29 August 2007 (http://www.nrk.no/nyheter/okonomi/1.3045394; http://www.nrk.no/nyheter/okonomi /1.3063808, accessed 23 May 2011).
10. *E24*, 30 July 2007 (http://e24.no/boers-og-finans/article1911510.ece#AF, accessed 23 May 2011).
11. *E24*, 31 July 2007 (http://e24.no/boers-og-finans/article1913037.ece#VG, accessed 23 May 2011).
12. *E24*, 1 August 2007 (http://e24.no/boers-og-finans/article1914548.ece, accessed 23 May 2011).
13. For example, former Minister for the Labor Party Hallvard Bakke, "Kasinoøkonomi," *Klassekampen*, 21 September 2007.
14. *E24*, 25 July 2007 (http://e24.no/boers-og-finans/article1903743.ece#AF, accessed 23 May 2011).
15. *Dagbladet*, 1 August 2007 (http://www.dagbladet.no/nyheter/2007/08/01/507684.html, accessed 23 May 2011; *E24*, 29 July 2007 (http://e24.no/boers-og-finans/article 1910416.ece#AF, accessed 23 May 2011).
16. *E24*, 31 July 2007 (http://e24.no/boers-og-finans/article1913043.ece#VG, accessed 23 May 2011).
17. *E24*, 31 July 2007 (http://e24.no/naeringsliv/article1911840.ece#VG, accessed 23 May 2011).
18. *E24*, 27 July 2007 (http://e24.no/naeringsliv/article1907562.ece#AF, accessed 23 May 2011).
19. *E24*, 25 July 2007 (http://e24.no/boers-og-finans/article1903977.ece, accessed 23 May 2011).
20. *Dagbladet*, 1 August 2007 (http://www.dagbladet.no/nyheter/2007/08/01/507734.html, accessed 23 May 2011).

21. *Dagbladet*, 2 August 2007 (http://www.dagbladet.no/nyheter/2007/08/02/507822.html, accessed 23 May 2011).
22. *E24*, 30 July 2007 (http://e24.no/naeringsliv/article1911027.ece#VG, accessed 23 May 2011).
23. *Aftenposten*, 1 August 2007 (http://www.aftenposten.no/meninger/debatt/article 1914640.ece, accessed 23 May 2011).
24. *Aftenposten*, 31 July 2007 (http://www.aftenposten.no/meninger/kronikker/article 1912570.ece, accessed 23 May 2011).
25. See for example *Aftenposten*, 4 August 2007 (http://www.aftenposten.no/meninger/ debatt/article1920264.ece, accessed 23 May 2011).
26. *E24*, 3 August 2007 (http://e24.no/boers-og-finans/article1918921.ece#VG, accessed 23 May 2011).
27. *E24*, 5 August 2007 (http://e24.no/naeringsliv/article1921795.ece, accessed 23 May 2011).
28. *Stavanger Aftenblad*, 5 August 2007 (http://web3.aftenbladet.no/innenriks/article 491226.ece, accessed 23 May 2011).
29. *Aftenposten*, 6 August 2007 (http://www.aftenposten.no/nyheter/iriks/politikk/article 1923420.ece, accessed 23 May 2011).
30. *E24*, 7 August 2007 (http://e24.no/naeringsliv/article1924303.ece, accessed 23 May 2011).
31. *E24*, 8 August 2007 (http://e24.no/opsjonssaken/article1925784.ece, accessed 23 May 2011).
32. E.g., *Dagens Næringsliv*, 8 August 2007.
33. *Dagbladet*, 8 August 2007 (http://www.dagbladet.no/nyheter/2007/08/08/508227.html, accessed 23 May 201).
34. *Dagens Næringsliv*, 7 August 2007.
35. *Dagens Næringsliv*, 8 August 2007.
36. *E24*, 7 August 2007 (http://e24.no/naeringsliv/article1924303.ece, accessed 23 May 2011).
37. *E24*, 8 August 2007 (http://e24.no/naeringsliv/article1926874.ece, accessed 23 May 2011).
38. *Dagbladet*, 9 August 2007.
39. *Klassekampen*, 16 August 2007.
40. *Aftenposten*, 11 August 2007, and *Dagens Næringsliv*, 18/19 August 2007. By a stroke of unfortunate coincidence, in terms of Hydro's reputation, the front page of this issue of *Dagens Næringsliv* featured the tax fraud case of the Ditlev-Simonsen family. It spurred major media attention and featured both Mayor of Oslo Per Ditlev-Simonsen and his daughter, the executive vice-president and chief communications officer of Hydro. Later both left their offices.
41. *Dagen Næringsliv*, 18/19 August 2007.
42. As outlined by Knut N. Kjær, the manager of the Norwegian "Oil-fund" (renamed "Government Pension Fund Global") in an essay with the illustrative title "Highest Possible Returns for the Petroleum Fund" (2002): "The Petroleum Fund will act as an financial investor in the international capital markets" (my trans.). Warned by the experiences of the Kuwaiti Oil Fund, the Norwegian fund wanted explicitly *not* to act as a strategic and demanding investor in companies, instead remaining a pure financial investor (with ethics constraints).
43. "Å være toppleder i den type selskaper handler ikke bare om egne inntekter og gevinster. Det handler om å forvalte tillit på vegne av hele det norske folk. Derfor er det å være toppleder et tillitsverv. Det betyr at det må stilles særskilte krav til slike

toppledere. Det handler om klokskap og respekt." *E24*, 13 August 2007 (http://e24
.no/opsjonssaken/article1933957.ece, accessed 23 May 2011).

44. By the end of 2010 the total market value of the Government Pension Fund Global
was NOK 3,077 billion (USD 525 billion). "A robust investment strategy with good
results", Ministry of Finance press release, no. 13/2011, 8 April, 2011.
45. NRK, "Redaksjon EN," 16 November 2006.
46. B. S. Tranøy, *Dagbladet*, 20 November 2006.
47. In a letter to the shareholders of Berkshire Hathaway Inc. Available online.
48. Gabriel Kolko, "Finansielle trolldomskunster," *Le Monde Diplomatique*, 8 November
2006. Can be accessed at LMD here: http://www.lmd.no/index.php?article=1075, accessed 23 May 2011.
49. Jamil Anderlini, "Prudence guides China's outlook," *Financial Times*, 24 September
2008, http://www.ft.com, accessed 19 May 2011.
50 Paul Krugman, "Innovating Our Way to Financial Crisis." *The New York Times*, 3
December 2007, http://www.nytimes.com/2007/12/03/opinion/03krugman.html, accessed 19 May 2011.
51. Hydro Annual Report 2006.
52. Hydro Annual Report 2006.

Chapter 6

MONEY MANAGER CAPITALISM AND REVERSE REDISTRIBUTION

> If class warfare is being waged in America,
> my class is clearly winning.
> —Warren Buffet, Letter to Shareholders of
> Berkshire Hathaway, Inc.

> … here should exist among the citizens neither extreme
> poverty, nor, again, excess of wealth, for both are
> productive of both these evils [faction and distraction].
> —Plato, *The Laws, Book V.*

> There's an evenin' haze settlin' over the town
> Starlight by the edge of the creek
> The buyin' power of the proletariat's gone down
> Money's gettin' shallow and weak
> —Bob Dylan, "Workingman's Blues #2"

A brief note on some of the commonplace ideas and widespread misconceptions about the idea of "global capitalism" is appropriate before proceeding with the inquiry. Indeed, in many respects capitalism is now organized on a global scale, as indicated by the existence of so-called transnational or global companies worldwide. Most of these companies, however, have originated in a few of the wealthiest countries on earth. Indeed, this reflects some basic realities about capitalism as perceived globally. Although companies like, for example, Hydro must in many ways be considered to be global actors, and although the markets for goods, services, capital, and labor in many respects are global in reach, there are fundamental asymmetries, idiosyncrasies, and specific constraints to the conception of the globalized economy.

Some of the more fundamental misconceptions are that (a) global capitalism is a recent invention, when instead it has deep historical roots; (b) that global capital circulates globally, while it in reality moves mainly between a small group of wealthy countries; (c) that the importance of nation-states and international differences has diminished, when in fact differences abound and nation-states are as much a key in the functioning of capitalism and so-called global companies today as ever before, as illustrated by the case of Norway above, so that capitalism is differentially constituted, and (d) that global capitalism is converging and is becoming homogeneous, and thus works as an integrating force, when in truth the more global capitalism has become the more dramatically the international inequalities of wealth have increased (Fulcher 2004: 103).

Nonetheless, contemporary global capitalism, or neoliberal globalization, signifies a shorthand for some fundamental processes that have transformed the world in various ways in recent years, connecting increasingly new parts and actors of the world. Capitalism's institutions and practices are today the world's unquestionably dominant economic system, unrivaled by any alternative. Most of the global capital flows between North America, Europe, and Japan. Castells showed that in 1998 emerging markets accounted for only 7 percent of the world's capital, while these countries contained 85 percent of the world's population. An indication of the uneven flow of money can be illustrated by the amount of foreign direct investments to poor countries. Almost nothing goes to Africa; instead the concentration is on a few countries, prominently China, Brazil, and Mexico. In the year 2000 the whole of Africa received less than 1 percent of the total world foreign direct investment—approximately the same amount as received by Finland (referred to in Fulcher 2004: 97). Hydro's "global corporation" reflects these international patterns of distribution. Hydro's global physical presence is also uneven, with a concentration in the wealthiest countries in the world. Let us now more specifically characterize the form of globalized financial capitalism that presently defines the world economy, an economy in which Hydro and its investment projects are asymmetrically and ambiguously situated.

Financialization and International Economic Relations

"The financial markets have taken the world economy hostage," wrote the *Financial Times*'s chief economist Martin Wolf on 11 September 2007.

The assertion pertained to the real estate mortgages and subsequent bank crisis as it manifested itself in 2007, when the central banks of several countries "bailed out" several of the troubled banks. By late 2007, a host of more or less catastrophic-sounding messages poured out of the financial press and financial institutions. Most of the major Wall Street companies, from Goldman Sachs to JP Morgan, now voiced concern about a "hard landing" for the US economy. On 12 November Richard Berner of Morgan Stanley entitled one of his analyses "A Perfect Storm for the American Consumer."[1] Possibly even more discomforting was the forecast made by Nouriel Roubini, Professor at the Stern School of Business at New York University. In his regular economic analysis, published on his blogsite Global EconoMonitor, he made the following comment in November 2007: "It is increasingly clear by now that a severe U.S. recession is inevitable in next few months.... I now see the risk of a severe and worsening liquidity and credit crunch leading to a generalized meltdown of the financial system of a severity and magnitude like we have never observed before."[2] As shown in the introduction to this volume, the magnitude of the numbers in the financial expansion and overall financialization of the global economy since the 1970s has also been remarkable, reaching its peak in 2008, and the global financial crisis unfolding from 2007 on has more easily brought to light both the causes and the consequences of financialization.

Global financial assets increased *ninefold* from 1980 to 2007. Comprised of equity, public and private bonds, and bank deposits, these assets grew from US $26.6 to us $241 trillion (Palma 2009: 834). Moreover, from the relatively modest number of about US $100 million in 1980 (LiPuma and Lee 2004: 74), the amounts outstanding of over-the-counter derivative contracts reached a quite remarkable US $684 trillion in 2008 (BIS 2009). Even after having grown gargantuan in size, in just the ten years prior to 2009 these amounts increased by a factor of 7.5, while their gross market value increased tenfold (Palma 2009: 834). As reported above, as early as 2002 Warren Buffet, then the world's richest man, wrote that derivatives are "financial weapons of mass destruction," describing them as a "megacatastrophe risk" and as "time bombs, both for the parties that deal in them and the economic system."[3] This means that in the last ten years the gross market value of these "catastrophic weapons" grew about eight times faster than global GDP (Palma 2009).

There were obviously multiple enablers for this radical increase in the circulation of money. The immediate starting point was a fundamental change in global monetary policy upon the complete abandonment of the gold standard in 1971, and thus the termination of the post–World War II Bretton Woods system of regulated exchange rates. Since that time, variations of floating exchange rate regimes and thus floating currencies have been norm in the global monetary system. Central banks have first and foremost sought regulation via various inflation targets (Norges Bank 2004).

As argued by, for example, leading central bank economist Murray Rothbard (1983, 1994) and the chairman of the Federal Reserve from 1987 to 2006, Alan Greenspan ([1966] 1986), the abandonment of the gold standard uprooted the fundamental anchoring of the financial economy in the "real" productive economy.[4] They, among others (Norges Bank 2004), argue that the "impossible" pressure to keep the dollar pegged to gold (and other currencies again pegged to the dollar), was caused to a large extent by running huge deficits on the balance of payments, and the constraints provided by the gold standard preventing the accumulation of huge national debts.

The financialization of the economy in developed as well as developing economies is visible in that the ratio of financial assets to GDP made a remarkable jump in the period from 1980 to 2007. In the US financial assets approached 450 percent of GDP, in the EU nearly 600 percent (particularly high in Iceland and Ireland), and in the UK nearly 700 percent, while the ratio in Asia approached 400 percent, and Africa, Latin America, the Middle East, and Eastern Europe all were in the range of 150 to 200 percent by 2007 (Palma 2009). The new deregulated monetary regime, coupled with the principles of "fractional-reserve banking," enabled another critical factor in the financialization of the economy: the radical increase in the total money supply in the economy since the 1970s. Let us first look at the development of the Norwegian money supply from 1819 to 2004, illustrated by the development and divorce between the monetary base (coins and notes) and broad money (see fig. 12).

The long time series used in the figure masks the fact that the M0 and M2 have been divorcing since the mid nineteenth century. However, we see that a dramatic acceleration of the separation process set in during the 1970s. We can specifically locate the years when the separation of M0 and M2 really picked up speed: 1970–1973. These years are, not coincidentally, related to the year 1971, the year the Bretton Woods system broke down and the final step in the abandonment of the gold standard was implemented throughout the world monetary system. In the thirty-four years since 1970, the total Norwegian money supply, M2, increased from close to NOK 40,000 million to more than NOK 900,000 million. This is an increase of more than 2,000 percent. In the preceding 34-year period (from 1936 to 1970), the increase of the money supply was about 1,200 percent. In the 34-year period before that (1902–1936), the increase in the money supply was nearly 450 percent. Thus the rate of growth (of the separation of M0 and M2) since the turn of the twentieth century

Figure 12. Development of the Money Supply in Norway, 1819–2004
The black line represents M0, the monetary base of coins and notes; the gray line represents M2, broad money.

Norway's money supply

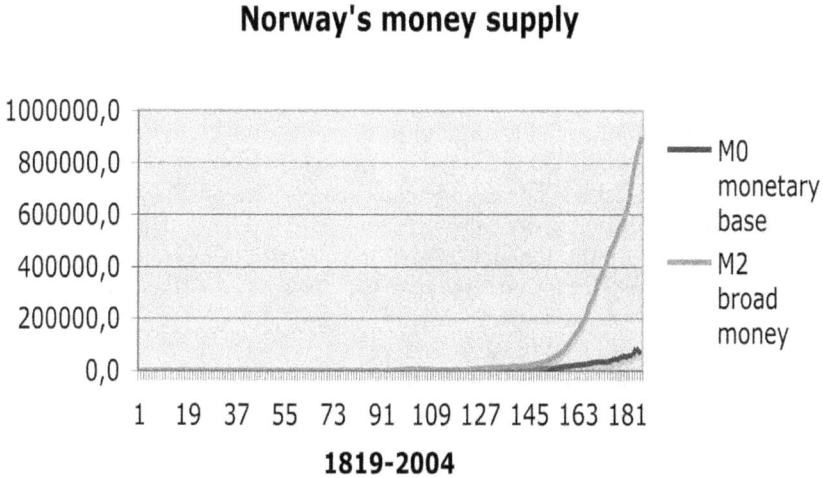

Source: Klovland 2004.

has been approximately proportional and of the second order (quadratic), rather than linear. And by May 2011 Norwegian MZ had increased to more than NOK 1.6 billion.

The US dollar supply, as well as most other money supplies in developed economies, displays a similar pattern. In all cases the increase of the money supply since the 1970s has come in terms of money forms other than physical currency and other forms of relatively "concrete" money. This is significant. The major portion of the rise has come in various forms of virtual or digital money. Among the enabling factors of the new financialized economy has been the overall deregulatory political ideological climate of neoliberalism, the technological advances in information and communication technologies, and innovations in financial instruments and products. But where does all this money come from? How is it created?

Qatalum Money Creation

Let us use the example of the Qatalum project to illustrate the "money multiplier" mechanism of the banking system, a system that links debt creation with money creation. On 23 August 2007, Hydro announced in a press release that the Qatalum project had "successfully closed a project finance package with lending institutions for the construction of the new aluminium plant in Qatar." Under the headline "Qatalum closes USD 2.6 billion project finance deal," the announcement briefly described the finance package in the following manner:

> The USD 2.6 billion limited recourse financing is comprised of a USD 2,250 million commercial bank term loan facility and a USD 350 million export credit agency facility with the Norwegian Guarantee Institute for Export Credits (GIEK). The commercial bank term loan facility was joined by 30 banks and the Export Development Canada. The initial request for proposal issued by the Financial Advisor in April 2007 resulted in over USD 3.5 billion offer for underwriting commitments for the commercial bank term loan facility alone.[5]

Using these loan figures, we can now, on the basis of "fractional reserve" banking principles, calculate an approximation of how much money the lending institutions can "create" or "originate" and release into circulation in the economy. In fractional reserve banking (Rothbard 1983, 1994; El Diwany 2003) the principle is that the bank only needs to hold a small fraction of the money as reserves, compared to the amount it may lend out. The reserve ratio sets the minimum reserves each bank must hold to customer deposits and notes. The ratio differs both among countries and for different types of deposits. The conventional notion is that the more risk entailed in the loan, the higher is the reserve requirement. "Under the Basel accord, banks are expected to maintain a minimum 8 percent buffer" (Lawson 2009: 771). In 2006, for example, the US reserve requirement was 10 percent on so-called "transaction deposits" and zero on all other deposits. In Jordan, as a significant example of Islamic banking, the required reserve ratio was 80 percent, while in China it was 12 percent, in Switzerland 2.5 percent, and in Australia, Sweden, Mexico, Canada, the UK, and Norway it was "more or less" zero.[6]

The finesse of fractional reserve requirements is that it enables the banking system to originate "new money" and by implication expand the money supply. If the reserve requirement is 10 percent, for example, a bank that receives a $100 cash deposit can lend up to $90 of that deposit, keeping only a $10 cash deposit within the bank. If the borrower then writes a check to someone who deposited the $90, the bank receiving that deposit can lend out $81. As this fractional-reserve banking process continues, the banks can expand the initial deposit of $100 into a maximum of $1,000 of money ($100 + $90 + $81 + $72.90 + ... = $1,000). In contrast, with a 20 percent reserve requirement, the banking system would be able to expand the initial $100 deposit into a maximum of $500 ($100 + $80 + $64 + $51.20 + ... = $500). Thus, higher reserve requirements should result in reduced creation of transaction deposits.

However, for the present illustration it is worth noting that also in countries with reserve requirements, those do usually not apply to the virtual forms of money M2 and M3 (but only to M0 or M1). Deposits such as savings accounts and time deposits such as CDs have no reserve requirements and therefore can expand without regard to reserve levels. So, for countries without reserve requirements and for the majority of money forms in countries that do, the central banks operate in a way that permits banks to acquire the reserves they need to meet their requirements from the money market. And the regulatory mechanism is the banks' willingness to pay the rents for their borrowed reserves at the central bank. Consequently, reserve requirements currently play a relatively limited role in money creation also in countries that have (some) requirements. This is ultimately the reason why the rate of interest is such a big issue in public discourse.

For the Qatalum case we thus have the following situation. The reserve requirements of the lending institutions that provided the finance deal are at best a fraction of the amount they lent to Qatalum. Let us assume that the reserve requirement for the loan is on average 5 percent. Using the commercial bank loan figure of $2,250 million, the banks needed to back up the loan by holding $112.5 million in reserves. Assuming that the banks' only business was this loan to Qatalum, and thus that this was all the reserves the bank in fact held because it did not need hold more, the result is that the borrowing made by Qatalum enabled the financing institutions to create $2,250 million in "new money"—this to meet the investment demand of the project, and it was backed only by $112.5 million. That this particular money creation is also backed by the values invested in the project in terms of technology and so on and so forth, is irrelevant to the present focus on the money supply and its creational mechanisms. This key "money multiplicator" mechanism accounts to a large extent for the drastic increase in the global circulation of money. By these forms of money creation the noncurrency part of the money supply is dramatically increased without needing to be backed by other physical assets such as gold. Instead these virtual forms of money created are backed by loans, mortgages and, to a small extent, other bank assets.

In the evolution of money Keynes distinguishes between "money of account" (the *expression* of debts, prices, or purchasing power), and "money proper" (what is actually *discharged* or *held*), and already in its early form money is identified with debt.[7] Underscoring the importance of debt in the creation of forms of money, Giddens writes:

A basic transition is initiated when acknowledgements of debt can be substituted for commodities as such in the settlement of transactions. This "spontaneous acknowledgement of debt" can be issued by any bank and represents "bank money." Bank money is recognition of a private debt until it becomes more widely diffused. This movement to money proper involves the intervention of the state, which acts as the guarantor of value. Only the state ... is able to transform private debt transactions into a standard means of payment—in other words, to bring debt and credit into balance in respect of an indefinite number of transactions. Money in its developed form is thus defined above all in terms of credit and debt. (1990: 23–24)

And while acknowledging that the relation between money and debt is far from new, the relationship as further described below seems to have been configured in new ways in the present.[8] The understanding of the casual relationships between debt and money has also changed and is contested. Economist Steve Keen, for example, has recently argued that the creation of debt by banks precedes the creation of government money. This contradicts the causality chain as promoted in conventional neoclassical economics, where infusion of money into the banks (from government and private deposits) that create excess reserves in the banks precedes the creation of loans, debt, and credit money.[9]

In the current situation we might arguably say that money is "borrowed into existence" through a process where the meaning of "acknowledgement of debt" has changed, while the (inter)state system has to some extent, through deregulation policies, "retracted" as a guarantor of value. If this holds true, its measure is the extent to which states are failing to fulfill their role in bringing debt and credit into balance. Furthermore, the banks produce money to lend not only to private companies and individuals, but also to governments. It is important to notice that this money creation logic is almost entirely privatized. The vast majority of the money supply is created through accounting entries, by private commercial banks and central banks as *private* corporations,[10] lending to governments and private actors alike. In the US, for example, the only money created by the government is coins, comprising one one-thousandth of the total money supply. Moreover, as illustrated by the money supply figures, Federal Reserve notes (dollar bills) and government coins together comprise less than 3 percent of the money supply; the other 97 percent is created by private commercial banks (Brown 2007). Similar arrangements apply for most Western countries. As economist James K. Galbraith recently stated: "Banks are not money-lenders. Banks are money-creators. They do that by making loans" (2009: 65). Money creation is indeed the most important product of banking.

The Dance of Debt

Concomitant with the radical financialization, the accumulation of debt since 1980 by the globally systemic core economy of the US has been remarkable, with total debt as a percentage of GDP soaring from 168 percent to over 350 percent by 2007. Notably, the former highest historically debt ratio was recorded during the Great Depression. In the early 1930s the total debt as a percentage of GDP reached a peak of 265 percent.[11] By the end of 2009 the ratio was closing in on about 393 percent ($55 trillion in total debt to $14 trillion GDP).

In their empirical documentation of historical banking crises—of "eight centuries of financial folly"—Reinhart and Rogoff (2009) highlight the critical role of debt accumulation and credit bubble drunkenness of both financial actors and policy makers. Their study found that historical banking crises have been accompanied, in emerging and advanced economies alike, by a surprisingly dramatic rise in debt. "The true legacy of banking crises is greater public indebtedness—far over and beyond the direct headline costs of big bailout packages" (2009: 171). The world's governments have initiated historically unprecedented bailout and stimulus package measures during the current crisis, and the accumulation of debt is similarly unprecedented. The core message from Reinhart and Rogoff's extensive empirical data is the "concept of the financial fragility in economies with massive indebtedness. All too often, periods of heavy borrowing can take place in a bubble and last for a surprisingly long time" (2009: 292). The reason for this they assign to the pervasive and historically persistent syndrome that says "this time is different," a belief that dismantles the critical faculties that might detect and prevent the buildup of new bubbles that sometimes reach a complexity and (anti)gravity that inevitably leads to large-scale collapse and crisis.

To comprehend the extent to which the decoupling of the financial from the productive economy has developed today, we need to compare the description of the "financial casino" with measures of the productive economy. Is the dramatic increase in financial transactions and of the world money supply matched by a similar increase in economic growth, an economic growth that might explain the demand for more means of payments to be injected into the economy? Although several profound problems render it imperfect, arguably our best measure of "real" economic production is the GDP (Gross Domestic Product), and variants like the GNP (Gross National Product).[12] The most widely accepted empirical work on long-term economic growth is that of Angus Maddison (2001: 126) made for the OECD (Organization for Economic Co-operation and Development). The work shows that the annual rate of growth in real global GDP fell from 4.9 percent in the period 1950–1973 to 3 percent in 1973–1998. Using another procedure of measurement, the United Nations confirms the development when they estimate that the world GDP grew at an annual rate of 5.4 percent in the 1960s, 4.1 percent in the 1970s, 3 percent in the 1980s, and 2.3 percent in the 1990s (Crotty 2005).[13]

Another estimate calculates other figures, but illustrates the same overall trend. It shows that the aggregate global growth rates have continued to fall, after the 3.5 percent of the 1960s, to 2.4 percent in the 1970s, while the 1980s and 1990s displayed growth rates of 1.4 percent and 1.1 percent. It also states that this trend has continued in the years since 2000 (Harvey 2005: 154). These numbers do not take into account the surging global inequalities. Neoliberalized globalization has thus not delivered growth in real GDP. It has instead enabled a dramatic increase in the financial economy. Major regions of the world, many of them under neoliberal "shock therapy," have seen catastrophic economic results. Only in East and Southeast Asia, and to some degree India, has neoliberalization been related to positive growth records. Here, however, the developmental states of a not-so-neoliberal outlook have played a significant part (ibid.). The reason that the proportion of global poverty has fallen is almost exclusively due to the positive developments in China and India.

We may now compare the scale of the productive economy with that of the financial. Although the growth rates of real GDP have steadily fallen under neoliberalization, according to the World Bank the world total GDP for 2006 was approximately US $48 trillion.[14] High-income countries accounted for $36 trillion of this. This figure can then be compared with the US $7 trillion or so in *daily* turnover in the financial markets and the impression of the decoupling of the productive and financial economy, and the imbalances are highlighted—especially in light of an estimate that only approximately US $800 billion a year would be required to sustain international trade and productive investment flows (Harvey 2005: 161).

As we have seen in the case of Hydro, however, the company also uses various forms of derivatives, hedging, and taking on large debts to finance their projects, thus subsequently enabling financial actors to create huge amounts of virtual money, contributing to the expansion of the "financial casino." The task of strictly separating that which is "pure finance" from the part that is directly linked to production is therefore far from straightforward. We might propose that all wealth origination is in the last instance linked to production (GDP), though to a larger or lesser extent. Metaphorically we might picture a pyramid turned upside down, with the production economy at the bottom and ever expanding floors of wealth origination on top of it. Hydro is positioned fairly close to the bottom, as it were, firmly grounded in the realities of nature and productive economic activities, but it also contributes to inflating the more detached levels of finance capitalism above them. Other financial actors still operate more or less exclusively in this "decoupled" and inflated area.

In September 2006 the Federal Reserve commented on the relationship between the money supply and real economic performance thus:

> For decades, the Federal Reserve has published data on the money supply, and for many years the Fed set targets for money supply growth. In the past two decades, a number of developments have broken down the relationship between money supply growth and the performance of the U.S. economy. In July 2000, the Federal Reserve announced that it was no longer setting target ranges for money supply growth.[15]

In this statement we can read some of the new relationship that connects money with debt in recent times. As described above, along with the complete abandonment of the gold standard, the decisive role of the state in transforming private debt into standard means of payment (by bringing debt and credit into balance) seems to have become frailer or partly broken under the regime of neoliberal financialization. Central banks are increasingly trying to manage the global economy solely through interest and inflation measures. The perspective is that as long as inflation rates are "reasonable," new virtual money can "soundly" be injected into the system. The problem here, of course, is that inflation is a result of a series of more or less autonomous factors and thus is not only dependent upon the "isolated" money supply of various countries' currencies. In a globally integrated economy, where large parts of "the workshop of the world" have moved to Asia, especially China in recent years, the rise in cheap imports keeps the purchasing power strong in the import countries (the rich countries), even in the face of huge increases in the money supply. The inflation-driving mechanism of the dramatically increased money supply is masked, and thus kept in check, for the time being at least, by the exploitation of cheap labor and natural resources from developing countries, which produce cheap products for the rich countries to purchase.

Another confusion is the notion that the money supply is increased because of the "demand" for means of payments, liquidity, by the market. This contention is difficult to maintain in light of the statistical data presented above. The growth in the money supply does not correlate at all with economic real growth measures like GDP. It is, rather, contingent on the dramatic increase in pure finance transactions and activities in the financial markets. Thus we have a self-reinforcing process, whereby the growth in the financial markets creates an ever increasing demand for more liquidity, which in turn drives the financialization of the economic system, which in turn creates more demand for liquidity: a spiral of enchantment, as it were.

As several authors have indicated, our contemporary predicament can be described as a "casino culture," fueled by a finance capitalism that fosters the notion of speculation and gambling—a casino capitalism (Strange 1986). For example, Comaroff and Comaroff put some of the recent trends together: "the explosion of popular gambling, its legitimate incorporation to the fiscal heart of the nation-state, the global expansion of highly speculative market 'investment,' and the changes in the moral vectors of the wager." Then they ask what has happened and answer themselves by way of paraphrasing a reflexive Fidel Castro: "'The world has become a huge casino.' He [Castro] refers to the fact that the value of stock markets has lost all grounding in materiality and has as such finally realized the dream of medieval alchemy: 'Paper has been turned into gold'" (Comaroff and Comaroff 2000: 297).

Applying the same metaphor, it is rather abstract money digits that have been turned into gold, we might add. As Hardt contends, the gaming room has become iconic of capital, of its "natural" capacity to yield value without human input (1995: 39). Jameson proposes that finance capital brings into being a play of monetary entities that need neither production nor consumption (1997). These perspectives hark back to Keynes's famous statement, quoted above, that when "the capital development of a country becomes a by-product of the activities of a casino, the job is likely to be ill-done" ([1936] 2008: 159). As the historical constant of deep, recurrent and system-changing financial crisis testifies (Arrighi 1994; Appendix), however, there is no such thing as capitalism without production or value creation without human input; thus the neoliberal, and by implication the neoliberalized social theories' stress on market mechanisms (supply and demand, consumption, circulation, and exchange) as the key in economic value considerations is deeply problematic. The chapter will conclude with some of the social implications of neoliberal financialization both nationally and globally.

The "Ancien Régime" Reinvented

It is well documented that in the 1970s two of the performing arms of the "Wall Street-Treasury complex" (Bhagwati 2004), the World Bank and the International Monetary Fund, began imposing a set of "conditionalities" on loans to poor debtor countries, requiring them to open up their capital markets, cut spending on social welfare, and privatize their industries. Whatever possible other benign motives these policies might have had, only in this way did the lenders get their interests. Joseph Stiglitz, former chief economist of the World Bank and winner of the so-called

Nobel Prize in Economics, has extensively criticized these conditionalities from an insider perspective (2002). For example, he describes the TRIPS (the WTO's intellectual property rights treaty) as part of a new global order that has "condemned people to death," and World Bank plans as "undermining democracy" (Palast 2003: 157). The developing countries that have escaped these "steps to economic damnation," as Palast describe them, have largely done so by not adopting their measures (ibid.: 152; Reinert 2007).

Another insider account of these practices was provided by John Perkins in his 2005 international bestseller *Confessions of an Economic Hit Man*. Perkins was employed by an international consulting firm that worked to convince poorer countries to accept enormous development loans, and to make sure that the development projects were contracted to US companies. Once they were loaded with debt, the US government would request their favors, including access to natural resources, military cooperation, and political support. As Perkins writes:

> Economic hit men are highly paid professionals that cheat countries around the globe out of trillions of dollars. Their tools include fraudulent financial reports, rigged elections, payoffs, extortion, sex and murder.... People like me are paid outrageously high salaries to do the system's bidding. If we falter, a more malicious form of hit man, the jackal, steps up to the plate. And if the jackal fails, then the job falls to the military. (2005: xiii)

The above exposition illuminates that both financialization and the global financial crisis must be analyzed within the broader cultural, political, and distributive climate in which financialization has thrived. Many mechanisms have been identified, but as Palma rightly points out, "ultimately, the current financial crisis is the outcome of something much more systematic, namely an attempt to use neo-liberalism (or, in US terms, neo-conservatism) as a new technology of power to help transform capitalism into a rentiers' delight ... to transform the state into a major facilitator of the ever-increasing rent-seeking practices of oligopolistic capital" (2009: 833).

It is by now documented that it is highly doubtful that neoliberalism has contributed to "real economic growth" in any reasonable sense of the expression. Rather, as described above, and as put forward as the central thesis of scholars of neoliberalism (Duménil and Levy 2004; Epstein 2005; Harvey 2005), neoliberalism constitutes the remaking of world economies and societies in the image of restoring elite class revenues and power. The elites in question are those collectively referred to as "finance," whose power was partly lost in the Great Depression, during World War II, and in the post–World War II order. A glimpse of the heights of their former power, and an anticipation of the temporary loss of it, is highlighted in a letter from Franklin D. Roosevelt to Colonel E. M. House in 1933: "The real truth ... is, as you and I know, that a financial element in the larger centers has owned the Government ever since the days of Andrew Jackson" [the seventh president of the US, from 1829 to 1837] (Scott 2007: 1).

Let us use some key statistical measures to identify the "world society" in terms of economic distributions. In 1989 there were 66 billionaires and 31.5 million people living below the poverty line in the US. In 1999 the number of billionaires had increased to 268 and the number of people below the poverty line was now 34.5 million. This same year, at the height of a decade-long economic boom, one in six American children was officially poor and 26 percent of the workforce earned poverty-level wages. And during the same decade, not surprisingly, stock market gains went mostly to the wealthiest (Mintzberg et al. 2002: 72). In Norway a similar trend emerged. From year 2000 to 2010 the number of billionaires in Norway increased about four times, from 43 to 168. In only one year, from 2006 to 2007, the 400 richest people in Norway, holding values of approximately NOK 762 billion, increased their wealth with NOK 168 billion.[16] Moreover, since 1990 the growing inequalities in income distribution between the richest one percent and the national average have been *more* pronounced in Norway than for example in the US, and the inequalities when comparing the richest one percent against the average are in Norway back at pre-1930 levels (Gunnesdal and Marsdal 2011: 4).

As noted by Hallvard Bakke, a former minister of Norway and a commentator in the debate, whereas 19 percent of the total income went to the 10 percent of the population with the highest incomes in 1990, the percentage had increased to 24.5 by 2003. This increase amounted to NOK 70 billion (more than one billion dollars).[17] This means that if the 10 percent of people with the highest incomes had still accounted for "only" 19 percent of the total incomes in 2003, their income in that year would have been NOK 70 billion less than it actually was. This trend was also connected to an increase in the number of poor people in Norway, although judging by rhetoric it is difficult to believe that in "the world's richest country," a favorite expression among politicians of parties across the political spectrum, there is a significant portion of poor people. Statistics indicate that 11 percent of the population lives below the limit of what is defined as poor, according to the definitions provided by EU (Lysestøl 2006: 20).

Moreover, these trends in the US and in Norway are far from unique. Looking at wealth distribution in a global perspective, the statistics unequivocally illustrate the present predicament. The authoritative reports on global inequalities from the United Nations Development Program draws a depressing picture (UNDP Human Development Report 2005). In 1998 the world's 225 richest people owned more than one trillion dollars, the equivalent of the total income of the bottom 47 percent of the world's income earners. Three of these wealthy individuals held assets that were greater in worth than the forty-eight least developed countries combined. In terms of consumption, Hart contends that "[w]orld consumption has increased six times in the last twenty years; but the richest fifth account for 86 per cent of it" (2002: 28). The striking asymmetries in the global income distribution can be pictured, somewhat ironically, as a champagne flute. According to numbers from the year 2000, the richest 20 percent of the world's population holds 75 percent of the world's total income. The poorest 40 percent, the roughly 2 billion people living on less than $2 a day, hold 5 percent of world income. The poorest 20 percent of the world population, the roughly 1 billion living on less than $1 a day, hold 1.5 percent of the world's total income (UNDP Human Development Report 2005: 36). Indeed, a metaphor of a "champagne culture" seems to be appropriate.

To put the asymmetries in perspective, we can look at the cost of ending extreme poverty, as stated by the UNDP: "Measured in 2000 purchasing power parity terms, the cost of ending extreme poverty—the amount needed to lift 1 billion people above the $1 a day poverty line—is $300 billion" (UNDP Human Development Report 2005: 38). This amount, as the report underscores, is equivalent to less than 2 percent of the income of the richest 10 percent of the world's population. As clearly demonstrated by the UNDP reports, the gap between the richest and the poorest countries is also increasing dramatically. It has been estimated that in 1750 the rich countries were twice as rich as the poor (Reinert 2007: xvii). Furthermore: "In 1820 the five richest countries in the world were three times as rich as the five poorest. By 1950, they were 35 times as rich; by 1970, 44 times; and by 1992 72 times" (Fulcher 2004: 98).

In the rhetoric of "economic globalization" it is easy to jump to the false conclusion that the world economy is converging and that it is integrating the world, when in fact "[t]he world has become steadily more *divided* by international differences in wealth" (Fulcher 2004: 98). Indeed, Hart compares the contemporary world situation in terms of economic inequality with that of the ancien régime in France during the 1750s, at the centers of agrarian civilization before the modern revolutions of political struggle and economic development swept them away (2002: 27). It is not, then, inadequate to restate a conclusion Albert Einstein reached in his essay "Why Socialism?" published in the first issue of *Monthly Review* in 1949: "nowhere have we really overcome what Thorstein Veblen called 'the predatory phase' of human development."[18] Recently James K. Galbraith has described the emergence since the early 1970s of the new "predator state" (2008).

As the New Deal institutions and especially the Bretton Woods system were dismantled by neoliberal (neoconservative) policies, finance took control from industry. "By dismantling rules, regulations, institutions and safety nets, the predator state assisted the rise of money managers (Wray 2009: 809). The result was the emergence of a particular form of capitalism that Hyman Minsky has described as "money manager capitalism." As Wray notes, it was accompanied by rising inequality also because in the "predator state" government policy was directed and subsumed to the benefit of the elite predators (ibid.).

Financial Neo-imperialism

Minsky describes the rise of a new stage of capitalism in the US as "money manager capitalism," in which "the proximate owners of a vast proportion of financial instruments are mutual and pension funds. The total return on the portfolio is the only criteria used for judging the performance of the managers of these funds, which translates into an emphasis upon the bottom line in the management of business organizations" (1996).[19] The creation of "money manager capitalism" was initiated because of the development in the 1960s and 1970s of a diverse set of financial mechanisms and institutions, accompanied successively by deregulation, that circumvented New Deal constraints on finance, including many of the issues described earlier: "securitisation of mortgages, derivatives to hedge interest rate (and exchange rate) risk, and many types of 'off balance sheet' operations (helping to evade reserve and capital restraints)" (Wray 2009: 814).

An issue that has been somewhat more overlooked, possibly due to the intellectual hegemony of neoclassical economic theories and especially the Chicago school monetarists, is the redistributive effect caused by the *increase in money supply*. As Rothbard contends, "the big error of all quantity theorists, from the British classicists to Milton Friedman, is to assume that money is only a 'veil,' and that increases in the quantity of money only have influence on the price level, or on the purchasing power of the money unit" (1994: 25). According to Rothbard, Friedman's fallacy is the notion that the increase in money supply and the subsequent dilution of the money unit is somehow magically "showered" by a "helicopter effect" symmetrically and instantaneously on every person proportionally to his or her money stock. Notably, Chairman of the US Federal Reserve

Ben Bernanke referred to Friedman's notion of the helicopter effect in a speech about deflation and has since been called "helicopter Ben" by critics.

On the contrary, Rothbard explains, owing the insight to the eighteenth century Irish-French economist Richard Cantillon and the economists of the Austrian school to which he himself belongs, that in addition to this quantitative effect, "an increase in the money supply also changes the distribution of income and wealth" (1994: 25). This occurs because the effect of the increased money supply does not magically affect everybody at the same time but rather "ripples through the economy" in a process transmitting the new money "from one pocket to another." Because it is a process in time, the compound effect is that "[w]ealth then moves to those market participants who gain early access to this newly created fiat money. Who loses? Those who gain access to this fiat money later in the process, after the market effects of the increase of money have rippled trough the economy" (Gary North, Foreword to Rothbard 1983: 6). Thus the dramatic increase of the money supply also reproduces elite power relations by redistributing wealth *upward* in the system.

On the level of global money flows and the management thereof, there is one further highly relevant, and seldom acknowledged, consequential implication in terms of the reproduction of asymmetrical relations. As outlined in detail and depth by Michael Hudson (2003) and popularly summarized by Niall Ferguson (2005), the monetary system of today works in effect as an imperial tool for the United States. This came about through the adoption, late in World War II, of the "U.S. Treasury bill standard"—the dollar as the key world reserve currency—and the inception of a worldwide monetary logic based on dollars through the "Washington consensus" (IMF, World Bank, US Treasury Department, Wall Street). Also, this dollarized monetary logic has been hardwired into the world's domestic economies through global trade, capital markets, and central banks interlinked in international economic relations. One of the effects has been that other nations have been paying huge "empire tributes" to the United States. Since the 1970s and the complete abandonment of the gold standard, the US has even been able to rule in the position not of world creditor, but of world debtor. As mentioned by Ferguson, Nixon's Treasury secretary once told his European counterparts: "the dollar is our currency, but your problem" (2005).

As I have described earlier, the US economy is running and accumulating huge debts in the form of "twin deficits"; that is, both the budget deficit (the difference between federal tax revenues and expenditures) and its balance of payments deficit (the difference between what Americans earn from foreigners from exports, services, and investments abroad and what they pay out to foreigners for imports, services, and loans). When a government runs up debt, it can tap public savings by selling government bonds. However, as Ferguson notes: "Perhaps the most amazing economic fact of our time is that between 70 and 80 percent of the American economy's vast and continuing borrowing requirement is being met by foreign (mainly Asian central banks)" (ibid.). In political terms this means in effect that the US administration's combination of tax cuts and "global war on terror" is to a large extent financed by other countries. Paul Craig Roberts, the assistant secretary of the Treasury in the Reagan administration and former associate editor of the Wall Street Journal, puts it like this: "The macho super patriots who support the Bush regime still haven't caught on that US superpower status rests on the dollar being the reserve currency, not on a military unable to occupy Baghdad.... When the dollar ceases to be the reserve currency, foreigners will cease to finance the US trade and budget deficits, and the American Empire along with its wars will disappear overnight." The US government's multibillion-dollar excess expenditure is thus to a large extent a free ride on the global monetary system. China and Japan are the foremost owners of US debt, denominated in government bonds, debt the US seems to have little intention of paying back. Opposite to the way Britain ruled the world economically in the third "systemic cycle of accumulation" by taking responsibility for keeping the international financial system in order, the US uses it from a debtor position to fund its increasing debt (Arrighi 1994).

Norway too plays a role here and might also serve as an example of money manager capitalism. Norway has become a substantial world creditor and financial player, especially through the Government Pension Fund Global. By 2006 it held values of about NOK 2 trillion, by the end of 2010 it held values of more than NOK 3 trillion. In 2006, 40 percent of the values were invested in stocks and 60 percent in rent instruments, mostly government bonds. Of the stock investments 30.4 percent were invested in US stocks, and as for the bonds, 32.6 percent of these values were invested in US rent instruments, that is, mostly Treasury bonds.[20] Thus, in 2006 roughly NOK 400 billion was invested in US government bonds. That is to say, Norway is in part financing the US deficit, and by implication its free ride, by about NOK 400 billion. In this way, troubling to the moral idiom of Norway as a "peace nation," it is indirectly financing the US military spending on the war in Iraq and the global "war on terror." In fact, Norway is in this line of argument arguably Europe's biggest financial contributor to the illegitimate war in Iraq.

As Arrighi (1994) and others have shown, however, all earlier capitalist empires have collapsed, and they did so in periods of extensive "financial expansion" of the economy—periods resembling that of contemporary millennium capitalism. How long the US can sustain its debtor-positioned political and economic hegemony remains to be seen. Today the fear in Asia and Europe is that changing the financial and payments system, "getting off the dollar," would harm their own economies to a great extent as well. Removing the monetary imperialism of today would, they fear, crash the whole system as long as the whole system is upheld by what Hudson calls a "superstructure of dollar debt" (2003: 387). As history's lesson shows, however, it is when your power wanes that owing a fortune in your own currency, as the US does today, become a real problem for you—that is, as opposed to being a problem for someone else. The question for the creditor nations is to calculate when the problems of the current financial system outweigh the problems of changing it.

Radical Reverse Redistribution

Thus the most substantive contribution of neoliberal financialized globalization since the 1970s, from the "finance capital takeover" to the inherent workings of the present monetary system itself, is the *redistribution*, and not the creation, of wealth and real incomes. The redistributive mechanisms performed under neoliberalization have been described by Harvey as "accumulation by dispossession" (2005), that is, accumulation by the wealthy through dispossession of the public, the poor, and increasingly the middle class. This conceptualization of government policies under neoliberalization resembles Galbraith's notion of the "predator state" (2008). Harvey sees the mechanisms of dispossession as the continuation and proliferation of a set of accumulation practices comprising four main features: (1) privatization and commodification, (2) financialization, (3) management and manipulation of crisis, and (4) state redistributions. Some of the more specific redistribution practices included in the concept of "accumulation by dispossession" are the following:

> the commodification and privatization of land and the forceful expulsion of peasant populations ... conversion of various forms of property rights (common, collective, state, etc.) into exclusive private property rights ... suppression of rights to the commons; commodification of the labor power and the suppression of alternative (indigenous) forms of production and consumption; colonial, neocolonial, and imperial processes of appropriation of assets (including natural resources); monetization of exchange and taxation, particularly of land; the slave trade ... and usury, the national debt and ... the use of the credit system as a radical means of accumulation by dispossession ... [and] extraction from patents and intellectual property rights and the diminution or erasure of common property rights (such as

state pensions, paid vacations, and access to education and health care). (Harvey 2005: 159)

The state, with the judicial system's definition of legality and the brute force entailed in its monopoly of violence, is both backing and promoting these processes, Harvey argues. These processes are antagonistic also toward "the essence" of the capitalist mode of production, which is obviously to *produce and generate* wealth. As development economist and historian of capitalism Erik Reinert notes, though widely ignored by mainstream economics the key issue in escaping poverty, as testified by all countries that have done so, is to "get the economic activities right" (2007: 216). But as the documentation above shows, globalized neoliberal financial-iziation has failed in this crucial sense. Herein lies a core reason for the current crisis. And because of its incapacity to provide a framework to foster productive investments and increase the generation of real wealth, neoliberalism is already dead (Hardt and Negri 2009).

The anthropologists Holmes and Marcus have referred to the cultural formations created by the wide-ranging program of neoliberal change as "fast-capitalism": "We have argued that the most distinctive feature of fast capitalism is its propensity to subvert the science, political economy, and metaphysics of solidarity upon which modernist conceptions of society rest" (2005: 238). This "unchallenged capitalism," notes Palma, "nearly brought to an end the specific culture in which it developed: the Enlightenment" (2009: 863). The irony in our case with Hydro is that, while Hydro in some respects struggles to resist and overcome the cultural formations that are produced under neoliberal financialization, to counter the subversion of the social, it is simultaneously adding "to the financial casino" itself, mostly by the practices of "risk management." It is thus fueling "fast financial capitalism" while simultaneously working to subvert it through its tenacious main corpus of modernist production practices.

In a similar vein Comaroff and Comaroff identify and explore three key corollaries of "millennial capitalism": "the shifting provenance of the nation-state and its fetishes, the rise of new forms of enchantment, and the explosion of neoliberal discourses of civil society" (2000: 293). In the enchanted economy of appearances, signs of finance have moved to the center of the value-creating processes of capitalism itself. Production is transformed into "value creation," and value creation increasingly takes on a virtual meaning of "value appreciation" and "value origination" through various innovative ways of leveraging a debt-based economy. As early as 1993 Hyman Minsky, who coined the term "money manager capitalism," saw what was developing when he wrote that:

A peculiar regime emerged in which the main business in the financial markets became far removed from the financing of the capital development of the country. Furthermore, the main purpose of those who controlled corporations was no longer making profits from production and trade but rather to assure that the liabilities of the corporations were fully priced in the financial market. (1993: 112)

The only way to make sense of the contemporary economic predicament is by investigating it in the contexts of the political and ideological circumstances, as well as the redistributive outcomes, within which it takes place. This total "neoliberal culture complex" of global reach came to a fundamental crisis by 2008. Enabled by the "predator state," money manager elites moved to the center stage, captivated the global economy, and while dispossessing the public at large through radical reverse redistribution steered the whole system off the cliff.

Notes

1. See http://www.morganstanley.com/views/gef/archive/2007/20071112-Mon.html# anchor5785 (accessed 23 May 2011).
2. Access Roubini's blog here: http://www.roubini.com/ (accessed 23 May 2011).
3. In a letter to the shareholders of Berkshire Hathaway Inc. Available online.
4. Greenspan's support of the gold standard is expressed in a chapter in Ayn Rand's "Capitalism: The Unknown Ideal" (1966). Greenspan's continued support for the gold standard, arguably a marginal position among contemporary economists, has been discussed as somewhat ironic given his role in the Federal Reserve, which regulates the current fiat money system.
5. See www.hydro.com press room news archive 23 August 2007, http://www.hydro .com/en/Press-room/News/Historic-news-archive/2007/08/Qatalum-closes-USD-26-billion-project-finance-deal/ (accessed 16 May 2011).
6. For particularities of the Norwegian system see Kran and Øwre (2001).
7. In Keynes's work *Treatise on Money*. For an illuminating graphical outline of Keynes's classification and evolutionary scheme of money forms, see Hart (2000: 247).
8. This discussion leaves the huge field related to the "the philosophy of money" relatively untouched. In general we might note that the development described here in some senses can be interpreted in terms of Keynes's classification of money forms and an "evolutionary scheme emphasizing the gradual replacement of an objective standard of value (commodity-money) with symbols of no intrinsic value (token or representative money)" (Hart 2000: 247). This move was described as an evolution from *substance to function* by Simmel. Simmel also held that money provided stability in a volatile world of commodity exchanges, because of its feature as a common measure uniting independent acts of exchange. This idea has earlier in this volume

been described as one key element of the "abstraction package" (abstract value) that constitutes the "infrastructure" of the modernization processes, which standardizes and thus commensurates cross-cultural communication.

9. See http://www.debtdeflation.com/blogs/2009/09/19/it's-hard-being-a-bear-part-five-rescued/ (accessed 5 November 2009).

10. Despite what the name connotes, the status of the Federal Reserve banks as "independent, privately owned and locally controlled corporations," was confirmed for instance in a court ruling (*Lewis v. United States*, 680 F.2d 1239) in 1982. See *Global Research*, 2 April 2008 (http://www.globalresearch.ca/index.php?context=va&aid=8518, accessed 2 April 2008).

11. Gabelli Mathers Fund, using as source of data for the period 1916–1951: *Historical Statistics of the United States: Colonial Times to 1970* (Bureau of Census; 2 volume set edition (29 April 2003); and for the period 1952–2004: Federal Reserve Board.

12. The inventor of GDP, Simon Kuznets, acknowledged the serious flaw in the GDP measure of not taking into account qualitative differences in growth, of not indicating "+ and –" of the growth accounting, and stated in 1962: "Distinctions must be kept in mind between quantity and quality of growth, between costs and returns, and between the short and long run. Goals for more growth should specify more growth of what and for what" ("How To Judge Quality," *The New Republic*, 20 October 1962). Likewise, former Senator Robert F. Kennedy allegedly stated: "The gross national product includes air pollution and advertising for cigarettes and ambulances to clear our highways of carnage. It counts special locks for our doors and jails for the people who break them. GNP includes the destruction of the redwoods and the death of Lake Superior. It grows with the production of napalm, and missiles and nuclear warheads" ("Measuring Progress: Annex 1-What's wrong with the GDP?" *Friends of the Earth*, 13 March 2003).

13. UN *World Economic Survey*, various issues.

14. World Development Indicators database, World Bank, 1 July 2007.

15. See http://www.newyorkfed.org/aboutthefed/fedpoint/fed49.html (accessed 1 December 2008).

16. Norwegian business magazine *Kapital* 37, no. 16. 2007, and *Kapital* no. 16. 2010, p. 65.

17. *Klassekampen*, 17 November 2006.

18. Albert Einstein, "Why Socialism?" *Monthly Review* (May 1949). Accessible here: http://www.monthlyreview.org/598einstein.php (accessed 5 November 2009).

19. Quoted in Wray (2009: 814).

20. See the pension fund reports, found at Norges Bank Investment Management (NBIM), who manages the Norwegian Government Pension Fund Global: http://www.nbim .no/ (accessed 23 May 2011).

Part III

In Good Company?

Chapter 7

DIRECTORS AND DIRECTIONS
OF CREATION

... it is almost a general rule that wherever the ways of man are
gentle (*mœurs douces*) there is commerce.... Commerce... polishes
and softens (*adoucit*) barbarian ways as we can see every day.
—Montesquieu, *Esprit des lois*

Hurrah! Today marks the end of the
doux commerce, and I am a free man.
—Engels in a letter to Marx, 1 July 1869

The dichotomy between pleasure and pain is
socially constructed to make the economy work.
—Norman O. Brown, *Apocalypse and/or Metamorphosis*

Reprise and Review

From a diverse set of angles and idioms, managing actions in a series of investment projects have been explored. I have positioned these projects in
the broader contexts of corporate and capitalist social and historical realities. In so doing a description of some important aspects of contemporary
capitalist conjunctures has been offered. Contingent upon the presently
dominating accumulation processes of neoliberal financialization, qualitatively different from the processes constituting the main Hydro activi-

ties but nevertheless providing constraints upon them, the production of wealth and the reproduction of economic inequality and asymmetries of power has also been investigated. Hydro's "glocal" (Robertson 1995) "assemblage" investment projects have proved to be an apt case for exploring what I believe to be some of the core dynamics of contemporary global culture, due to the fact that they are ambiguously positioned along a range of fundamental dimensions that underscores the present predicament.

The contemporary Hydro project practices and organization are the offspring of several distinct historical trajectories. First, the corporate capitalist organization emerged and conquered the world in the free enterprise system from the turn of the twentieth century onward with its vertically integrated, bureaucratically managed, multi-unit business enterprise (Arrighi 1994: 294). Today's Hydro is also a product of a second path, however, staked out by the most fervent rival of the US capitalist corporation, namely the German model of corporate capitalism: the horizontally integrated, nationally oriented business form with active involvement from the government in support of the "cohesion, modernization, and expansion of the resulting technostructure" (ibid.: 290). Thirdly, Hydro practices are characterized by the conditions of national culture pertaining especially to the "Norwegian democratic and cooperative industrial work life model," with its sociotechnical perspectives, democratic ideals of work life relationships, participative design of work processes, and psychological job demands (Emery and Thorsrud 1976).

As highlighted by the social reality of investment projects, Hydro encompasses a tension between its pecuniary and technological rationality. In the neoliberal age of high finance this tension has been reconstituted in new ways. By investigating technology and its realm of knowledge configurations, forms of causality, and instrumentality, we came to see the "social reality of construction" as a deep interconnection between technology and art. Harking back to the Aristotelian notion of Poiesis (*tekhne*), which included everything profanely "artificial" and "creational" and from what today is considered both "fine arts" and "industrial production," it was shown that technology, in its present constitution in Hydro projects, is a much more polysemic notion than implied in popular conceptions like technology as machinery or "applied science." "Technology" in Hydro was seen as both morally and aesthetically embedded, connected both to the present realms of the somewhat sacred "arts" domain and the political and normative. And at the heart of project genesis was an unconcealed ontology of "*situated potentiality*." This potentiality was at once consonant and in strong tension with the Hydro "turn to finance" and the pecuniary rationality of "money managing" with the priority on shareholder return and the bottom line.

This relationship has been present in Hydro throughout its century-old history, since its inception as an industrial, entrepreneurial company (represented by Sam Eyde, one of its three cofounders,) with its basis in fundamental and ingenious science (represented by Norway's arguably most prominent scientist ever, Kristian Birkeland) and with the introduction of a new type of financial actor in Norway (represented by Marcus "*häradshövdingen*" Wallenberg and his finance family dynasty). Through its German-oriented approach to technology, "*teknisk*" and "*teknikk*," which it arrived at via both its NTH relationship and, later, its acquisition of the aluminum company Årdal and Sunndal Verk (ÅSV) and the large German aluminum company VAW, it also inherited a "Norwegian/German" tradition of technological rationality.

We might furthermore interpret Hydro projects and wider practices in a British/American tradition in their formal and pecuniary aspects, organizational form, and market orientation—that is, to a large extent, its efforts to suspend and supersede the market through its "vertically integrated," professionally "managed" multi-unit business approach (Arrighi 1994: 288–304), and in terms of its external pressures (e.g., "high finance," shareholder returns, internal rents, etc.). On the other hand it can be seen more as German/Norwegian in its production- and knowledge-based industrial "content" aspects, and possibly also in its metaphysical orientation, that is, in its particular technological or instrumental rationality, its *Homo faber* orientation, its productive creational approach, and its activities that promote cultural and moral values conducive to "democratic capitalism's" wealth and welfare creation logic, with the aim of contributing to the progress of society—a modernist, rational, but likewise morally spirited obligation.

The discussion has highlighted the necessity of differentiating quite sharply between fundamentally different activities in the capitalist system. As reflected both in Veblen's ([1904] 1975) distinction and opposition between "the captains of finance" and the "engineers," and in Schumpeter's difference between the financial (or economic) and the entrepreneurial function ([1939] 1982: chap. 3), production and finance capital are based in two very separate sets of motives and criteria under which various actors function within the capitalist system. Following Perez (2002), the purpose of finance capital is to make money from money (MM') and thus to serve as agents for reallocating and *redistributing wealth*. As our discussion has shown, the particular form of this redistribution in the globalized, neoliberal age of financialization is aptly termed "accumulation by dispossession" by Harvey (2005) and "super imperialism" by Hudson (2003). By contrast, the term "production capital," again following Perez, "embodies the motives and behaviors of those agents who generate *new* wealth by producing goods or performing services" (2002: 71, italics in original). A key finding, then, is that *redistribution*, a core concept in economic anthropology, though used mainly to characterize "archaic," noncapitalist societies, is also a most adequate label to describe the constitutive dynamics of contemporary global capitalism. Indeed, the contemporary capitalist form of redistribution is directed toward producing economic inequality with great force, and might thus be described as *radical reverse redistribution*.

As shown above, Hydro investment projects are more or less "pure" instantiations of a production capitalist logic. As production capital, their purpose is to create production capacities in order to produce—and in turn to be able to produce more. This conforms to the MCM' variant of the Marxian formula for capital. As an embodiment of production capital, Hydro investment projects are moreover at the commanding heights of an essentially knowledge-based "creational" tradition. For production capitalists, knowledge about processes, products, and markets is the basis of its success, while the knowledge of finance capital needs only to be linked to profitability concerns. In line with the knowledge-based production tradition, the objective of Hydro investment projects is to increase their profit-making capacities by investing in technological innovations and the expansion of production. Here finance is an absolutely necessary enabling mechanism, but it can easily be separated from the actual processes of wealth creation in which their investment projects are positioned at the core. A possible distinction could be made between a knowledge-based "creational" capitalist logic (of production), and a "creationist" logic of captivating finance capital.

Throughout historical capitalism the necessary relationship between production and finance capitalism has taken on various configurations, from symbiosis at one end to parasitism at the other (Reinert and Daastøl 1998). The spirit of our neoliberal capitalist age seems to be that of parasitic and kleptocratic finance capital. Referring to the neoliberal (or neoconservative) policies that captured the state and enabled the current crisis, Wray states: "Much more could be said about predators ... and rampant insider deals, corruption, fraud and cleptocracy that rivals anything the Russian Mafia could produce" (2009: 817). While paraphrasing Gore Vidal, Palma states that the political and economic system was transformed into "socialism for the rich and capitalism for the rest" (2009: 862). And the extractive redistributors came to be perceived as the wealth creators akin to the tail wagging the dog.

Hydro is a true offspring of the fourth systemic cycle of accumulation (Arrighi 1994; Appendix). It was born at the beginning of a long period of material expansion, an MC capitalist phase in terms of the main types of capitalist accumulation forms, and thus of welfare production. What I have studied is what has happened with Hydro projects, and the Hydro organization, in the neoliberal age of high finance in the CM' phase. Several elements characteristic of a "turn to financialization" clearly have been embedded in the Hydro organization's approach to investment projects (and other processes), for example the designation CVP (capital value process) to identify its prime decision support methodology for managing investment projects. The focus since the late 1990s on profitability, on shareholder returns, the "value-based management" model, the plethora of financial and accounting control concepts, financial risk management, financial incentive models, the expanding use of market mechanisms internally (e.g., the trading of engineering hours), and the relative objectification or "entification" of their cultural practices, illustrated by their "culture-building" project being directed away from worker-management relations toward management-investor relations, and of the "invention of identity" through their Hydro Way corporate culture program (see Røyrvik 2008a). These efforts could all be seen as partial answers to the emergence of a neoliberal culture complex, with its finance-led "economy of signs and appearance."

However, Hydro has not switched into a financial MM' corporation. It has not become financialized in the sense that Hydro does not invest its stock of money in financial speculation or in the credit system (other than to a limited degree as a risk moderator to secure its productive investments from volatile changes in the market). The company is still routinely reinvesting the major part of its surplus of capital in creating new "projects for production." As we have seen, concerns have been voiced about the return requirements, as expressed in the "internal rent" of profitability of projects. As documented, in recent years Hydro has been strategically directing its project investments toward the up and midstream areas of its business, where they yield the highest returns. Nevertheless, its economic activities are clearly marked by focusing on what it calls "source business." This is business morally legitimated as central to and deeply embedded in the infrastructural functioning of society. As one manager said: "Hydro could never produce toothpaste." Source business does not sit particularly well with the contemporary version of "high finance" and consumer culture.

Furthermore, Hydro's projects and production activities focus on both innovation and "optimization." The latter targets areas that under mainstream, "dismal" economic science logic would reap the lowest return on capital and a falling rate of profit, due to decreasing returns. However, by employing inventions (knowledge), innovations (technological change), and synergies Hydro creates value-added activities in these "barren zones" of economic resource space. *Homo faber*, man the creator, transforms them into increasing returns activities that might yield profitable return on capital, and then in turn capital accumulation for reinvestment in new projects. This last point of innovative optimization also has moral underpinnings. A morality of moderation and frugality has been and seems still to be constitutive of Hydro cultural notions. That is one reason why the stock options case of managerial compensation excesses caused such a stir.

Hydro and the Right Kind of Globalization

The analysis sought to explain some of the consequences of the liberalization of finance since the complete abandonment of the gold standard in 1973. A political regime of deregulation since the late 1970s, enabled by the revolution in information and communications technology, has together with other significant developments led to widespread innovation and expansion in finance instruments and finance's overall role in the economic, societal and cultural relations. Clegg et al. (2004) has characterized this accelerating development as finance capital taking on a hyper-real quality. Many authors have suggested that the finance system now has achieved a degree of autonomy from real production, and as Harvey notes, that under conditions of postmodernity capitalism has become dominated by an economy of signs rather than things (1992: 102). As I have documented, the present predicament of the globalized and financialized economy has been more of a process of a *belief* in a relative autonomy of the financial system from "real" production. It is simulated in the sense that its expansion and redistributive effects are indeed real, and it has been inflated by real faith in addition to greed and other factors. As social reality always is based in some form of belief and trust in relations, we might say that belief was transformed, that we moved from some forms of beliefs to others, or from belief to "belief." However, as shown by both historical and contemporary statistical data on "extractive redistribution" and economic inequality, finance wealth without production is a projection of an enchanted fantasy.

We have also seen that another of the presently popular terms of capitalism, that of "innovation," needs to be qualified. In recent times it is the financial sector that has delivered innovations at the highest speeds. Although undoubtedly a portion of these innovations could be seen as beneficial to the economy and society, a large part have projected capitalism into the realm of the hyper-real and delusional. For innovations to be socially beneficial in terms of wealth creation and distribution, they need to be linked with increasing, transforming, and dispersed productive capacities, expanding the economic horizon. In order to succeed, the political settlements with which they are linked, and the distributive implications of their activities, must be taken into account. Modern-day financial innovations seem mainly to have been vital in enabling a redistribution of wealth from both the "have-somethings" and the "have-nots" to the "have-too-muchs." Hydro has used these new finance measures as "risk management" devices to reduce the risks involved in its productive investments. However, even ardent "risk management" advocates such as Alan Greenspan have by now recanted and acknowledged that the current crisis shows that the basic premise of traditional financial risk management theory is wrong (2009).

In this light we can reassess the neoliberal financialization adjustments and adaptations made by Hydro in quite another light. While both production and finance capital constantly face various types and forms of risks at different junctures, the two forms of capital are radically differently positioned to escape them. Thanks to its liquidity, finance capital can choose more or less unlimitedly how to invest and withdraw its money, and thus avoid risks. Production capital, however, is path-dependent to historical trajectories. For example, the Hydro Qatalum project is a long-term investment that needs to develop robust strategies for facing risks. Most relevant here, however, is Hydro's need to "lure financial capital" because of the development that led to the domination of industry by finance. If the company does not succeed in this enterprise it can do nothing but face failure. As our description above testifies, Hydro has managed this luring of finance to a remarkable degree, while overall keeping to the creational virtues of production capital. In the last thirty years or so of excessive casino-style financialization, this balancing act performed by Hydro must be interpreted as impressive. Hydro has managed to keep hold of the inherently uncommitted, "disloyal" finance capital even in an environment where finance increasingly has been investing in finance.

As Perez notes, "Financial capital is footloose by nature; production capital has to face every storm by holding fast, ducking down or innovating its way forward or sideways" (2002: 73). This is exactly what Hydro has done throughout its hundred years of continuous history. In the contemporary atmosphere of the combined falling rate of profit and financialization pressure, it is something of a feat to have kept to its innovative industrial production mandate. One indication of this focus is that it seems safe to estimate that the company has been the single largest corporative spender of money for research and development in Norwegian history. On the other hand, it is not evidently certain, although some of its own traders were confident of the issue, that Hydro could have achieved an even higher profit rate if it indeed had (partly) shifted into pure financial (MM') business. International megacorporations like GE and large Norwegian companies like Orkla, both long-term strong industrial actors, have indeed moved into various forms of "financial business."

Anti-market Capitalism

Hydro's robust resilience suggests some quite consequential implications. In light of the fact that the profit rate for financial corporations has exceeded that of nonfinancial corporations in the rich world in the last decades (Duménil and Lévy 2004; Palma 2009), the premises on which the production economy of Hydro is constituted must be reassessed. A possible conclusion is that Hydro's determined focus on investment projects for production, in an age of high finance, more or less disqualifies it from being defined as a capitalist corporation in the strongest or most "purist" sense of the term. Arrighi, who more often than not uses the terms "production" and "trade" interchangeably, states:

> An agency that reinvests routinely the profits of trade in the further expansion of trade as long as the returns to capital so invested are positive cannot be defined as "capitalist" by any stretch of the imagination. A capitalist agency, by definition, is primarily if not exclusively concerned with the endless expansion of its stock of money (M).... An agency of capital accumulation is capitalist precisely because it reaps large and regular profits by investing its stock of money in trade and production or in speculation and the credit system depending on which formula (MCM' or MM') endows that stock with the greatest power of breeding. (1994: 229–230)

Following this analysis Hydro needs essentially to be considered a *noncapitalist* corporation, in this radical sense of the word. However, as I have been arguing, using Hydro as an example and more broadly advocating the concepts of "the other canon" (Reinert 2007), capitalism comprises uneven, multiple, ambiguously contradictory and conflicting trajectories and tendencies. In the present atmosphere of capitalist accumulation, the production capitalism of Hydro may be seen to be under pressure both from "above" and from "below." From above comes the pressure applied by the financial investor community to uphold a rate of profit that is comparable with purely financial speculation. From "below" comes the pressure of the structural crisis in the current phase of capitalism, which rests on a material and technological base that is in crisis, with the overall result of a falling rate of profit in nonfinancial corporations.

Adopting Braudel's (1984) view of capitalism as the "anti-market" top layer of a three-tier structure with the "material" base at the bottom, the market in the middle, and capitalism at the top, we see that Hydro, as a free market–oriented, industrially based technology company, must face this double pressure by "luring" finance from above, while continuing to create *new* wealth through taming nature (and culture) by ingenious use of knowledge and technology "below." This is a balancing act, an art of considerable proportions. While invoking both Veblen's distinction between industrial and pecuniary pursuits (1904) and Keynes's notion of the domination by speculation over enterprise, Braudel's anti-market capitalism layer on top of the system resembles the Marxian concept of "monopoly capitalism." This is a term that is widely used among Marxist economists to denote the stage of capitalism dating from the last quarter of the nineteenth century and reaching full maturity in the period after the Second World War (Sweezy 1987). After Marx and Engels it was Rudolf Hilferding who pioneered this line of theory with his *Das Finanzkapital*, published in 1910. It set out to analyze the "latest phase of capitalist development," as stated in the subtitle of the book. Arguing that the characteristic feature of finance capitalism is rising concentration, he expanded upon the theme of monopolization (centralization and concentration of capital) from Marx and concluded that monopoly spreads in all directions from every point of origin, and that there are no limits on "cartelization" (used synonymously with monopolization).

Another related and significant post-Marxian contribution in this vein was provided by Michal Kalecki, who theoretically linked the theme of monopolization on the one hand and that of class distribution of income on the other (Kalecki 1938). He concluded that a system where the degree of monopoly determines the distribution of national income is a system far removed from a pattern of free competition. A further step was achieved by Sweezy, who integrated monopolization on the one hand and crisis theory on the other (1987). With other significant contributions adding to a rich body of literature,[1] monopoly capitalist theory has shown among other things that monopolistic (or oligopolistic) organization gives capital an advantage in its struggle with labor, and therefore tends to raise the level of profits; and *ceteris paribus* the level of income and employment under monopoly capitalism is lower than it would be in a more competitive organized capitalism (Sweezy 1987).

In this picture Hydro's "other canon" tradition of market-oriented (although oligopolistic in the sense of quite few and large corporations) knowledge based industrial capitalism could be positioned. Hydro's continuing industrial commitment in an overall global and finance-based economy attests to that. Hydro's adaption, in the last decade or so, to the neoliberal tenets characteristic of our time of "high finance" nevertheless illuminates fundamental ambiguities—Hydro's own approach to contemporary industrial capitalism on one level, and on another the tensions and paradoxes embedded in the global system of accumulation itself, in which, as it is already clear, the worst crisis since the Great Depression is unfolding and moreover threatens to become the most fundamental crisis in the entire near 600-year history of capitalism (Arrighi 1994; Appendix).

Financial "Entification"

In terms of the concept of "management," we might say in view of Hydro's recent history that it was actually not until the late 1990s and the turn of the century that the democratic and participatorily endowed technocratic, engineering-based managing culture in Hydro was seriously challenged. Its major efforts since 1999, at all levels and pertaining to major aspects of their practices, have challenged the engineering-based technocratic managing hegemony and partly supplanted it with a finance control regime. Finance control mechanisms have been introduced to steer both project work and other types of corporate work and functions, including the "capital value process" for managing investment projects, key performance indicators, and personnel policy in terms of compensation incentives like the stock options program.

Thus we might see that engineering-based managerialism has been partly transformed by finance hegemony into what Hyman Minsky described as "money manager capitalism," where "the total return on the portfolio is the only criteria used for judging the performance of the managers ... which translates into an emphasis upon the bottom line in the management of business organizations" (1996).[2] At present what seems to reign is a mixture of a technocratic and what we might label an *accountocratic* "money manager" rationality (to coin a term derived from the finance world's arguably most persistent discipline) that legitimizes managing. In a self-reinforcing cycle, accounting has climbed to the high peaks of corporate management, more or less globally in concurrence with the emerging neoliberalization the last thirty years or so, and has in turn been enabling a shift from "production" to "finance" controls.[3]

Nevertheless, other managing practices and knowledge trajectories are still maintained in Hydro. As we have also seen, the managing practices in Hydro continue to be characterized by the particularities of the "Norwegian model" of moral *eigenvalues* of "democratization," "humanization," and "participation," as forged among other things through the Norwegian Industrial Democracy Program since 1962. This was particularly well illustrated in the Xi'an project, where such Hydro values were highlighted in the effort of establishing a plant in China. Although "hybridized" in actual cross-cultural project practices, we have in these cross-cultural managing crossroads been able to trace a managing trajectory in Hydro that constitutes an idiosyncratic tradition of managing in contemporary conditions, one that in some aspects resembles the American, German, French, and British traditions even as it differs from them in other ways. If we leave out the obvious problems of homogenizing national cultures of managing, the Norwegian tradition, instantiated and "mongrelized" in particular cross-cultural, disciplinary, and historical trajectories by Hydro also in its contemporary global project "assemblages," serves as an alternative that to a large extent has been overlooked in management studies. As such, I have also sought to "mongrelize" conventional ideas about "management" and managing rationality.

In managing Hydro investment projects, the experience gained through project work and aluminum production, through creations and destructions and transformations, moreover builds up a repertoire of realizations, tacitly or otherwise, of fundamental reality as undivided movement and flow. This movement can be "tapped into" in various ways, and from it cultural creations of great power and potency for wealth creation and societal progress can be abstracted and materialized. This form of ontological grounding fits with the quantum reality view of nature briefly outlined in Chapter 3 and is summarized in the concept of an *ontology of situated potentiality*. It describes the *social reality of construction* in the domain of managing investment projects as processes of bringing forth and realizing potentials in projects and plants as combined abstracted/materializing wholes in new forms of increasing density, robustness, and durability.

Against this fundamental background we have seen, consistent with the historical legacy of the "managerial revolution," that managing actions in projects are much concerned with conceptualizing, standardizing, and formalizing aspects of reality. The main objective of projects is in a sense the making of the thing (the plant) before the thing is made. At least this applies to the first phases, up to Decision Gate four of the CVP process. From then on the project is "execution," i.e., the making of the "real thing." However, as the foregoing presentation indicates, rather than any dichotomized notion of abstract work being materialized in the plant, a more dynamic model of unfolding this abstracting/materializing from the implicate order is advocated. Conceptualizations of early phases are also "thinglike" and imbued with "thinghood."

Western cultural tradition can significantly be described in terms of its "things" orientation (Paglia 1990). The thing-making acts in the early phases of projects are directed at endowing various qualitative and conceptual flows with enough "thinghood" to prepare the ground for the materialized "execution" of the project to produce the finished plant. However, in projects qualities are never attached and detached in the more or less accidental way that circumstances and strategies, or some person's will, can bring about. Natural and cultural "realities" pronounce sentences and convict, keeping the objectification "in check," so to speak, within an "unfolding" project logic that defines the "social reality of construction."

As discussed earlier, standards are ways of measuring that make particular events and things commensurable and comparable. As Larsen has argued: "Processes of modernization are mainly about the development of new 'measuring' standards for the commensuration of particulars: writing, monetarization, individualization, codification of customary law, quantification of time and space" (2008: 221). As such the "managing revolution" from the turn of the twentieth century added another level to the modernization process. The engineering-based managerial revolution followed the scientific and the industrial revolution, and introduced a whole set of new measures and standards that objectified new realms of life and reality in the language of "systematization," "productivity," "efficiency," and "organizing." As literature has shown, managerial rationality soon expanded its technical realm and conquered the whole organization and ever-expanding areas of society, indeed becoming "the unquestioned pacemaker of the modern social order" (Shenhav 1999: 2). A Taylorist component, fused with neoliberal measures of finance control, is presently found in almost all areas of life, from the private sector to New Public Management (NEP) and civil society.

As we have seen, the knowledge economy has added yet another level to the managerial revolution. In the at least partial switch from a technocratic, engineering-based managerialism to an "accountocratic," finance-based money-managerialism, the managing of knowledge in terms of "managing management" has been accompanied by a thorough financialization of everything. We have seen how Hydro's project and other corporate activities, in conquering more and more areas of corporate professional life, are increasingly managed by financial control mechanisms. This demands a preparation of particular qualitative domains by what we might label "financial entification." As a continuation of Weber's notion of the disenchantment of the world, new areas are continuously included where wholes are divided into smaller, manageable units. Incentive systems, key performance indicators, best practices, innovative financial "products," and so on and so forth.

In the "acts of entification" (Larsen 2008) the objectified sign usurps the object. In this conception objectification has gone so far that qualities can be attached to and detached from objects, the self included, by strategy and will. Entification, seen as a process of making something inchoate into a "thinglike conceptual entity," is a precondition of thing-making and might be considered a premise for managing. A resistance to entification has been pointed out in Hydro, even if entification is considered to be a precondition of managing. The managing in Hydro is skeptical of conceit. Managing practices here should be dealing with the "serious stuff" close to the core processes of nature and culture. Launching fancy management slogans, "just words," would bring down even the president and CEO, he himself mused—much as the "heavenly mandate" was revoked from the emperors of China if the people became disgruntled enough. In sum, at a deeper level Hydro has also resisted the transformation of the abstract creational potential of the industrial arts into financially enchanted bubbles of money manager capitalism.

Qualifying Capitalism

By unearthing the characteristics of managing actions in Hydro investment projects we have revealed, both at Hydro and in general, a movement from engineering management to money managing. Not only has managing been differentially legitimated historically, cross-culturally, and in the present day, but capitalist economic activities more generally are also *qualitatively* different in terms of their wealth-creating potential and moral underpinnings. Thus both capitalist corporations and the managing of them *are* different, and they can be normatively assessed differently. There is a difference between financial and nonfinancial corporations, each linked with two radically different processes of contemporary capitalism—production and financial capitalism—and there are also huge differentiations both inside and in the relationships of these two broad categories.

Anthropologists of capitalism have recorded a variety of diverse cultures' different responses to capitalism's challenges, and they have done this by also analyzing systemic features of capitalism as a world system. Unfortunately, in doing so they often implicitly or explicitly endorse a singular view of "global capitalism." As Anna Tsing has argued, "it is easy to lose track of the specificity of particular capitalist niches.... Even as critics, we are caught in the hyperboles imagined by advocates of neoliberalism, structural adjustment, and transnationalization" (2002: 446). I have tried to avoid that problem, and rather sought to unfold some of the key internal differentiations and frictions within capitalism at some levels, and their more common features and overall deeper development at other levels.

Anthropology has documented how economic activities in small-scale or so-called premodern societies are of qualitatively different characteristics and are often relegated to different value spheres (Bohannan and Dalton 1965; Barth 1967). As discussed earlier, a frequently cited classification is that of Polanyi's three main forms of exchange ([1944] 2001): market (synchronous exchange), redistribution (delayed and asymmetrical or vertical exchange), and reciprocity (delayed and symmetrical or horizontal exchange). Although in Polanyi's conceptualization the three main forms are dynamic in the sense that each contains components of the others[4] and thus avoids being a mere classification, it seems that economic anthropology, almost as an unintended consequence of its favored economic objects of study, has unfortunately lumped modern capitalist activities together in all-encompassing categories like "market exchange."

Although at some level this is arguably warranted, I have shown the necessity of differentiating qualitatively between types of economic activities, based on various value considerations, in the "core" capitalist economy as well. Contemporary capitalism as it is embodied by neoliberalized financialization is, for example, arguably anti-market both in its foundations and implications. As noted above, it is rather particular forms of radical and reverse *redistribution* that constitute the hallmark of contemporary capitalism. The chief reasons for our lack of an extensive and shared vocabulary to describe these qualitative differences are the formalism and orthodoxies of mainstream economics. The current crisis illustrates the urgent need not to leave the advanced capitalist economy alone in the hands of economists, and rather for all scholarly disciplines to engage with this vital dimension of reality.

As discussed earlier, underlying most economic theorizing of capitalism, Marxist as well as liberal or bourgeois theories of value, is the purely quantitative concept of labor-time (excluding the Schumpeterian entrepreneurial function). Economic activities are measured and made commensurable by labor time accounting. However, as we have seen, different economic activities vary fundamentally in their potential to absorb new knowledge and technology, in their learning potential, and thus in their overall *potential* for "value creation"; to use the Hydro term designated specifically for the early phases of investment projects and more generally being a strong managerial and Hydro representative idiom.

Hydro's industrial business is situated exactly in those "source" activities that have vast potential for creating much wealth. In the moral discourse at Hydro, its "source" wealth-creating activities and their implications for society are a major justification of the company's existence and self-identification. On the macro level, on the one hand, it has been argued that it is not possible for a country in a capitalist economy to prosper through, for example, farming or simple services. On the other hand, we have shown that the whole capitalist logic of accumulation is in jeopardy when it reaches its own "wuthering heights"—when it reaches stages of such self-suggestiveness as to believe it is able to create value without productive input. With regard to such a stage, reached just prior to the recent collapse, history shows that a recurring theme is the finance economy's expansion and more or less decoupling from the "real" economy. For Braudel and Arrighi, this is a sign of "autumn" in the capitalist accumulation, and continuing the metaphor, the current crisis instantiates the unfolding of "winter."

Incidentally, the current crisis also coincides with the turning point crisis in the Schumpeter-Freeman-Perez techno-economic paradigm shifts (Perez 2002; Appendix). In the empirical material presented in the foregoing, the phase of high finance was marked by a rhetorical shift away from a focus on production toward concepts of value creation, and finally to "value assessment" or "value appreciation" and "value origination." When the practice of assessing and originating values takes on its own life, seen as more or less independent from the productive realities, we may talk about an "age of enchantment." Analyzing the contemporary capitalist predicament, as it is formed in the image of finance, we are forced to conclude, in opposition to notions of the "disenchantment of modernity," that it indicates the allure of capitalism, where the whole capitalist system was increasingly characterized by the "waving of the enchanter's wand," to paraphrase Comaroff and Comaroff (2000)—dramatic economic inequalities being a result.

With Hydro as an example, it has been illustrated how the nonfinancial industrial corporation, the Schumpeter-Chandlerian firm at the core of the twentieth century capitalist wealth-creating machinery, at the millennium moment has become the dog being wagged by the finance tail. The sometimes symbiotic relationship between finance and production has become asymmetrical and parasitic. Many of the socially detrimental effects of this form of "capitalism unleashed" have been recorded in the foregoing presentation. Hydro's activities can thus be positioned at a middle level of knowledge- and production-based, technology- and innovation-driven activities, where moral and cultural considerations are taken into account. They are indeed "directors of creation," but not creators of *any* creation—neither toothpaste, nor decoupled fantastically reified and "entified" finance innovations. As such Hydro constitutes in some respects an alternative force in a contemporary situation where the economics of the "world system" is analogous to the polarization between a rich elite and the poor masses of the ancien régime in France during the 1750s (Hart 2002: 27). Hydro is thus to some extent at odds with this rising of a "new feudalism" akin to pre-industrial society (Comaroff and Comaroff 2001: 291).

As documented earlier, the "thingified" sign abstractions do material work. They have profound effects of producing inequality and asymmetrical economic relations in "real life." The replacement of economic reality with its imitations and even by the simulacrum of financialization, to use postmodern language, produced an ethos or euphoria of enchanted beliefs at the millennium moment. The euphoria, now arguably cooling down quite dramatically as the crisis unfolds, is consistent with the historically recurring pattern of financially induced economic crisis in capitalism. At the height of potential crisis, before the breakdown, a spirit conducive of a "wonderful moment" has been found at the capitalist centers (Arrighi 1994; Braudel 1984; Appendix). The result, however, has been reenchanted delusional finance economy dominating economies and society alike through radical reverse redistribution.

Although Hydro, since about the millennium shift, has been changed in many ways by the increasing finance hegemony in the global economic system, it still stands out as an exemplary manifestation of the Schumpeterian-Chandlerian real wealth–creating corporation. When the capitalist logic reached its captivated moment of value origination and appreciation— creating money out of thin air, as it were—Hydro has, through subtle balancing acts, managed to both "hang on" and "surf the wave" of financialization, while still not abandoning reality. The value of Hydro had increased sixfold in just a few years after the millennium, and although it was responsible for parts of this value increase itself, what is more important is that Hydro competently have been riding the global wave of financialization while keeping with its industrial mandate. Despite soaring shareholder returns, the wave of finance has created severe operating constraints on investment projects and the operations of the company. Nevertheless, Hydro has stuck to its industrial and productive capitalist guns, carrying out investment projects for creating productive capacities, as well as corporate and societal wealth, by interpreting and mastering both nature and culture with the immaterial powers of the mind (and money) and the material powers of the body and the machine: of knowledge, technology, and money capital.

As such, Hydro and similar corporations can be seen to be working "real magic" by utilizing its silent and "spiritual" powers, which are based in what I have identified as an ontology of situated potentiality. In this fusion of nature and culture, its productive creations are continuously reproduced and transformed anew. Coupled with notions of social values and contingent moral conceptualizations, it contributes substantially to wealth and welfare creation at the societal level. In view of the actual practices performed in the name of the company, its brand slogan, "Progress of a different nature," is a fitting one.

Incarnations of a Different Nature

The interpretation and mastery of both nature and culture has been a recurring theme in this volume. The picture tells something about the notions of the human and nonhuman, about creatura and pleroma (Bateson 1979), that prevails in Hydro's project practices and corporate cultural artifacts and idioms. It tells a story about a view of nature, tapping into not only the romantic Rousseauist naturism that has dominated Western debate in many disguises, but also the cultural tradition of paganism, which portrays nature also in terms of its cruelty, evilness, and darkness, the diabolical and dangerous. Hydro's favorite slogan emphasizes this point: "Progress of a different nature." Nature is to be mastered and changed. In this way cultural progress might be brought forth. In the "Hydro Way" corporate culture profiling material, nature is portrayed as wild oceans and strong forces to be aesthetically enjoyed, interpreted, and technologically mastered (Røyrvik 2008a).

The beauty of nature is not unacknowledged, but it is not an innocent beauty; it is a beauty also of devastating allure and power. Hydro's cultural technology and products are perceived as saving and creating powers and are held to be comparable to products of art, placed in museums as well as in the everyday life of humans as cultural beings. The company's focus on environmental issues in recent years does not discard this picture. Rather, the saving power, as reflected upon by Heidegger (1977), of its "technologies" is highlighted at a time when nature has become cultured, when the distinctions between culture and nature have blurred again. Hydro seems to recognize also the danger, in Heidegger's sense of technology, inherent in its technological practices. At a time of environmentalism and personal self and identity constructivism, when nature has been objectified as a cultural product to be re-stored and remade, Hydro has been able to adapt its narrative to also come to the aid of, rather than just tame, this objectified and cultured nature.

Before the environmentalist and poststructuralist movements, when distinctions between nature and culture were stronger, the Hydro cultural Apollonian struggling with, tapping, and taming the forces of a "wild" Dionysian nature was more straightforward. It tamed the frowning waterfalls and cataracts of nature and conjured food out of thin air. Nature was up for a fight, and Hydro paved the way for the large-scale machine revolution and industrialization process of Norway, and thus for wealth and welfare production in the emerging industrial welfare state of Norway. As noted by one Hydro member: "The very premise of our existence was to help found a nation, not just make money." In the present public discourse nature is perceived as fragile and in need of cultural care. Nature's supreme danger, nevertheless, is found not far below the surface. If it is not cared for, and even if it is, it might come crashing down upon humanity with all its devastating force. This slight change of perception in recent years has been accompanied by a change in Hydro managerial rhetoric.

If leadership can be considered as embodied or personified *incarnations of organizational processes*, this change is understandable. The management anthropologist Sørhaug proposes this characteristic as a transhistorical and cross-culturally universal feature of leadership (2004: 31), although leadership is performed in a multiplicity of ways in highly heterogeneous contexts. As an implication of this change in managerial incarnation, Hydro's environmental impact—its danger versus saving power—is compared and assessed on a balance sheet of morals. And in addition to its corporate reporting on its environmental impact and "viability performance," Hydro has also embarked upon new adventures in alternative and renewable energies like solar and wind power.[5] In addition to its continuously increasing productivity, it has also reduced its greenhouse gas emissions per kilo of aluminium produced at its Norwegian smelters by 65 percent in the last fifteen years.[6] In its corporate communications it highlights the assertion "Climate matters." Related to such a shift, we might with Wagner say that "pollution is Culture viewed from the standpoint of nature" (1981: 70). The struggle and relationship between nature and culture is thus cast as a wider cultural drama.

On the moral side, referring to changes that have taken place since the Great Depression, Carl Kaysen spoke of a "qualitative break" in corporate goals and behavior in 1956, declaring that "the modern corporation is a soulful corporation" (Ho 2009: 195). Given the current predicament such statements might easily be brushed aside, but let us here use it to indicate that corporations are different, and that they even possibly "*could* be soulful, that profit maximization for 'owners' should not be the only guiding principle of business" (ibid.: 196). As shown, although successful in financialization up until the full unleashing of the crisis, Hydro has found itself ambiguously positioned within this framework, still imagining itself to be a permanent social institution committed to producing for the public good and the growth of both economy and society. Although shareholder value became the dominant liturgy even among industrial corporations such as Hydro, the death of the "good corporation" seems not to have been fully accomplished. The crisis has potential to help in the processes of its resuscitation and resurrection.

Notes

1. See Foster and Szlafjer (1984) for an overview.
2. Quoted in Wray (2009: 814).
3. This is not to imply, however, that accounting is a novel invention. In his magisterial four-volume work *The Social History of Art*, first published in 1951, Arnold Hauser discusses the emergence of capitalism and some fundamental changes that had already come about in the Renaissance: "The enterprising spirit of the pioneers lost its romantic, adventurous, piratical character and the conqueror became an organizer and an accountant, a carefully calculating merchant, managing his business with prudent circumspection" (1999: 19). On this note we might suggest that three elements—adventurous entrepreneurial spirits along with technocratic and "accountocratic" rationality—have been constituting characteristics in various configurations since capitalism's inception. I argue that Hydro in its current incarnation comprises all three of them. Hydro could as such be described as "quixotic and circumspect."
4. To be more precise, in Polanyi's scheme primitive or tribal societies, which are seen to be mainly reciprocal, also often show elements of redistribution. And on the other hand, in archaic societies that are mainly characterized by the redistributive form of exchange, reciprocity occurs. Furthermore, these two main forms are likewise still continuing under "market exchange" capitalism, reciprocity, e.g., in types of gift giving, and redistribution in terms of, e.g., state tax revenues that are redistributed through the various branches of the government.
5. Investing, e.g., in projects developing "ocean windmills" and in the solar company Norsun. See http://www.hydro.com/en/Press-room/News/Historic-news-archive/2006/November/Hydro-invests-in-solar-energy-company-Norsun/ (accessed 23 May 2011).
6. Eivind Reiten, "Askeladden og den globaliserte økonomien—Hydro i endring" [Askeladden and the globalized economy—a changing Hydro", my trans.] Kristofer Lehmkuhl lecture, Norges Handelshøyskole, Bergen, 26 September 2007.

Chapter 8

MANAGING IN A TOTAL CONTEXT OF CRISIS

... it was almost as if the global economy fell off a cliff.... It is time
to take finance back from the clutches of Wall Street's casino.
—L. Randall Wray, "The Rise and Fall of Money Manager Capitalism"

In nature we never see anything isolated,
but everything in connection with something else
which is before it, beside it, under it and over it.
—Johann Wolfgang von Goethe, *Conversations Of Goethe*

The foregoing presentation might in one sense be summarized as an exposition of "directors and directions of creation," as the former chapter
is titled. Its immediate focus has been the reproduction of relations in
the practices and conceptions constituting investment projects in Hydro.
It has investigated the managing actions of diverse "directors" and their
drive to make something, to create projects and new plants. In this sense
Hydro's managers are "directors of creation" in both technological and
economic, and thus cultural, aspects of this reality. The phrasing alludes
to a saying about God as the "Director of Nature." The analogy is fitting,
in at least two ways. First, the projects of Hydro are intimately related to
nature in a variety of ways. Hydro thrives upon knowledgeable technical
specialists' processing and creative transformation of nature's, and culture's, resources. They are dependent upon nature's "blessings" for provid-

ing some of these resources, even as they concurrently challenge, tame, and master nature, setting themselves "upon" nature and, belatedly, seeing themselves increasingly as custodians or caretakers of nature. In all of this they are continually interpreting and "creating" nature. In this interpretative quest, people and their relations are also made into objectified manifestations of nature, and thus the epic struggle and reinvention of nature and culture, both as differentiated and united, is instantiated and reproduced in particular capitalist trajectories. The explicit engagement of interpreting and mastering not only nature but also culture is strongly evident in the "cultural management" of projects. This is especially the case in the China projects as well as in Hydro's own considerable apparatus and means of communicating and representing its self-image, and thus its "presentation of self," in terms of "native" concepts of corporate culture and values, and—attuned to the sign of the times—through "branding" (see Røyrvik 2008a).

Secondly, the analogy fits because the knowledge tradition in which I argue Hydro projects situate themselves, the "knowledge and production-based other canon" tradition of economic theories and practice (Reinert 2007),[1] projects an image of man different from the purely maximizing and animal-like economic man. Rather, the image in which Hydro perceives itself is first that of *Homo faber;* "man the maker," man the producer, man the creator. As noted earlier, this is an image of man as potentially godlike, as active, creative, and compassionate, in contrast to the reactive, maximizing, and consuming economic man. *Homo faber* is humanity depicted as controlling the environment through tools, defining intelligence in terms of creating artificial objects, in particular tools to make tools, and indefinitely varying its makings. It is man as the intelligent tool-making animal, and it is conceptually related to notions about "deus faber," god the creator or the "making god."

A second, and arguably not so pronounced image of man that is an alternative and complement to both economic man and *Homo faber* in which Hydro partly sees itself is that of *Homo ludens,* the playing man. At Hydro, however, play is a serious business. It is not "playing around" with accidental amusements, but play as the joy of *making* something, creating something. It is serious play in the modernist sense, with a seriousness that I find serves as an antidote to the relativization of culture. Thus these images are reflective of the notion of the joy (and pain) of creation. Economic man is, of course, also a part of the picture. Also in the creational delusions of hyper-real, captivated capitalist relations do we find a potent yet detrimental blend of all these images of man. Before concluding with some reflections on the present predicament of deep crisis and the future of capitalist organizing and social relations, some main points to be drawn from the above exposition in terms of discourses on value spheres, modernity, and rationality will be briefly summarized in the following.

Managing, Reasons, and Rationalizations

It seems that Habermas's perspective on the modern rationalization of society can be criticized in the exact same manner in which he criticized Weber. It can be argued that it is not the *capitalist* realization of modernity per se that has determined a route to loss of meaning, anomie, and psychopathology. This image is but a mirror of the mainstream standard canon's representation of economic history and theory as a "dismal science" with a generally pessimistic outlook, and of animal-like economic man. This can be contrasted with the alternative trajectory of economic history, as portrayed in the optimistic outlook of the "other canon" in its tenet of the spiritually inspired producing man with *Schöpfungslust* and *Schöpfungskraft* (the power, pain, desire and joy of creation), and the "never ending frontier of knowledge." This alternative cannot simply be discarded as the "modern myth of progress" (von Wright 1994). Thus, a homogeneous view of the instrumental economic rationality system needs to be differentiated, in the first instance at least into the two idealized "canons." The Habermasian critique of Weber, that the latter is guilty of projecting an inevitability (an alternativelessness) into the historical trajectory he investigates (Vetlesen 2006), can thus also be applied to Habermas himself. He can be said to project inevitability into the capitalist trajectory he is investigating, while in the factual economic history and the history of economic thought and policy, several major and competing possibilities have existed.

The second major trajectory has at its core the potential for a vastly different route for society and humankind than that which currently is most extensively realized. In the "other canon," as exemplified by Hydro projects and managing, the value spheres are indeed integrated in diverse ways, and discourses on morality are a premise for economic activities, both rhetorically and practically. The full horizon of possibility is thus not taken into account when the historical analysis is based upon the rationalization of a capitalist society, when the latter is conceptualized as a version more or less reified as the "standard canon." As for Weber with the differentiation of the value spheres in general, for Habermas it is capitalism—the impersonal market forces accentuated by the profit motive, the alienating machine forces and exploitation of labor—that characterizes the path taken by modernity. This is seen as a path that by historical necessity has led to the colonization of the lifeworld, with its implications of loss of meaning in terms of cultural reproduction, anomie in terms of social integration, and psychopathology in terms of individual identity formation (Vetlesen 2006).

At Hydro, the profit motive as it is expressed in investment project managing is constituted in line with an MCM' logic (and not MM'), but is furthermore complemented with wider moral and societal concerns. Profit is to a large extent perceived as a means to and end rather than as an end in itself. Some significant quotes from Hydro executives and employees, gathered through a major culturally self-reflexive "brand process" in the company, illustrates this quite well:

> For better, for worse, we've used profit in ways that let us contribute more over time—not just to customers and shareholders, but to people generally.

> Our structure is complicated because we wanted to ensure that there was interesting industrial activity for our people. Our evolution is not driven solely in pursuit of profit.

> We have a hard time arguing for profitability alone, as though that's all that counts. Our history looks at money as a way to ensure self-sufficiency for others as well as ourselves.

> I think on a certain level people do not comprehend this constant drive for more profitability. We think to ourselves, well, we have enough profits to serve our purpose.

Seen in such a light, in the perspective of the wider empirical descriptions above and bearing in mind different attitudes toward the profit motive, Hydro is a somewhat illustrative exemplar of what has been described as the capitalist spirit of the Renaissance: "the profit motive and the so-called 'middle-class virtues,' acquisitiveness and industry, frugality and respectability" (Hauser 1999: 20). My argument in the discussion here is that the tradition of the "other canon" provides an alternative capitalist historical route that demonstrates the limits of the colonization thesis. It provides a basis for the argument that it was neither the rationalization of society per se (the differentiation of the value spheres), as was Weber's argument, nor the selectivity dictated by the historical trajectory of capitalism per se, as Habermas argues, but rather the hegemony of the "standard canon," the barter, trade, exchange, finance, and consumer tradition of capitalism, that might be accountable for the colonization thesis.

It is not the profit motive or the machinization of society per se, but the specific culturally contingent capitalist ethic(s), or lack thereof, that guide the emergence of these phenomena and dress them up in particular clothing that should be the focus of analysis. Shenhav (1999), for example, argues questionably that managing emerged homogeneously as totally separated from morality and the sphere of politics. The Norwegian tradition and Hydro examples show such generalizations to be historical reifications. More credibility is to be found in Schumpeter's ([1942] 2008) view that imperialism is not a *necessary* feature of capitalism. In this respect I am in agreement with Habermas's description of modernity as an inconclusive, unfinished project. A capitalist trajectory based upon the "other canon" provides an alternative, a powerful force of resistance coming from within the capitalist economic system itself and directed, at least to some degree, against the colonizing powers of the "standard system." As has been illustrated throughout the book, Hydro exemplifies tendencies of capitalist rationalization of both the standard and the other canon type, but fundamentally, I argue, its social organization and cultural legacy as instituted in its "social reality of construction" and its particular type of managing practices and economic activities, underpinned by specific values, show its profound belonging to and embeddedness in the other canon.

This outline may immediately raise some objections. If neoliberalized fiancialization is indeed a triumph of the last quarter of the century, how can it possibly be accountable for the trajectory produced by capitalism? One answer is to reject the core tenets of both Weber and Habermas concerning the differentiation of the value spheres and the subsequent domination of the instrumental system. Another possible solution is to argue that, seen through the lens of the other canon, the differentiation of the value spheres would not necessarily lead to disassociation of the "big three," but to a possibility of differentiation accompanied by integration. This is to say, again, that it is the dominance of the "standard canon" that has increasingly led to the disassociation from the subsequent colonization trajectory, a path that realized its full "potential" during the last quarter-century or so.

Mixed Regimes of Rationality

In such a perspective, the main faculties of rationality, as outlined in Aristotle's concepts of Theoria (*sophia*), Praxis (*phronesis*), and Poiesis (*tekhne*) and since then discussed and changed both in content, relationships, rank and position, make an interesting contribution. I have argued that in one sense the practices of industrial investment project managing at Hydro, and by empirical generalization Hydro corporate cultural practices, are instantiations of modernity at its "height," as it were. On the other hand, to paraphrase Latour's quote-friendly title, the same practices and relations that constitute them "have never been modern" (1993). I have shown

that in certain respects the Hydro case also illuminates a strong historical continuity of Western cultural thought and practice reaching back to
antiquity and notions of, most importantly, Poiesis (*tekhne*).

Moreover, a space for both Praxis and Theoria was found in the midst
of Hydro's "most modern" of practices, exemplified not least by its research-based industrial project managing practices, i.e., its scientific, industrial, and managerial legacies' alliance between theory and skills-based,
or metaphysical and physical, production. In the practices of managing
investment projects, arguably defined as capitalist "oikos"-activities par
excellence—at the core, as it were, of instrumental, economic object rationality—pockets of activities of goal-*finding*, of collective and communicative interactive wit and will formation, and forms of "self-legislation"
were discovered. These aspects bear stronger affinity to the moral value
domain of modernity, and also to the Praxis and Theoria domain of antiquity (Øfsti 1999). In Hydro's various emphases on creational aspects of its
work, strong legitimation has also been found in the aesthetic-expressive
value domain, to use Habermas's conceptualization. In the Hydro case we
found empirical illustrations of both diasynchronous continuity and dramatic changes in the reconfigurations of rationality and validity claims
to knowledge. Thus, in the midst of practices of capitalist, industrial, and
profane production, ostensibly clear and unambiguous instantiations of
Habermas's cognitive-instrumental value domain, we find alternative
spaces bringing forth other types of rationality and validity claims.

The rationality shift accompanying the turn to finance—a turn I argue
underpins fundamentally the legitimation of managing at the millennium
moment—has important significance for the debate on contemporary modernity. I have shown that from its technocratic engineering foundations,
neoliberalization transformed the legitimating basis of management to a
large extent into economics, finance, and accounting. This "money manager capitalism" is significant as both a cause and effect of the neoliberal
culture complex. We have seen managing as another, crucial and dominating discourse in the globalization of modernity, adding to the medium
machinery of the Western-produced abstract package of cross-cultural
intercommunications infrastructure (which makes worldviews comparable and commensurable), of abstract autonomous individuals, abstract
time and work, abstract value, and abstract space. Managing has created
and disseminated a new nomenclatural layer of standardization, systematization, classification, productivity, efficiency, etc., fueling modernity.
However, as we have seen, these processes have not been absolutely mo-
nological and all-embracing. Hydro in some respects instantiates alternatives and, to some extent, counter-constructive managing trajectories.

The neoliberalized shift in managing legitimation from engineering to economy, finance, and accounting has brought about changes in both managing practices and ideology. We have witnessed a shift of emphasis in the managing elites, indicating an underlying turn from technocratic to "accountocratic" rationality. The particular accountocratic rationality of neoliberalized modernity is an aspect or phase, however, transformed by a financialized economy of signs, of "virtualism" and "hyperreality." We might appreciate that the crisis "called the bluff" of that economy and laid bare some of the mechanisms of turning "virtual paper" into gold and/or shit: a socialism for the rich, with gold for the few and shit for the many. This is what I have chosen to describe as a reenchantment of modernity, a captivating and *captivated* capitalism that distributes values upward in the system. It also signifies, however, that in the midst of the cognitive-instrumental machinery, which according to Habermas and others is colonizing the lifeworld, validity claims based in both the morality and the aesthetic-expressive value domains have been discovered, in sum comprising what I call "mixed regimes of rationality." Here morality, aesthetics, the good, and the beautiful, notions with affinity to the Theoria, Praxis (*phronesis*), and Poiesis (*tekhne*) conceptualizations of antiquity, are also enacted in practice—in some senses radically changed, but nevertheless carrying with them continuity.

The Medium-Range View: Levels in Capitalism

In his analysis of the decline of capitalism, Schumpeter stresses the important factor of the change in the bourgeois kind of profit motive—the family as an important means of the capitalist engine of production. The family-oriented profit motive of bourgeois values kept up the long-term view, as benefits were perceived to be harvested by the lineage rather than for immediate consumption. In fact, he notes that

> the capitalist order entrusts the long-run interests of society to the upper strata of the bourgeoisie. They are really entrusted to the family motive operative in those strata. The bourgeoisie worked primarily in order to invest, and it was not so much a standard of consumption as a standard of accumulation that the bourgeoisie struggled for and tried to defend against governments that took the short-run view. ([1942] 2008): 160)

Possibly realizing the potentially controversial aspect of this argument, he adds the following footnote: "It has been said that in economic matters 'the state can take the longer view.' But excepting certain matters outside of party politics such as conservation of natural resources, it hardly ever does" (ibid.: 161). Schumpeter's argument is that with the decline of the family motive, the time-horizon of the businessman shrinks, roughly to his life expectation.

In a research interview Reiten promoted the position that he and Hydro indeed are taking societies' long view, while politics too frequently is concerned with narrow interests. As a custodian of a century-old continuous wealth-generating corporation, his words cannot be dismissed out of hand, not least since he also knows top-level politics as an insider. In relation to specific investment projects, the time horizon is considerably shorter than the time frame imagined by Schumpeter's family motive–driven capitalist society of bourgeoisie entrepreneurs. However, as I have shown, in this scheme projects represent the reproduction of capitalist relations on all levels, from project to corporation to "system."

Of particular importance is Hydro's claim that it represents societies' long-term view. This might be seen as a specific version of capitalist society, at odds with the financialized economy and consumer culture. Also, if we take into account the substantial difference in the overall conception of time in the present globalized economic order of the transport- and ICT-enabled, interconnected, "time-compressed" planet, with its real-time market transactions and public media galore, there might be even more truth in the Hydro CEO's contention. Considering Hydro's hundred-year history as Norway's leading industrial company and an important global actor, which is a highly unusual long-term resilience in the world of corporate life cycles, the assertion seems to have even more legitimacy.

Restating also Schumpeter's prediction of the obsolescence of capital's entrepreneurial function and the consequence that capital cannot survive for long either, the implication for the middle-class bourgeois function in society is also striking. If the entrepreneurial function fades, in the end "it also expropriates the bourgeoisie as a class which in the process stands to lose not only its income but also what is infinitely more important, its function" ([1942] 2008): 134). Schumpeter concludes that the bourgeoisie depends on the entrepreneur economically and sociologically, and as a class "lives and will die with him, though a more or less prolonged transitional stage—eventually a stage in which it may feel equally unable to die and to live—is quite likely to occur, as in fact it did occur in the case of the feudal civilization" (ibid.). The question we must ask is whether we have reached this stage in the present day.

A cross-cultural review of "pre-capitalist" notions of "money and the morality of exchange" found that "the vast majority of cultures make some space for exchanges which display many of the features which are sometimes, as in our own society, associated with monetary exchange" (Bloch and Parry 1989: 29). Nevertheless, a recurring cross-cultural pattern of two related but separate "transactional orders" emerged, comprising "on the one hand transactions concerned with the reproduction of the long-term social or cosmic order; on the other, a 'sphere,' of short-term transactions concerned with the arena of individual competition" (ibid.: 24).

Although arguably interdependent, the first is typically linked with morality and the second with political economy. The articulation of the two spheres shows that they need to be both separate and related, and thus transformative processes of conversions between them become imperative. Conversions from the short-term individualistic cycle to enable the reproduction of the long-term cycle are morally evaluated in positive terms, while the opposite, acquisitive individuals' diversion of resources from the long-term cycle for their own short-term interests, is morally sanctioned negatively and in stronger terms. Bloch and Parry speculate that the ideology of capitalism reflects something completely different from the logic of the two transactional orders, or possibly that the values of the short-term order have expanded to the long-term cycle. Indeed, echoing neoclassical economics thought and ideas traced back to Adam Smith and the wider philosophical debate about passions and interests, capitalism in this view has possibly developed into an all-encompassing order and theory "in which it is *only* unalloyed private vice that can sustain the public benefit" (ibid.: 29).

Thus again, we see the dominance of the "standard canon" in assessing capitalist economic activities, and the image of man and social relations constituted within it. Taking both the recurring and consistent pattern of the two transactional orders of precapitalist societies and the "other canon" capitalist tradition into consideration might help to better explain the heated and morally charged public discourse surrounding, for instance, the Hydro managers' stock options compensation schemes. When they diverted a small portion of value from the company, seen as a vehicle for societal reproduction, into managers' own individual pockets, it seems that the political and public reaction to a large extent interpreted the options schemes as converting value from the long-term cycle to the short-term. Indeed, the prime minister of Norway described President and CEO of Hydro Eivind Reiten as a "representative" (*tillitsmann*) of society. In this picture, we might possibly conclude that Hydro and its managers incarnate more accurately modern society's "medium-range view." And in this sense we might appreciate that while corporate managers had become powerful and representative of "vested interests," they had also become trustees for society as a whole (Ho 2009), an image that resisted the neoclassical, and neoliberal, dictates of the corporation as solely a financial entity. Corporate managerialism still retained an image, and a self-image, of organizational and social responsibilities.

Deep Crisis in Contemporary Capitalism

Corporations like Hydro, and their managers, are both hailed and demonized, seen as positioned somewhere between the short and the long-term orders. Just as the contradictory representations of money universally as both "devilish acid or as instrument and guarantor of liberty" (Bloch and Parry 1989: 30) can be explained from the two different perspectives of the transactional orders, so can Hydro and its managers' ambiguous public positioning. Perceived as an agent of acquisitive short-term grasping for the "love of gain" or the "love of lucre"—strong moral themes in capitalism's inception (Hirschman [1977] 1997)—or as "avarice," the latter a term frequently used to characterize Hydro managers' motives in the stock options debate, Hydro represents the devilish nearsightedness. Perceived as a custodian of society's long-term welfare and development, Hydro represents a saving power of moral valor and respect. Indeed, in light of the perspective of differential ontologies and implicate orders advocated here, we might also discard the notion of *two* transactions orders and rather imagine a landscape of multiple interconnected levels or orders of capitalism.

Furthermore, it is a highly questionable tenet that finance capital in its contemporary constitution should embody the long-term view. It seems very difficult to align the present financialized system of "accumulation by redistributive dispossession" with a long-term view for the common good. For Schumpeter, a critical sign toward a change into a more short-term time horizon is when the capitalist "drifts into an anti-saving frame of mind and accepts with an increasing readiness anti-saving *theories* that are indicative of a short-run *philosophy*" ([1942] 2008): 161, italics in original). As discussed above, the age of neoliberalization is constituted on anti-saving theories and short-run philosophies and frames of mind. The crux of the neoliberal financialized global economic system can be described as a debt economy, a pyramid-game of "virtuous" financial cycles, of "borrowing virtual money into existence" in new and innovative ways—and thus in direct opposition to a saving view. Indeed, it has been termed a gigantic Ponzi scheme (Wray 2009: 821).

How has Hydro acted in this respect? Varying to some extent during its history, Hydro has always been a financially solid company. It has never ventured upon hugely debt-financed adventures. This path was chosen in the face of often considerable scorn from investors and other opinion makers, who characterized Hydro as a conservative, overly careful, boring company. Hydro thus seems, when it comes to its own financial situation and despite the other "enchanted adjustments" in the name of shareholder value and value-based management, to have bought relatively little into the "casino capitalism" of the last quarter of a century. At a time when the Norwegian state, as outlined earlier, is managing one of the world's largest investment funds and has become a financial speculative state of considerable proportions, by the end of 2010 holding values in its pension fund surpassing NOK 3 trillion (USD 525 billion), Hydro has still continued to invest circumspectly in industrially productive projects, at home and abroad.

In a neoliberalized age of short-term profits, financially driven "casino capitalism," self-interested nearsightedness, and speculation as the spirit of the age, from the capital market state through to the "gambling individual" (Comaroff and Comaroff 2000), the Hydro projects and corporate strategy of productive investments can be reframed and in one sense reassessed as rather somewhat risky and bold. We might say that the image of individualistic utilitarianism is alien to the context of a modern corporate capitalist ethic that enjoys working for the future more or less irrespective of the possibility of harvesting the crops "instantly." While seen as positioned somewhere in the "medium-range view" with its industrial investment projects, in Hydro's boldness and "riskiness" we thus also find, in the midst all of its modern rationality, a kind of life-inspiring madness.

State capitalism was cast in a new form by the global neoliberal culture complex. Emerging from the breakdown of the Bretton Woods system in the early 1970s, it came to a captivated climax when the formation of a neoliberal (neoconservative) predatory state enabled an "unlimited" financialized takeover of the economy. In several senses one might say that a neoliberal plutocracy was formed, a government by and for the wealthy strata of society, largely by dispossessing the public at large and creating large-scale patterns of economic inequalities. The state was transformed, to varying degrees across the globe, into a facilitator for finance and its ever-increasing and innovative rent-seeking practices. It was a capital takeover, in the sense of both a major takeover and dominance of finance over politics and culture and a takeover of capital itself. Capital at large was reconstituted in its "purest" MM' finance form—captivated. The neoliberal triumph of finance was arguably a reinvention and transformation of the mercantile Anglo-Dutch banking and finance tradition, as distinct from several traditions of more industrially oriented banking that focused on how to best finance a "higher economic horizon".

Enabled by the structural crisis of the 1960s and 1970s and the formation of the neoliberal state, the economic system was pushed toward accelerating "virtuous cycles" of financial accumulation. It developed through the structural phases that "Minsky labeled hedge, speculative and finally Ponzi" (Wray 2009: 821). The allure of the captivated system was suddenly repelled in 2008. When discussing the bank bailouts, the Ponzi character of the system in its collapsing phase was succinctly noted by Eliot Spitzer, the former governor and attorney-general of New York who built a reputation as "the Sheriff of Wall Street" for his prosecutions of corporate crime: "You look at the governing structure of the New York [Federal Reserve], it was run by the very banks that got the money. This is a Ponzi scheme, an inside job."[2] A new type of capitalism emerged where large segments of the capitalist elite created, successfully for a while, a neoliberal cultural complex along political, economic, and social dimensions in which they "could have their cake and eat it" (Palma 2009: 863). Indeed, neoliberal financialization became in large parts a *racket* in which the few misled and exploited the many on a scale "too big to believe" (Røyrvik 2009; Krugman 2010).

In some senses we might say that the Las Vegas–style cocktail of gambling, gangsters, government, and greed became an open model not only of America, but of capitalism itself: "The city [Las Vegas] was not only a reflection of culture and values and the near-complete rule of money in American life.... By the millennium, the national surrender of democracy to oligarchy in the United States ... had simply come into the open, where it had long been in Las Vegas" (Denton and Morris 2001: 391–392). However, as the above documentation shows and the current crisis instantiates, a capitalist system characterized by predatory accumulation by dispossession seems "doomed to self-destruct" (Palma 2009: 864). Adding to the established neoliberal new ancien régime of inequality, since the eve of the global economic crisis in 2007 about 30 million more people worldwide had become unemployed by 2010, according to the International Labor Organization (ILO 2011).

As shown in the historical analysis of the waning of US hegemony provided by Giovanni Arrighi (1994; 2007), the *signal* crisis of the American empire occurred in the 1970s with the decoupling of the dollar from the gold standard, the Vietnam War, and the first oil crisis, while the *terminal* crisis of the US political economic hegemony can be identified by the invasions of Iraq and Afghanistan and the global military "bases of empire" (cf. Lutz 2009) on the one hand, and the systemic financial crisis on the other. As the history of failing empires shows, in the final stages militarism and economic decline go hand in hand (Kennedy 1989).

Two options seem readily available for continuing capitalist control in the face of a structural crisis: war and finance (Hardt and Negri 2009: 288). The war option was strongly pursued, especially in the post-9/11 wars with the invention of the "global war on terror." As demonstrated, it has failed miserably and inflicted horrors and suffering. The US invention of the so-called global war on terror was a desperate measure to fabricate enemies, thus creating cultures of fear that in turn would justify protection by continuing and expanded US global political dominance and unilateralism, allowing the US to preserve its waning economic hegemony through political means and military force. But as the history of falling empires reveals, "military 'security' alone is never enough" (Kennedy 1989: 696). The financialization option was much more effective, for a long time, until it was also exhausted. Warmongering and financialization both reached their interconnected climax of racketeering and crisis in the first part of the new millennium (Røyrvik 2009). The immediate question is whether the unprecedented rescue efforts by the interstate system to get everything "back to normal" will reinstate the basic tenets of the neoliberal culture complex on yet a more dangerous level, reinflate another delusional bubble, and reinvigorate new ways of racketeering, or whether the state system, and capitalism along with it, will transform itself out of its current predatory condition.

Downfall, or a Phoenix for the Future?

The preceding presentation leads to some final reflections, intended to enable creative and transformational thinking going forward, on the centuries-old discussion of the characteristics and relationships between the passions, interests, and reason of human nature, and their impact upon economy, society, and humanity. The current crisis illuminates the prospect of substantial and quite immediate changes in the capitalist system, of a possible downfall at least of the present form of financialized money manager capitalism, or of capitalist history, or worse. Contemplating the possibilities of both a future postcapitalist world empire and a postcapitalist world market, Arrighi warns about the possible grave implications of the escalating violence that has accompanied the collapse of the Cold War world order in the concluding sentence of his *The Long Twentieth Century*: "Whether this would mean the end of just capitalist history or of all human history, is impossible to tell" (1994: 356). Is the current crisis pointing toward a fundamental downfall of capitalist society as we know it, or will the crisis serve as a transition to reproduce and transform the system on yet another scale, as it has done for about six hundred years? If we choose to see opportunity and potentiality in the crisis, a new form of economic system, however radically new, can possibly rise like a phoenix out of the ashes of the current predicament. At such a critical juncture, lessons from the arguments and conflicting perspectives at the birth of capitalism are highly relevant.

In his fascinating review, Albert O. Hirschman (1997) described the complex philosophical discourse accompanying the emergence of capitalism, where the economic "interests" came to be constructed as the way destructive passions were tamed and transformed to become custodians of the public good. He shows how private vices related to the "love of lucre" and the acquisitive instinct involved in commercial activities mingled self-seeking with rationality in the concept of "interested affection," or simply "interests." As long as they defeated other and more deadly sins and passions of human nature, such as ambition, lust for power, or sexual lust, these vices of greed and avarice could be transformed into collective virtues to the benefit of society as a whole. Moneymaking and commerce became a calm passion, innocent and *doux*. This is a position revealingly illustrated by a remark of Dr. Johnson from 1775: "There are few ways in which man can be more innocently employed than in getting money" (quoted in Hirschman 1997: 58). In a similar vein, advocating the acquisitive drive as a calm but simultaneously strong passion, the leading philosopher of the time, David Hume, hailed capitalism in his essay "Of Interest": "It is an infallible consequence of all human industrious professions, to … make the love of gain prevail over the love of pleasure" (ibid.: 66). Hume saw capitalism as enabling and activating some benign human proclivities while also able to repress and perhaps, as Hirschman notes, "atrophy the more destructive and disastrous components of human nature" (ibid.).

This view is echoed in another language in the thesis adhering to Adam Smith, today the premise followed in mainstream standard economics, that the basic relationships between humans are competitive and driven by self-interest, yet through the division of labor individually ego-oriented acquisitions in sum produce cooperation and the common good. The contemporary crisis has initiated a long-awaited mainstream questioning of these premises, as exemplified for example by Samuel Brittan writing for the *Financial Times:* "The most difficult issues, however, arise on the moral side. The assumption that the pursuit of self-interest within the rules and conventions of society will also promote the public interest is not likely to survive."[3]

Positive and negative denotations of international commercial activities and the management of such have been evoked throughout history in a long train of Western thought. Indeed, cross-culturally and transhistorically, money and commercial activities display patterns of doubleness, of denunciation and idolization (Bloch and Parry 1989). The contemporary delusional hyperreality of financialization brings the amazing Freudian connection between money, psychopathology, and anality to the forefront. Harvey notes, in relation to the "passage from modernity to postmodernity": "Baudrillard depicts postmodern culture as an 'excremental culture,' and money = excrement both in Baudrillard's and Freud's view (some hints of that sentiment can be found in Marx)" (1992: 102). Indeed, in his early writings Marx talked about money as the "universal whore" (Giddens 1990: 22). Moneymaking as devilish "filthy lucre" is a recurring philosophical theme of historical capitalism (Brown 1991; Hirschman 1997). The timeless conclusion of Ferenczi's "The Ontogenesis of the Interest in Money" vividly illustrates the point: "After what has been said money is seen to be nothing other than deodorized, dehydrated shit that has been made to shine" (1950: 327). This might arguably be the unbeatable height of psychoanalytical analysis of the "dirty business" of moneymaking.

On the other hand, Jacob Viner, for example, traced the idea of a favorable interest of providence in international trade back to the fourth century A.D. (Hirschman 1977: 60). In a similar vein we might interpret Paglia's contention that capitalism, "gaudy and greedy" but also glorious, can trace its roots through aesthetics back to ancient Egypt (1990: 37). As Paglia's statement also signifies, regarding the omnipotent contemporary economic force best known today as "the corporation," businessmen, politicians, academics, and the "common people" alike have been highly suspicious of this organizational form since its emergence in the late sixteenth century. In fact, following the collapse of the South Sea Company and tired of the stockbroker tricksters swarming in London's Exchange Alley, the English Parliament banned the corporation for fifty years in 1720 (Bakan 2004). Why could it not happen again? As Adam Smith himself noted in *The Wealth of Nations*, "The pretence that corporations are necessary for the better government of the trade, is without any foundation" ([1776] 2003: 178).

While a company seen as a form of purposeful organization engaged in economic transactional activities might arguably be said to have been a hallmark institution in every society throughout cultural history, the economic organization of the corporation has a very specific cultural process of origin and trajectory of development. The two decisive moments in its genesis that have concerned us here were, first, the idea conceived in the mid eighteenth century of separating company ownership, the shareholders, from directors and managers, and second, the victory of the idea of "limited liability" on behalf of investors, and subsequently the creation of the "limited-liability joint-stock company" as a legal person (that can be sued) in the mid nineteenth century (Micklethwait and Wooldridge 2003; Bakan 2004). And not only can the corporate body be sued, but it comes seemingly with full-blood emotions. In the period when the media focus related to the Hydro options case raged at its worst, Reiten allegedly announced in a newspaper interview: "The biggest burden is nevertheless to see that our employees and Hydro as a company are in pain" (my trans.).[4]

A Tragedy or Triumph of the Commons?

At its inception, the idea of separating owners and managers was believed by many to be a recipe for corruption and scandal. As noted earlier, Adam Smith warned of this in *The Wealth of Nations* because managers could not be entrusted to "steward other people's money." "'Negligence and profusion' would inevitably result when businesses organized as corporations" (quoted in Bakan 2004: 6). And indeed, while managers had the upper hand in corporate affairs throughout much of the period of "organized capitalism" in the twentieth century, power has changed hands again with neoliberalism and the financialized shareholder surge. To a large extent managers were at least "bought" by incentive schemes like stock options, which caused the managers to become owners themselves. Engineering managers were to a large extent transformed or substituted by "money managers," and capitalism at large transformed into an enchanted, financialized money manager capitalism that ultimately was doomed to fail. The imminent collapse was signaled not least by the derivatives "death star." Overshadowing planet Earth with its size ten times that of global GDP, it symbolized the opulence and spectacle, and arguably the imminent demise, of Man the money manager. To be sure, had there been political will the derivative bubble could have been quite easily disposed of. Even Myron S. Scholes, one of the economists who won the "Sveriges Riksbank Prize in Economic Sciences in Memory of Alfred Nobel" (the so-called Nobel Prize in Economics) in 1997 for his contribution to finding "a new method to determine the value of derivatives,"[5] says that "the solution is really to blow up or burn the OTC [over-the-counter] market, the CDSs [credit default swaps] and swaps and structured products, and let us start over."[6] But it seems that this simple, yet possibly profound, solution to the derivatives problem is not being acted upon by politicians or regulators.

However, as the present work has documented, there are multiple trajectories in terms of managing corporations and in terms of capitalism, in both its diverse manifestations and as a world system. The question is what will take over after the failures of the financial takeover. One can hope for the formation of a more robust and stable economic system that serves democratic processes and distributive practices for increasing equality. Significantly, the finance crisis has spurred a widespread renewed interest in Islamic banking practices due to their relative success during the crisis. Both the US Treasury Department and the Vatican have recently shown interest in Islamic banking, and the French finance minister has announced France's intention to make Paris "the capital of Islamic banking" (Tobin 2009). Islamic banking and finance present alternatives to usury and a fundamentally debt-based economy. This system is described by, for example, British expert in Islamic finance El Diwany (2003). In a presentation at Cambridge University in 2002 he referred to a United Nations Human Development Report from 1997 that wrote that debt relief in Africa alone would save the lives of about 21 million children in three years. El Diwany is quoted as saying:

> The UNDP does not say that the bankers are killing the children, it says that the debt is. But who is creating the debt? The bankers are of course. And they are creating the debt by lending money that they have manufactured out of nothing. In return the developing world pays the developed world USD 700 million per day net in debt repayments.[7]

Alternative examples that might inspire a thorough reorganizing of the global economy do exist, both historically and cross-culturally. It is not overly pessimistic, however, to acknowledge that the present predicament leaves a huge open space for a more or less popular resurgence of right-wing, totalitarian, xenophobic, and fascist-like cultural formations. The political theorist Sheldon Wolin argues that the current political system in the US already is characterized by what he calls "managed democracy" and "inverted totalitarianism" (2008). While representing the antithesis of constitutional power, this is a system that represents the political coming of age of corporate power. The main argument is that it has been possible for a new form of totalitarianism, an inverted one different from the classical one, to evolve from an allegedly strong democracy. Inverted totalitarianism is totalizing in its obsession with "control, expansion, superiority, and supremacy" (ibid.: ix), but different from the classical versions in that it instead projects power "inward," by strategies of cooptation, the appearance of freedom, and political disengagement rather than mass mobilization. This system, argues Wolin, has emerged more or less unnoticed and in continuity with national politics. A tightening and strengthening of inverted totalitarianism is a likely product of the contemporary crisis, and I suggest that money manager capitalism and managed democracy can be seen as two sides of the same coin.

In closing I want finally to strike a note of optimism. The crisis also represents a potential for major changes and transformations in a constructive and positive direction. The circumstances of a total context of crisis are an invitation to dialogue and action for substantial rethinking and reshaping of the foundational premises upon which economy and society rest. Arguably Hardt and Negri provide the most refreshing and imaginative recent contribution to that respect in their book *Common Wealth* (2009). Providing a catalogue of possibilities for political action and resistance "within and against Empire," they seek to transcend the narrow space provided by dichotomies like socialism-capitalism and public-private, and rather unfold a much greater space of potentiality in a rethinking of the sociality of *the common*. Included in their notion of the common are sharing and participation, primarily in regard to all of the common wealth of the material world, that is, all of nature's resources that classical political texts consider an inheritance of humanity as a whole—"the air, the water, the fruits of the soil" (2009: viii). Secondly, their concept of the common includes "those results of social production that are necessary for social interaction and further production, such as knowledge, languages, codes, information, affects, and so forth" (ibid.). Their concern relates to the ecological and socioeconomic frameworks that might bring about the maintenance, production, and distribution of the common in both the above senses.

The two most central concepts for the realization a new paradigm of the common are "poverty" and "love." Neither is in scarce supply in the present day. In the concept of the poor, Hardt and Negri find opportunities to question traditional class designations, "investigate with fresh eyes how class composition has changed and look at people's wide range of productive activities inside and outside wage relations" (2009: xi). The challenge they seek to resolve is to find ways to translate the possibilities of the poor into power to make a common world. Love is the other conceptual leg investigated as a road to expand the power of the common. Reaching back to historically older notions of love, they investigate love as "a means to escape the solitude of individualism but not, as contemporary ideology tells us, only to be isolated again in the private life of the couple or the family" (ibid.: xii). The challenge also here is to translate a notion of love into a political concept that reorients it toward the recreation of social life in the image of the common.

The historical subjects and agents of the major political changes to come are still undecided. The cooptation of political elites by neoliberal ideology and money managers, and thus the "managed democracy" state of affairs, seems to deprive political power of both imagination and real will to advocate true change. Meanwhile the political challenges are considerable, given the balancing act of addressing the short-term need to prevent global depression by stopping the financial collapse, while simultaneously both directing a medium-term serious deleveraging of the financial economy (to get debt levels more in balance with GDP) and designing for the long term a robust new financial and economic architecture that serves productive, democratic, social, and egalitarian needs. Without a massively engaged, demanding, and active public, the fundamental changes that are needed are unlikely to be realized. However, this total context of crisis is a great moment for the mobilization of the common and a rethinking of all aspects of the common wealth. If this can be accomplished, the cultural *tragedy* of the commons reaching its climax of crisis under neoliberal financialization might, like a phoenix for the future, be transformed into a *triumph* of the commons. Critical to this end is a sincere and widespread recognition that human beings are all entangled "parts of the whole," as Albert Einstein put it.[8] A space of opportunity, open and vast, awaits its realization.

Notes

1. For publications and bibliographies documenting and extending the "other canon" tradition, see http://www.othercanon.org/ (accessed 19 April 2010).
2. D. Tencer, "Spitzer: Federal Reserve Is a 'Ponzi Scheme, an Inside Job'," *Raw Story*, 25 July 2009. http://rawstory.com/08/news/2009/07/25/spitzer-federal-reserve-is-a-ponzi-scheme-an-inside-job/ (accessed 5 December 2009).
3. S. Brittan, "A Catechism for a System that Endures," *Financial Times*, 30 April 2009. http://www.ft.com/cms/s/0/6e92328a-35b4-11de-a997-00144feabdc0,dwp_uuid=ae1104cc-f82e-11dd-aae8-000077b07658.html?nclick_check=1 (accessed 9 December 2009).
4. "Det som likevel er den største belastningen, er å se at våre ansatte og Hydro som selskap har det vondt," *Dagens Næringsliv*, 8 August 2007.
5. For both the correct name of the prize and the award in 1997 to Robert C. Merton and Myron S. Scholes, see http://nobelprize.org/nobel_prizes/economics/laureates/1997/index.html (accessed 27 April 2010). The content of the work awarded was, in a bit more detail, the following: "Robert C. Merton and Myron S. Scholes have, in collaboration with the late Fischer Black, developed a pioneering formula for the valuation of stock options. Their methodology has paved the way for economic valuations in many areas. It has also generated new types of financial instruments and facilitated more efficient risk management in society." http://nobelprize.org/nobel_prizes/economics/laureates/1997/press.html (accessed 27 April 2010).
6. "Scholes Advises 'Blow Up' Over-the-Counter Contracts," Bloomberg.com. http://www.bloomberg.com/apps/news?pid=newsarchive&sid=aNRppMJqgURA (accessed 27 April 2010).
7. Quoted in E. Brown, "Behind the Drums of War with Iran: Nuclear Weapons or Compound Interest," *Global Research*, 13 November 2007, http://www.globalresearch.ca/index.php?context=va&aid=7319 (accessed 16 May 2011).
8. See the first note in Chapter 3.

"SYSTEMIC CYCLES OF ACCUMULATION" AND TECHNO-ECONOMIC PARADIGMS

The figure below is an outline of Arrighi's four "Systemic Cycles of Accumulation" (1994); each constituted by a MC phase of material expansion and a CM' phase of financial expansion. Each cycle is named after the capitalist hegemon dominating the specific cycle:

1. The Genoese SCA: The genesis of "high finance" and the constitution of capitalist accumulation
2. The Dutch SCA: The rise of the interstate system and capitalism as world system
3. The British SCA: Free-trade imperialism
4. The US SCA: The free enterprise system

Included are also the "generally accepted" Schumpeter-Freeman-Perez five successive waves of "techno-economic paradigms," whose shifts, occurring every forty to sixty years, are named after the key technologies underpinning the new wave:

① The Industrial Revolution (Britain)
② The Age of Steam and Railways (Britain)
③ The Age of Steel, Electricity and Heavy Engineering (US, Germany, Britain)
④ The Age of Oil, Automobiles and Mass Production (US)
⑤ The Age of Information and Telecommunications (US)

The * in figure 13 indicates the major turning point of the techno-economic paradigm: from a "finance capital"–led installation phase, through a crisis, to a "production capital"–led deployment phase.

At the millennium moment we find the concurrence of crisis both in the current (4th) SCA and in the techno-economic paradigm.

Figure 13. Historical development of capitalism, including systemic cycles of accumulation, and techno-economic paradigms.

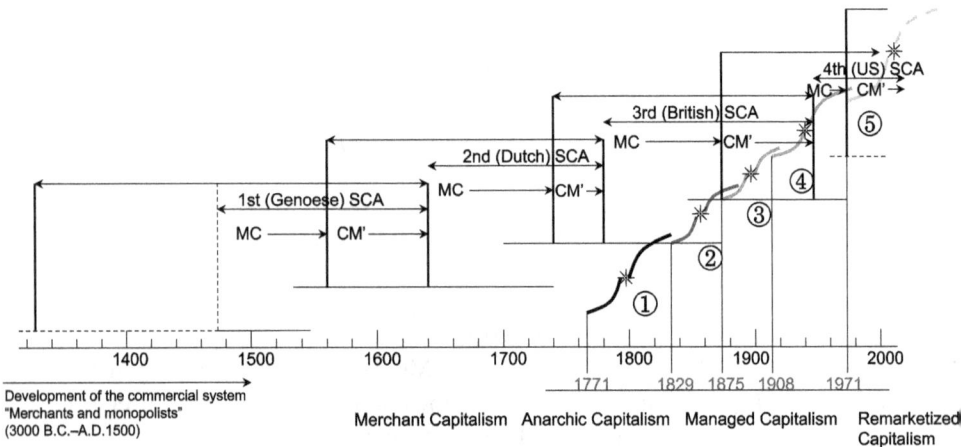

BIBLIOGRAPHY

Aczel, A. D. 2002. *Entanglement: The Greatest Mystery in Physics*. Chichester: Wiley.

Alexander, K., R. Dhumale, and J. Eatwell. 2005. *Global Governance of Financial Systems: The International Regulation of Systemic Risk*. New York: Oxford University Press.

Andersen, K. G. 2005. *Flaggskip i fremmed eie: Hydro 1905–1945* [Flagship in foreign hands: Hydro 1905–1945]. Pax Forlag.

Andersen, K. G., and G. Yttri. 1997. *Et forsøk verdt: Forskning og utvikling i Norsk Hydro gjennom 90 år*. Oslo: Universitetsforlaget.

Appadurai, A. 1996. *Modernity at Large: Cultural Dimensions of Globalization*. Minneapolis: University of Minnesota Press.

———, ed. 2001. *Globalization*. Durham: Duke University Press.

Armstrong, P. 1987. "The Rise of Accounting Controls in British Capitalist Enterprises." *Accounting, Organizations and Society* 12, no. 5: 415–436.

Arrighi, G. 1994. *The Long Twentieth Century: Money, Power and the Origins of Our Times*. London and New York: Verso.

———. 2007. *Adam Smith in Bejing*. London: Verso.

Arthur, B. W. 1994. *Increasing Returns and Path Dependency in the Economy*. Ann Arbor: University of Michigan Press.

Aspect, A., P. Grangier, and G. Roger. 1981. "Experimental Tests of Realistic Local Theories via Bell's Theorem." *Physical Review Letters* 47, no. 7: 460–463.

———. 1982a. "Experimental Realization of Einstein-Podolsky-Rosen-Bohm Gedanken-experiment: A New Violation of Bell's Inequalities." *Physical Review Letters* 49, no. 2: 91–94.

Aspect, A., J. Dalibard, and G. Roger. 1982b. "Experimental Test of Bell's Inequalities Using Time-Varying Analyzers." *Physical Review Letters* 49, no. 25: 1804–1807.

Auge, M. 1995. *Non-places: Introduction to an Anthropology of Supermodernity*. London: Verso.

Baba, M. L. 1986. *Business and Industrial Anthropology: An Overview*. NAPA Bulletin, No. 2. American Anthropological Association. Washington.

Bakan, J. 2004. *The Corporation: The Pathological Pursuit of Profit and Power*. London: Constable.

Barth, F. [1967] 1996. "Economic Spheres in Darfur." In *Themes in Economic Anthropology*, ASA Monographs nr. 6., London: Tavistock. In Norwegian: "Økonomiske sfærer i Darfur." In F. Barth, *Manifestasjon og Prosess*. Oslo: Universitetsforlaget.

———. 1975. *Ritual and Knowledge among the Baktaman of New Guinea*. Oslo, New Haven: Universitetsforlaget and Yale University Press.

———. 2002. "An Anthropology of Knowledge." *Current Anthropology* 43, no. 1: 1–18.

Bartlett, C., and S. Ghosal. 1989. *Managing Across Borders: The Transnational Solution*. Boston, MA: Harvard Business School Press.

Bate, S. P. 1997. "Whatever Happened to Organizational Anthropology? A Review of the Field of Organizational Ethnography and Anthropological Studies." *Human Relations* 50, no. 9: 1147–1175.

Bateson, G. 1979. *Mind and Nature: A Necessary Unit*. New York: Bantam Books.

Batteau, A. W. 2000. "Negations and Ambiguities in the Cultures of Organization." *American Anthropologist* 102, no. 4: 726–740.

Beck, U., A. Giddens, and S. Lash, eds. 1994. *Reflexive Modernization: Politics, Tradition and Aesthetics in the Modern Social Order*. Cambridge: Polity Press.

Bell, D. 2004. *Wealth and Power: Survival in a Time of Global Accumulation*. Walnut Creek: AltaMira Press.

Berger, P. L., and T. Luckmann. 1966. *The Social Construction of Reality: A Treatise in the Sociology of Knowledge*. New York: Doubleday.

Bergson, H. [1907] 2007. *Creative Evolution*. Bergson Press.

Berle, A., Jr., and G. Means. [1932] 1991. *The Modern Corporation and Private Property*. New Brunswick, NJ: Transaction Publishers.

Bhagwati, J. 2004. *In Defense of Globalization*. Oxford University Press.

Bijker, W. E., Hughes, T. P., and T. Pinch. 1987. *The Social Construction of Technological Systems*. Cambridge: MIT Press.

BIS (Bank for International Settlements). 2004. "BIS Quarterly Review" (December).

BIS (Bank for International Settlements). 2009. "BIS Quarterly Review" (June).

Bjerke, P. 2007. "Reiten vs. Røkke." *Klassekampen*, 16 August.

Blackler, F., M. Reed, and A. Whitaker. 1993. "Editorial Introduction: Knowledge Workers and Contemporary Organizations." *Journal of Management Studies* 30, no. 6: 851–862.

Blankenburg, S., and J. G. Palma. 2009. "Introduction: The Global Financial Crisis." *Cambridge Journal of Economics* 33: 531–538.

Blim, M. 2005. *Equality and Economy: The Global Challenge*. Walnut Creek: AltaMira Press.

Bloch, M., and J. Parry, eds. 1989. *Money and the Morality of Exchange*. Cambridge: Cambridge University Press.

Bohannan, P., and A. G. Dalton. 1965. *Markets in Africa*. New York: Doubleday.

Bohm, D. 1980. *Wholeness and the Implicate Order*. London: Routledge and Kegan Paul.

———. [1987] 2000. *Science, Order and Creativity*. Routledge.

Bohm, D., and B. J. Hiley. 1995. *The Undivided Universe*. Routledge.

Boltanski, L., and E. Chiapello. 2007. *The New Spirit of Capitalism*. London, New York: Verso.

Bourdieu, P. 1989. "Social Space and Symbolic Power." *Sociological Theory* 7, no. 1: 1–25.

Braudel, F. 1984. *Civilization and Capitalism, 15th–18th Century*, vol. 3: *The Perspective of the World*. New York: Harper and Row.

Brown, E. H. 2007. *The Web of Debt*. Third Millennium Press.

Brown, N. O. 1991. *Apocalypse and/or Metamorphosis*. Berkeley: University of California Press.

Burawoy, M. 1979. *Manufacturing Consent: Changes in the Labor Process under Monopoly Sapitalism*. Chicago: The University of Chicago Press.

———. 1998. "The Extended Case Method." *Sociological Theory* 16, no. 1 (March): 4–33.

———. 2009. *The Extended Case Method. Four Countries, Four Decades, Four Great Transformations, and One Tradition*. Berkeley: University of California Press.

Byrkjeflot, H., S. Myklebust, C. Myrvang, and F. Sejersted, eds. 2001. *The Democratic Challenge to Capitalism: Management and Democracy in the Nordic Countries*. Bergen: Fagbokforlaget.

Calaprice, A. 2005. *The New Quotable Einstein*. Princeton: Princeton University Press.

Carlsen, A., R. Klev, and G. von Krogh, eds. 2004. *Living Knowledge: The Dynamics of Professional Service Work*. London: Palgrave MacMillan.

Carrier, J. G. 1998. "Introduction." In *Virtualism: A New Political Economy*, ed. J. G. Carrier and D. Miller. Oxford: Berg.

Castells, M. 2000. *The Rise of the Network Society. The Information Age: Economy, Society and Culture*. Oxford: Blackwell Publishers.

Chang, J., and J. Halliday. 2005. *Mao: The Unknown Story*. New York: Alfred A. Knopf.

Chen, L. H., Zhao, H. J., and Liu, Z. 2001. "The Latest Development of Magnesium Industry in China." *Metall* 55, no. 9: 531–535.

Cicmil, S., and D. Hodgson. 2006. *Making Projects Critical*. Basingstoke: Palgrave Macmillan.

Clegg, S., M. Kornberger, and T. Pitsis. 2004. *Managing and Organizations: An Introduction to Theory and Practice*. London: Sage.

Cleverley, G. 1971. *Managers and Magic*. London: Longsman.

Clifford, J. 1997. *Routes: Travel and Translation in the Late Twentieth Century*. Cambridge, MA: Harvard University Press.

Cohen, R. S., M. Horne, and J. J. Stachel, eds. 1997. *Potentiality, Entanglement and Passion-at-a-Distance: Quantum Mechanical Studies for Abner Shimony, Volume Two (Boston Studies in the Philosophy of Science)*. Dordrecht: Kluwer Academic Publishers

Collier, S. J., and A. Ong. 2005. "Global Assemblages, Anthropological Problems." In *Global Assemblages: Technology, Politics, and Ethics as Anthropological Problems*, ed. A. Ong and S. J. Collier. Malden, MA: Blackwell Publishing.

Comaroff, J., and J. L. Comaroff. 2000. "Millennial Capitalism: First Thoughts on a Second Coming." *Public Culture* 12, no. 2: 291–343.

———, eds. 2001. *Millennial Capitalism and the Culture of Neoliberalism*. Duke University Press.

Coyle, D. 1999. "The Weightless World." Conference presentation, *Telework99*, Århus, 22 September.

Crotty, J. 2005. "The Neoliberal Paradox: The Impact of Destructive Product Market Competition and 'Modern' Financial Markets on Nonfinancial Corporation Performance in the Neoliberal Era." In *Financialization and the World Economy*, ed. G. A. Epstein. Cheltenham: Edward Elgar.

Czarniawska, B. 2003. "This Way to Paradise: On Creole Researchers, Hybrid Disciplines and Pidgin Writing." *Organization* 10, no. 3: 430–434.

Czarniawska-Joerges, B. 1992. *Exploring Complex Organizations: A Cultural Perspective*. London: Sage.

Dalton, M. 1959. *Men Who Manage: Fusions of Feeling and Theory in Administration*. New York: Wiley.

Davies-Floyd, Robbie E. 1998. "Storying Corporate Futures: The Shell Scenarios." In *Corporate Futures*, ed. G. E. Marcus. London: The University of Chicago Press.

Denton, S., and R. Morris. 2001. *Money and the Power: The Making of Las Vegas and Its Hold on America*. New York: Vintage Books, Random House.

Desrosiéres, A. 1998. *The Politics of Large Numbers: A History of Statistical Reasoning*. Cambridge, MA: Harvard University Press.

Dickens, E. 2005. "The Eurodollar Market and the New Area of Global Financialization." In *Financialization and the World Economy*, ed. G. A. Epstein. Cheltenham: Edward Elgar.

Dodd, R. 2005. "Derivatives Markets: Sources of Vulnerability in US Financial Markets." In *Financialization and the World Economy*, ed. G. A. Epstein. Cheltenham: Edward Elgar.

Douglas, M., and B. Isherwood. 1996. *The World of Goods: Towards an Anthropology of Consumption*. Routledge.

Drucker, P. F. 1954. *The Practice of Management*. London: Heinemann.

———. 1993. *Post-Capitalist Society*. New York: HarperCollins.

Dubinskas, F. A., ed. 1988. *Making Time: Ethnographies of High-Technology Organizations*. Philadelphia: Temple Univeristy Press.

Duménil, G., and D. Levy. 2004. *Capital Resurgent: Roots of the Neoliberal Revolution*. Cambridge, MA: Harvard University Press.

Easterby-Smith, M., and M. A. Lyles, eds. 2003. *Handbook of Organizational Learning and Knowledge Management*. Oxford: Blackwell.

Edelman, M., and A. Haugerud, eds. 2005. *The Anthropology of Development and Globalization: From Classical Political Economy to Contemporary Neoliberalism*. Malden, MA: Blackwell.

Einstein, A. 1949. "Why Socialism?" *Monthly Review* (May).

El Diwany, T. 2003. *The Problem with Interests*. Kreatoc Ltd.

Ellen, R. F., ed. 1984. *Ethnographic Research: A Guide to General Conduct*. London: Academic Press, Harcourt Brace and Company.

Emery, F., and E. Thorsrud. 1976. *Democracy at Work*. Leiden: Martinus Nijhoff.

Epstein, G. A., ed. 2005. *Financialization and the World Economy*. Cheltenham: Edward Elgar.

Eriksen, T. H., ed. 2003. *Globalisation*. London: Pluto Press.

Evans, T. M. S., and D. Handelman, eds. 2006. *The Manchester School: Practice and Ethnographic Praxis in Anthropology*. New York and Oxford: Berghahn Books.

Featherstone, M., ed. 1990. *Global Culture: Nationalism, Globalization and Modernity*. London: Sage.

Fei, X. 1992. *From the Soil: The Foundations of Chinese Society*. Berkeley and Los Angeles: University of California Press.

Ferenczi, S. 1950. *Sex in Psychoanalysis*. New York: Robert Brunner.

Ferguson, J. 2006. *Global Shadows: Africa in the Neoliberal World Order*. Durham and London: Duke University Press.

Ferguson, N. 2005. "Our Currency, Your Problem." *The New York Times*, 13 March.

———. 2008. *The Ascent of Money: A Financial History of the World*. London: Penguin Books.

Flyvbjerg, B., N. Bruzelius, and W. Rothengatter. 2003. *Megaprojects and Risk: An Anatomy of Ambition*. Cambridge: Cambridge University Press.

Foster, J. B., and F. Magdoff. 2009. *The Great Financial Crisis: Causes and Consequences*. New York: Monthly Review Press.

Foster, J. B., and H. Szlajfer, eds. 1984. *The Faltering Economy: The Problem of Accumulation Under Monopoly Capitalism*. New York: Monthly Review Press.

Fulcher, J. 2004. *Capitalism: A Very Short Introduction*. Oxford: Oxford University Press.

Fullbrook, E. 2007. "Economics and Neo-liberalism." In *After Blair: Politics After the New Labour Decade*, ed. G. Hassan. London: Lawrence and Wishart Ltd.

Furre, B. 1992. *Norsk Historie 1905–1990* [Norwegian history 1905–1990]. Oslo: Det Norske Samlaget.

Galbraith, John K. 1967. *The New Industrial State*. London: Penguin Books.

Galbraith, James K. 2008. *The Predator State: How Conservatives Abandoned the Free Market and Why Liberals Should Too*. New York: Free Press.

———. 2009. "Statement by James K. Galbraith." Before the Committee on Financial Services, U.S. House of Representatives, Hearings on the Conduct of Monetary Policy, 26 February. *Real-World Economics Review* 49: 62–72.

Gell, A. 1988. "Technology and Magic." *Anthropology Today* 4, no. 2: 6–9.

———. 1992. "The Technology of Enchantment and the Enchantment of Technology." In *Anthropology and Aesthetics*, ed. J. Coote and A. Shelton. Oxford: Clarendon Press.

———. 1998. *Art and Agency: An Anthropological Theory*. Oxford: Clarendon Press.

Gellner, D. N., and E. Hirsch, eds. 2001. *Inside Organizations: Anthropologists at Work*. Oxford and New York: Berg.

Giddens, A. 1990. *The Consequences of Modernity*. Cambridge: Polity Press.

Gluckman, M. [1940] 1958. *Analysis of a Social Situation in Modern Zululand*. Manchester: Manchester University Press for Rhodes-Livingstone Institute.

Glyn, A. 2006. *Capitalism Unleashed: Finance, Globalization, and Welfare*. Oxford: Oxford University Press.

Gouldner, A. W. 1954. *Patterns of Industrial Bureaucracy: A Study of Modern Factory Administration*. Glencoe, IL.: Free Press.

Gowler, D., and K. Legge. 1983. "The Meaning of Management, the Management of Meaning: A View from Social Anthropology." In *Perspectives on Management*, ed. M. J. Earl. Oxford: Oxford University Press.

Grant, R. M. 1996. "Toward a Knowledge-Based Theory of the Firm." *Strategic Management Journal* 17 (Winter Special Issue): 109–122

Greenspan, A. [1966] 1986. "Gold and Economic Freedom." In A. Rand, *Capitalism: The Unknown Ideal*. New York: Signet.

———. 2009. "We Need a Better Cushion against Risk." *Financial Times*, 26 March.

Grønhaug, R. 2001. "Antropologi som arena for en ny enhetsvitenskap" [Anthropology as an arean for a new unity of science]. *Norsk Antropologisk Tidsskrift* 12, no. 1–2: 60–67.

Gudeman, S. 2008. "Economic Anthropology." In *Encyclopedia of Social and Cultural Anthropology*, ed. A. Barnard and J. Spencer. London and New York: Routledge.

Gunnesdal, L., and M. E. Marsdal. 2011. "Det nye Norge. Økonomisk maktkonsentrasjon i perioden etter 1990." *Manifest report*, no. 1(2011). Oslo: Manifest Senter for Samfunnsanalyse.

Habashi, F. 2005. "A Short History of Hydrometallurgy." *Hydrometallurgy* 79: 15–22.

Habermas, J. 1984. *The Theory of Communicative Action: Reason and the Rationalization of Society*, vol. 1. Boston: Beacon Press.

Handelman, D. 2006. "The Extended Case: Interactional Foundations and Prospective Dimensions." In *The Manchester School: Practice and Ethnographic Praxis in Anthropology*, ed. T. M. S. Evans and D. Handelman. New York and Oxford: Berghahn Books.

Hannerz, U. 1998. "Transnational Research." In *Handbook of Methods in Anthropology*, ed. H. R. Bernard. Walnut Creek, CA: AltaMira Press.

———. 2003. "Several Sites in One." In *Globalisation: Studies in Anthropology*, ed. T. H. Eriksen. London: Pluto Press.

———. 2007. "The Neo-liberal Culture Complex and Universities: A Case for Urgent Anthropology?" *Anthropology Today* 23, no. 5: 1–2.

Hardt, M. 1995. "The Withering of Civil Society." *Social Text* 45: 27–44.

Hardt, M., and A. Negri. 2000. *Empire*. Cambridge, MA: Harvard University Press.

———. 2009. *Common Wealth*. Cambridge, MA: Harvard University Press.

Hart, K. 2000. *Money in an Unequal World*. New York and London: Texere.

———. 2002. "World Society as an Old Regime." In *Elite Cultures: Anthropological Perspectives*, ed. C. Shore and S. Nugent. London and New York: Routledge.

Hart, K., and H. Ortiz. 2008. "Anthropology in the Financial Crisis." *Anthropology Today* 24, no. 6: 1–3.

Harvey, D. 1992. *The Condition of Postmodernity: An Enquiry into the Origins of Cultural Change*. Malden, MA: Wiley-Blackwell.

———. 2005. *A Brief History of Neoliberalism*. Oxford and New York: Oxford University Press.

———. [1982] 2006. *Limits to Capital*. London and New York: Verso.

Hauser, A. [1951] 1999. *The Social History of Art*, vol. 2: *Renaissance, Mannerism, Baroque*. London and New York: Routledge.

Hausman, D. M. 1994. *The Philosophy of Economics*. Cambridge: Cambridge University Press.

Heads Together Productions. 2004. *Meltdown: Words and Images from a Yorkshire Foundry*. Heads Together Productions Limited.

Heidegger, M. 1977. *The Question Concerning Technology and Other Essays*. Trans. William Lovitt. New York: Harper and Row Publishers.

Hellevik, O., and O. Knutsen. 2007. "Norske velgere og nyliberalisme" [Norwegian constituents and neoliberalism]. In *Nyliberalisme: ideer og politisk virkelighet* [Neoliberalism: Ideas and political reality], ed. P. K. Mydske, D. H. Claes, and A. Lie. Oslo: Universitetsforlaget.

Henwood, D. 2005. *After the New Economy*. New York and London: The New Press.

Herbst, P. G. 1976. *Alternatives to Hierarchies*. Leiden: Martinus Nijhoff.

Hermansen, T. 2007. "Hydroopsjonene: striden som alle tapte" [The Hydro options: The battle everybody lost]. *Samtiden* 3: 119–126.

Hernes, G. 2007. *Med på laget*. Fafo report 2007: 09. ISSN: 0801: 6143.

Hess, D. J. 2008. "Crosscurrents: Social Movements and the Anthropology of Science and Technology." *American Anthropologist* 109, no. 3: 463–472.

Hilferding, R. [1910] 1985. *Finance Capital: A Study in the Latest Phase of Capitalist Development*. London: Routledge & Kegan Paul.

Hirokazu, M., and A. Riles. 2005. "Failure as an Endpoint." In *Global Assemblages: Technology, Politics, and Ethics as Anthropological Problems*, ed. A. Ong and S. J. Collier. Malden, MA: Blackwell Publishing.

Hirschman, A. O. [1977] 1997. *The Passions and the Interests: Political Arguments for Capitalism before Its Triumph*. Princeton, NJ: Princeton University Press.

Ho, K. 2005. "Situating Global Capitalism: A View from Wall Street Investment Banks." *Cultural Anthropology* 20, no. 1: 68–96.

———. 2009. *Liquidated: An Ethnography of Wall Street*. Durham and London: Duke University Press.

Holmes, D. R., and G. E. Marcus. 2005. "Cultures of Expertise and the Management of Globalization: Toward the Re-functioning of Ethnography." In *Global Assemblages: Technology, Politics, and Ethics as Anthropological Problems*, ed. A. Ong and S. J. Collier. Malden, MA: Blackwell Publishing.

Homans, G. 1958. "Social Behaviour as Exchange." *American Journal of Sociology* 63: 597–606.

Hudson, M. 2003. *Super Imperialism: The Origin and Fundamentals of U.S. World Dominance*. London: Pluto Press.

Hydro. Annual Reports. Various editions [year range].

Hård, M., A. Kjærvik, S. Kvaal, P. K. Larsen, O. Lauritzen, E. Rødahl, eds. 1997. *Teknologi for samfunnet*. *NTH i en brytningstid 1985–1995*. Trondheim: Norges teknisk-naturvitenskapelige universitet.

ILO. 2011. "Global employment trends 2011: The challenge of a jobs recovery." Geneva: International Labour Office.

IMF. 2009a. "Global Financial Stability Report: Responding to the Financial Crisis and Measuring Systemic Risk." Washington D.C., April: IMF.

IMF. 2009b. "World Economic Outlook. Crisis and Recovery." World Economic and Financial Surveys, Washington D.C., April: IMF.

Ingold, T. 2007. "Anthropology Is not Ethnography." Radcliffe-Brown Lecture in Social Anthropology (14 March), London, The British Academy.

Jackall, J. 1989. *Moral Mazes: The World of Corporate Managers*. Oxford: Oxford University Press.

Jacques, R. 1996. *Manufacturing the Employee: Management Knowledge from the 19th to 21st Centuries*. London: Sage.

Jameson, F. 1997. "Culture and Finance Capital." *Critical Inquiry* 24, no. 1. (Autumn): 246–265.

Jameson, F., and M. Miyoshi, eds. 1998. *The Cultures of Globalization*. Durham and London: Duke University Press.

Jaques, E. 1951. *The Changing Culture of the Factory*. London: Tavistock.

Johannessen, F. E., A. Rønning, and P. T. Sandvik. 2005. *Nasjonal kontroll og industriell fornyelse: Hydro 1945–1977*. Oslo: Pax Forlag.

Johansen, S. E. [1990] 2004. *Grunnriss av en differensiell epistemology* [Outline of a differential ontology]. Bergen: Ariadne.

———, ed. 2005. *Anthropology and Ontology*. Trondheim Occasional Papers in Social Anthropology 11. Department of Social Anthropology, NTNU. NTNU-trykk. ISSN: 0802-1341.

Jordan, A. T. 2003. *Business Anthropology*. Long Grove, III: Waveland Press.

Juarrero, A. 1999. *Dynamics in Action: Intentional Behaviour as a Complex System*. Cambridge, MA: MIT Press.

Kalecki, M. 1938. "The Determinants of Distribution of the National Income." *Econometrica* 6, no. 2. (April): 97–112.

Kant, I. 1929 [2003]. *Critique of Pure Reason*. Basingstoke: Palgrave Macmillan.

Kapferer, B. 2006. "Situations, Crisis, and the Anthropology of the Concrete: The Contribution of Max Gluckman." In *The Manchester School: Practice and Ethnographic Praxis in Anthropology*, ed. T. M. S. Evans and D. Handelman. New York and Oxford: Berghahn Books.

Karlsen, A. 2008. "Tung forskning på lett metal" [Heavy research in light metals]. In *Norsk Aluminiumsindustri: Globalisering i et århundre* [Norwegian aluminium industry: A century of globalization], ed. H. O. Frøland, J. Henden, and A. Karlsen. Bergen: Fagbokforlaget.

Kennedy, P. 1989. *The Rise and Fall of the Great Powers: Economic Change and Military Conflict from 1500 to 2000*. London: Fontana Press.

Kern, M. 2000. "The Stele Inscriptions of Ch'in Shih-huang: Text and Ritual in Early Chinese Imperial Representation." *American Oriental Series* 85: 27. New Haven: American Oriental Society.

Keynes, J. M. [1936] 2008. *The General Theory of Employment, Interest and Money.* BN Publishing.

Kjær, K. N. 2002. "Høyest mulig avkastning for Petroleumsfondet" [Highest possible returns for the Petroleum Fund]. In *Hva gjør oljepengene med oss?* ed. A. J. Isachsen. Oslo: Cappelen Akademiske Forlag.

Klein, N. 2007. *The Shock Doctrine: The Rise of Disaster Capitalism.* London: Allen Lane.

Klovland, J. T. 2004. "Monetary Aggregates in Norway 1819–2003." In *Historical Monetary Statistics for Norway 1819–2003*, ed. Ø. Eitrheim, J. T. Klovland, and J. F. Qvigstad. Norges Bank Occasional Papers, no. 35, Oslo.

Kobberød, J. T. 2008. "Norsk oksid—en nøkkel til shuksess?" In *Norsk Aluminiumsindustri: Globalisering i et århundre* [Norwegian aluminium industry: A century of globalization], ed. H. O. Frøland, J. Henden, and A. Karlsen. Bergen: Fagbokforlaget.

Kolko, G. 2006. "An Economy of Buccaneers and Fanatists: Weapons of Mass Financial Destruction." *Le Monde diplomatique* (October).

Kolltveit, B. J., and K. Grønhaug. 2004. "The Importance of the Early Phase: The Case of Construction and Building Projects." *International Journal of Project Management* 22: 545–551.

Kran, L. C., and G. Øwre. 2001. "Norges Banks system for å styre renten." *Penger og Kreditt* 1: 43–48.

Krugman, P. 2009. "How Did Economists Get It So Wrong?" *The New York Times*, 6 September, p. MM36.

———. 2010. "Looters in Loafers." *The New York Times*, 19 April, p. A23.

Kunda, G. 1993. *Engineering Culture: Control and Commitment in a High-Tech Corporation.* Philadelphia: Temple University Press.

Larsen, T. 1996. "Den globale samtalen: Modernisering, representasjon og subjektkonstruksjon" [The global conversation: Modernization, representation and subject construction]. In *Norge. Museum eller fremtidslaboratorium*, Kulturtekster 8, ed. S. Meyer and M. Steffensen. Bergen: Senter for European Cultural Studies, University of Bergen.

———. 2008. "Acts of Entification: On the Emergence of Thinghood in Social Life." In *Human Nature as Capacity: transcending discourse and classification*, ed. N. Rapport. New York: Berghahn Books.

———. 2009. *Den globale samtalen. Om dialogens muligheter* [The global conversation. On the possibilities of dialogue.] Oslo: Scandinavian Academic Press.

Latour, B. 1991. "Technology Is Society Made Durable." In *A Sociology of Monsters: Essays on Power, Technology, and Domination*, ed. John Law. London: Routledge.

———. 1993. *We Have Never Been Modern.* Cambridge, MA: Harvard University Press.

———. 1996. *Aramis, or the Love of Technology.* Cambridge, MA: Harvard University Press.

———. 2005. *Reassembling the Social.* Oxford: Oxford University Press.

Lawson, T. 2009. "The Current Economic Crisis: Its Nature and the Course of Academic Economics." *Cambridge Journal of Economics* 33: 759–777.

Leys, C. 2001. *Market-Driven Politics, Neoliberal Democracy and the Public Interest.* London: Verso.

Li, S. 2004. "Why Is Property Right Protection Lacking in China? An Institutional Explanation." *Californina Management Review* 46, no. 3 (Spring): 100–115.

Lie, E. 2005. *Oljerikdommer og internasjonal ekspansjon: Hydro 1977–2005.* [Oil wealth and international expansion: Hydro 1977–2005]. Oslo: Pax Forlag.

Linstead, S. 1997. "The Social Anthropology of Management." *British Journal of Management* 8: 85–98.

LiPuma, E., and B. Lee. 2004. *Financial Derivatives and the Globalization of Risk*. Durham and London: Duke University Press.

Lutz, C., ed. 2009. *The Bases of Empire: The Global Struggle against U.S. Military Posts*. London: Pluto Press.

Lynd, R. S., and H. M. Lynd. [1929] 1959. *Middletown: A Study in American Culture*. Orlando: Harcourt Brace & Company.

Lysestøl, P. M. 2006. "I faresonen." *Klassekampen*, 15 November.

Lysgaard, S. 1961. *Arbeiderkollektivet*. Oslo: Universitetsforlaget.

Løken, E., G. Falkenberg, and T. Kvinge. 2008. "Norsk arbeidslivsmodell—ikke for eksport?" [Norwegian work-life model—not for export?]. *Fafo-report*, no. 32.

Maddison, A. 2001. *The World Economy: A Millennial Perspective*. Paris: OECD Development Center.

Marcikic, I., H. de Riedmatten, W. Tittel, H. Zbinden, M. Legré, and N. Gisin. 2004. "Distribution of Time-Bin Entangled Qubits over 50 km of Optical Fiber." *Physical Review Letters* 93, no. 18: 1–4.

Marcus, G. E., ed. 1983. *Elites: Ethnographic Issues*. Albuquerque: University of New Mexico Press.

———. 1986. "Contemporary Problems of Ethnography in the Modern World System." In *Writing Culture*, ed. J. Clifford and G. E. Marcus. Berkeley: University of California Press.

———. [1989] 1998. "Imagining the Whole: Ethnography's Contemporary Efforts to Situate Itself." In *Ethnography through Thick and Thin*, ed. G. E. Marcus. Princeton: Princeton University Press.

Marcus, G. E., and M. M. J. Fischer. 1986. *Anthropology as Cultural Critique: An Experimental Moment in the Human Sciences*. Chicago and London: The University of Chicago Press.

Marcus, G. E., and E. Saka. 2006. "Assemblage." *Theory, Culture and Society* 23, no. 2–3: 101–109.

Marx, K. [1867] 1990. *Capital, Volume I*. London: Penguin Classics, Penguin Books.

Morton. W. S., and C. M. Lewis. 2004. *China: Its History and Culture*. New York: McGraw-Hill.

Micklethwait, J., and A. Wooldridge. 2003. *The Company: A Short History of a Revolutionary Idea*. London: Phoenix.

Miller, D. 1997a. *Material Culture and Mass Consumption*. London: Wiley-Blackwell.

———. 1997b. *Capitalism: An Ethnographic Approach*. Oxford and New York: Berg.

Mintzberg, H. 1973. *The Nature of Managerial Work*. New York: Harper and Row.

Mintzberg, H., R. Simons, and K. Basu. 2002. "Beyond Selfishness." *MIT Sloan Management Review* 44, no. 1. (Fall): 66–74.

Minsky, H. 1993. "Schumpeter and Finance." In *Markets and Institutions in Economic Development*, ed. S. Biasco, A. Roncaglia, and M. Salvati. Basingstoke: St. Martin's Press.

———. 1996. "Uncertainty and the Institutional Structure of Capitalist Economies." Working paper no. 155, Jerome Levy Economics Institute, April.

Morris, B. 2007. "Wittgenstein Revisited." *Anthropology Today* 23, no. 1: 28.

Mumford, E. 1997. "The Reality of Participative Systems Design: Contributing to Stability in a Rocking Boat." *Information Systems Journal* 7, no. 4 (October): 309–322.

———. 2006. "The story of socio-technical design: reflections on its successes, failures and potential." *Information Systems Journal* 16, no. 4 (October): 317-342.

Mydske, P. K., D. H. Claes, and A. Lie, eds. 2007. *Nyliberalisme: ideer og politisk virkelighet* [Neoliberalism: Ideas and political reality]. Oslo: Universitetsforlaget.

Nadeau, R., and M. Kafatos. 1999. *The Non-local Universe, the New Physics and Matters of the Mind.* Oxford: Oxford University Press.

Ngai, P. 2003. "Subsumption or Consumption? The Phantom of Consumer Revolution in 'Globalizing' China." *Cultural Anthropology* 18, no. 4: 469–492.

Nonaka, I., and H. Takeuchi. 1995. *The Knowledge Creating Company.* Oxford: Oxford University Press.

Norges Bank. 2004. "Norske finansmarkeder, pengepolitikk og finansiell stabilitet." *Norges Banks Occasional Papers* 34: 1–110.

Øfsti, A. 1999. "Theoria, praxis og poesis." In *Den litterære maskin* [The literary machine], ed. A. K. Børresen and K. O. Eliassen. Nr. 1 i skriftserie fra forskningsprosjektet "Fabrikken". ISSN: 1501–9780.

Olssen, M. 2003. "Structuralism, Post-structuralism, Neo-liberalism: Assessing Foucault's Legacy." *Journal of Education Policy* 18, no. 2: 189–202.

Ong, A., and S. J. Collier, eds. 2005. *Global Assemblages: Technology, Politics, and Ethics as Anthropological Problems.* Malden, MA: Blackwell Publishing.

Øye, H., and N. Ryum. 1997. "Lettmetaller og materialteknologi" [Light metals and materials technology]. In *Teknologi for samfunnet,* ed. M. Hård et al. Trondheim: Norges teknisk-naturvitenskapelige universitet.

Paglia, C. 1990. *Sexual Personae: Art and Decadence From Nefertiti to Emily Dickinson.* London: Penguin Books.

Palast, G. 2003. *The Best Democracy Money Can Buy. The Truth About Corporate Cons, Globalization and High-Finance Fraudsters.* New York: Plume.

Palma, J. G. 2009. "The Revenge of the Market on the Rentiers: Why Neo-liberal Reports of the End of History Turned Out to Be Premature." *Cambridge Journal of Economics* 33: 829–869.

Patriotta, G. 2003. *Organizational Knowledge in the Making: How Firms Create, Use, and Institutionalize Knowledge.* Oxford: Oxford University Press.

Perez, C. 2002. *Technological Revolutions and Financial Capital: The Dynamics of Bubbles and Golden Ages.* Cheltenham: Edward Elgar.

Perkins, J. 2005. *Confessions of an Economic Hit Man.* London: Ebury Press.

Pfaffenberger, B. 1992. "Social Anthropology of Technology." *Annual Review of Anthropology* 21: 491–516.

Pieke, F. N. 2005. "Beyond Orthodoxy: Social and Cultural Anthropology in the People's Republic of China." In *Asian Anthropology,* ed. J. van Bremen, E. Ben-Ari, and S. F. Alatas. London: Routledge.

Plato. [360 BC] 2010. *The Laws.* Trans. Benjamin Jowett. Timeless Classic Books.

Polanyi, K. [1944] 2001. *The Great Transformation: The Political and Economic Origins of Our Time.* Boston: Beacon Press.

Porter, T. 1995. *Trust in Numbers.* Princeton, NJ: Princeton University Press.

Power, M. 1997. *The Audit Society Rituals of Verification.* Oxford: Oxford University Press.

Project Managment Institute. 2004. *A Guide to the Project Management Body of Knowledge.* 3d ed. (PMBOK Guide). Newtown Square, Pa.: Project Management Institute.

Radcliffe-Brown, A. R. 1940. "On Social Structure." *Journal of the Royal Anthropological Institute* 70: 1–12.

Rand, A. [1966] 1986. *Capitalism: The Unknown Ideal.* New York: Signet.

Rees, M. 2008. *Financial Modelling in Practice: A Concise Guide for Intermediate and Advanced Level.* Chichester: Wiley.

Reinert, E. S. 1997. "Exploring the Genesis of Economic Innovations: The Religious Gestalt-Switch and the Duty to Invent as Preconditions for Economic Growth." *European Journal of Law and Economics* 4: 233–283.

———. 2007. *How Rich Countries Got Rich… and Why Poor Countries Stay Poor*. London: Constable.

———, ed. 2004. *Globalization, Economic Development and Inequality: An Alternative Perspective*. Cheltenham: Edward Elgar.

Reinert, E. S., and A. M. Daastøl. 1998. *Production Capitalism vs. Financial Capitalism: Symbiosis and Parasitism. An Evolutionary Perspective*. Published online at http://www.othercanon.org/.

Reinert, H., and E. S. Reinert. 2006. "Creative Destruction in Economics: Nietzsche, Sombart, Schumpeter." In *Friedrich Nietzsche (1844–1900): Economy and Society*, ed. J. G. Backhaus and W. Dreschler. Boston, MA: Springer.

Reinhart, C. M., and K. S. Rogoff. 2009. *This Time Is Different: Eight Centuries of Financial Folly*. Princeton and Oxford: Princeton University Press.

Robbins, R. 2009. "Anthropologizing Economics. Lessons from the Latest Crisis." *Anthropology News* 50, no. 7 (October): 11–12.

Roberts, P. C. 2007. "Dollar's Fall Collapses American Empire." *Information Clearing House*, 11 August, http://www.informationclearinghouse.info/article18686.htm (accessed 16 May 2011).

Robertson, R. 1995. "Glocalization: Time-Space and Homogeneity-Heterogeneity." In *Global Modernities*, ed. M. Featherstone et al. London: Sage.

Rothbard, M. N. 1983. *The Mystery of Banking*. The Ludwig von Mises Institute.

———. 1994. *The Case Against the Fed*. The Ludwig von Mises Institute.

Rothstein, F. A., and M. L. Blim. 1992. *Anthropology and the Global Factory: Studies of the New Industrialization in the Late Twentieth Century*. New York: Bergin and Garvey.

Røyrvik, E. A. 2008a. "Directors of Creation: An Anthropology of Capitalist Conjunctures in the Contemporary." PhD diss., Norwegian University of Science and Technology (NTNU). ISBN 978-82-471-1301-1.

———. 2008b. "Lettmetall og Ledelse i Midtens Rike" [Light-metal and managing in the Middle Kingdom]. In *Norsk Aluminiumsindustri: Globalisering i et århundre* [Norwegian aluminium industry: A century of globalization], ed. H. O. Frøland, J. Henden, and A. Karlsen. Bergen: Fagbokforlaget.

———. 2009. "The Sociality of Securitization: Symbolic Weapons of Mass Deception." *iNtergraph: journal of dialogic anthropology* 2, no. 2 (online journal).

Sagafos, O. J. 2005. *Livskraft: På Norsk. Hydro 1905–2005*. Oslo: Pax Forlag.

Sand, G., P. M. Schiefloe, and T. M. B. Aasen. 2005. *Norge 2020: Industrielle og økonomiske fremtidsutsikter*. Bergen: Fagbokforlaget.

Schatzberg, E. 2006. "*Technik* Comes to America." *Technology and Culture* 47: 486–512.

Schinasi, G. J. 2005. *Safeguarding Financial Stability: Theory and Practice*. Washington, DC.: International Monetary Fund.

Schön, D. A. 1983. *The Reflective Practitioner*. Basic Books.

Schumpeter, J. A. [1942] 2008. *Capitalism, Socialism and Democracy*. New York: Harper Perennial.

———. [1939] 1982. *Business Cycles: A Theoretical, Historical and Statistical Analysis of the Capitalist Process*. New York: McGraw-Hill.

Schwartzman, H. B. 1993. *Ethnography in Organizations*. Newbury Park: Sage.

Scott, P. D. 2007. *The Road to 9/11: Wealth, Empire, and the Future of America*. Berkeley and Los Angeles: University of California Press.

Searle, J. R. 1969. *Speech Acts*. Cambridge: Cambridge University Press.

———. 1995. *The Construction of Social Reality*. London: Allen Lane.

Sejersted, F. 1993. *Demokratisk kapitalisme*. Oslo: Universitetsforlaget.

Sennett, R. 2006. *The Culture of the New Capitalism*. New Haven and London: Yale University Press.

Shenhav, Y. A. 1999. *Manufacturing Rationality: The Engineering Foundations of the Managerial Revolution*. New York: Oxford University Press.

Slagstad, R. 2001. *De Nasjonale Strateger*. Oslo: Pax Forlag.

Smith, A. [1776] 2003. *The Wealth of Nations*. New York: Bantam Books.

Stiglitz, J. 2002. *Globalization and its discontents*. London: Penguin Books.

———. 2010. *Freefall. America, Free Markets, and the Sinking of the World Economy*. New York, London: W. W. Norton & Company.

Strange, S. [1986] 1997. *Casino Capitalism*. Manchester and New York: Manchester University Press.

Strathern, M., ed. 2000. *Audit Cultures: Anthropological Studies in Accountability, Ethics and the Academy*. London: Routledge.

Summers, L. H., and V. P. Summers. 1989. "When Financial Markets Work Too Well: A Cautious Case For a Securities Transactions Tax." *Journal of Financial Services Research* 3: 261–286.

Sweezy, P. M. 1987. "Monopoly Capitalism." In *The New Palgrave Dictionary of Economics*, ed. J. Eatwell, M. Milgate, and P. Newman. London: Palgrave Macmillan.

———. 1994. "The Triumph of Financial Capital." *Monthly Review* (June).

Sørhaug, T. 1996. *Om ledelse: Makt og tillit i moderne organisering*. Oslo: Universitetsforlaget.

———. 2004. *Managementalitet og autoritetens forvandling: Ledelse i en kunnskapsøkonomi*. Bergen: Fagbokforlaget.

Taylor, F.W. [1911] 1967. *The Principles of Scientific Management*. Newton Library: Harper and Row.

Tett, G. 2009. *Fool's Gold: How Unrestrained Greed Corrupted a Dream, Shattered Global Markets and Unleashed Catastrophe*. London: Little, Brown.

The Editors. 2011. "Ethnography in the Context of Management and Organizational Research: Its Scope and Methods, and Why We Need More of It". *Journal of Management Studies* 48, no. 1: 198–201.

Thorsrud, E., and F. Emery. 1970. *Mot en ny bedriftsorganisasjon*. Oslo: Tanum.

Tittel, W., J. Brendel, B. Gisin, T. Herzog, H. Zbinden, and N. Gisin. 1998. "Experimental Demonstration of Quantum Correlations over More than 10 km." *Physical Review A* 57, no. 5: 3229–3232.

Tobin, S. 2009. "Islamic Banking in the Global Financial Crisis." *Anthropology News* 50, no. 7. (October): 13–14.

Tranøy, B. J. 2006. *Markedets makt over sinnene*. Oslo: Aschehoug.

Trist, E. 1981. *The evolution of socio-technical systems. A conceptual framework and an action research program*. Occasional Papers No. 2. (June). Toronto: Ontario Quality of Work Life Center.

Trouillot, M. R. 2003. *Global Transformations: Anthropology and the Modern World*. New York: Palgrave Macmillan.

Tsing, A. 2002. "Conclusion: The Global Situation." In *The Anthropology of Globalization: A Reader*, ed. J. X. Inda and R. Rosaldo. Malden, MA: Blackwell Publishing.

UNDP Human Development Report. 2005. "International Cooperation at a Crossroads: Aid, Trade, and Security in an Unequal World." New York: United Nations Development Programme (UNDP).

Van Maanen, J. 1988. *Tales of the Field: On Writing Ethnography*. Chicago and London: University of Chicago Press.

———. 2011. "Ethnogrpahy as Work: Some Rules of Engagement." *Journal of Management Studies* 48, no. 1: 218–234.

Veblen, T. [1904] 1975. *The Theory of Business Enterprise*. New York: Augustus Kelley.

Veggeland, N. 2007. *Paths of Public Innovation in the Global Age: Lessons from Scandinavia*. Cheltenham: Edward Elgar.

Vetlesen, A. J. 2006. "Habermas verk Theorie des kommunikativen handelns: en kritisk gjennomgang." *Sosiologisk tidsskrift* 3: 199–218.

Von Wright, G. H. 1994. *Myten om fremskrittet*. Oslo: Cappelen.

Wagner, R. 1981. *The Invention of Culture*. Chicago: University of Chicago Press.

Wallman, S., ed. 1979. *The Social Anthropology of Work*. London: Academic Press.

Warner, W. L., and J. O. Low. 1947. *The Social System of the Modern Factory. The Strike: A Social Analysis* (The Yankee City Series 4). New Haven: Yale University Press.

Watson, T. J. 1994. *In Search of Management: Culture, Chaos and Control in Managerial Work*. London: Routledge.

Weil, J. R., and W. T. Brannon. 2011. *"Yellow Kid" Weil: The Autobiography of America's Master Swindler*. Oakland: A.K. Press.

Whyte, W. F. 1969. *Organizational Behavior: Theory and Application*. Homewood: Richard D. Irwin.

———. 1984. *Learning from the Field*. Beverly Hills, CA: Sage.

Wilk, R. R., and L. C. Cliggett. 2007. *Economies and Cultures: Foundations of Economic Anthropology*. 2d ed. Cambridge, MA: Westview Press.

Wolin, S. S. 2008. *Democracy Inc.: Managed Democracy and the Specter of Inverted Totalitarianism*. Princeton and Oxford: Princeton University Press.

Wray, R. L. 2009. "The Rise and Fall of Money Manager Capitalism: A Minskian Approach." *Cambridge Journal of Economics* 33: 807–828.

Wulff, E. 1992. "Aluminiumsmiljøet i Norge i dag." Trondheim: SINTEF report, STFO5 A92010.

Zaloom, C. 2003. "Ambiguous Numbers: Trading Technologies and Interpretation in Financial Markets." *American Ethnologist* 30, no. 2: 285–272.

———. 2006. *Out of the Pits: Traders and Technology from Chicago to London*. Chicago: University of Chicago Press.

Zuboff, S. 1988. *In the Age of the Smart Machine*. New York: Basic Books.

INDEX

9 781782 380658